I0901104

IMAGES
of America

SOUTH CHARLESTON

On the Cover: South Charleston's first band was formed by Belgian immigrants who came to South Charleston, West Virginia, to establish the Banner Plate Glass Window Factory. The band was created to play for socials, picnics, concerts, and dances. (Courtesy South Charleston Museum.)

IMAGES
of America

SOUTH CHARLESTON

Judy Bowen Romano

ARCADIA
PUBLISHING

ISBN 978-0-7385-8649-6

Published by Arcadia Publishing
Charleston, South Carolina

Printed in the United States of America

Library of Congress Control Number: 2010925442

For all general information, please contact Arcadia Publishing:
Telephone 843-853-2070
Fax 843-853-0044
E-mail sales@arcadiapublishing.com
For customer service and orders:
Toll-Free 1-888-313-2665

Visit us on the Internet at www.arcadiapublishing.com

To my family for their support and unconditional love: Vicki Vaughan, Gina Billups, Dr. Paula Potter (Jerry), and Dr. Robert Romano (Amanda); to my grandchildren Vanessa, Lance, Audriana, Jeri DeAnn, Gabrielle, Genevieve, and Amelia; to my departed parents, F. L. "Tucker" Bowen and Audrey F. Duncan Bowen.

Contents

ACKNOWLEDGMENTS

Many individuals and organizations made this book possible. Many residents donated photographs to the South Charleston Museum, including Bob Anderson, Ben Paul, Richard Grimes, John and Betty Oakes, Ken Samples, Diana Salamie, Frank P. Carter, Carl Dolan, Phillis Shawver, the South Charleston Woman's Club, Linda Weekly, George Brown, Lucie Mellert, and Dan Blue. The South Charleston History Book Committee, consisting of Phyllis Fenwick, Jackie Pauley, Don Evans, Frances Price (deceased), Charles Gorby (deceased), Robert Layer (deceased), Dennis Deitz (deceased), Judy Romano, Naomi Mallory, and Donald Miller also contributed. Special thanks to Fred Armstrong of the West Virginia Cultural Center and to Gary Stogner who helped so much with the manuscript.

I would like to thank *Charleston Daily Mail* photographer Tom Hindman, who donated his picture of the new Belgian display at the Interpretive Center and also the *Daily Mail* Salamie article and bridge picture by Chet Hawes.

Thank you to the City of South Charleston, Mayor Frank Mullens, and the South Charleston City Council for their interest in preserving South Charleston's history.

Many thanks go to Amy Perryman, who guided me through the book writing process, and for her patience and being available for my many questions throughout this process. Unless otherwise noted, all images in this book are courtesy of the South Charleston Museum Foundation.

Introduction

South Charleston was known as Price's Bottom in 1782 and was listed on the deed books as being situated in Montgomery County, Virginia. In 1829, the Kanawha and James River Turnpike came to the South Charleston area, and in 1873, the C&O Railway was built through the area.

The Kanawha Land Company was organized in 1906 and bought 1,800 acres of mostly farms and bottomland. The streetcar line was extended to South Charleston, and Plus Levi conducted an auction selling lots in the new town. Banner Plate Glass Window Factory moved to South Charleston from Indiana in 1907 and then Dunkirk Window Glass Company located in the town. At the time, the city was just a field of broom sage with deep ravines through the bottom, cut by streams, and there were no railroads, paved streets, or streetcars.

In 1914, the Rollins Chemical Company opened in South Charleston. Warner Klipstein Plant opened in 1915 and was later purchased by the FMC Corporation. Construction was underway for a large ordnance plant in 1917, because the area had abundant water, energy, land, and transportation. When World War I ended, the project was mothballed. In 1939, the site was leased by Carnegie-Illinois Steel Company to facilitate a heat treatment that hardened armor plate. During World War II, the plant produced armor plate, naval gun barrels of all sizes, and thousands of torpedo flasks, and was also the first to produce air-to-ground rockets. The plant employed 7,400 people, half of whom were women, and earned an "E" award for "high achievement in the production of war equipment." In 1946, the plant closed again, and reopened for the Korean conflict. FMC Ordnance acquired the plant in 1962 and built armored vehicles and later railroad cars.

Raymond Park of the Park Corporation, headquartered in Nevada and Cleveland, Ohio, bought the plant in 1970. It is now an industrial park and the location of many businesses.

The Carbide and Carbon Chemical Corporation moved to South Charleston from Clendenin and acquired the Rollins Chemical Plant in 1925. It also acquired Blaine Island, once owned by Fleming Cobb, who sold it to Blaine for a rifle. With the Naval Ordnance Plant, South Charleston became a wartime boomtown. The post–World War I era was depressed, and many companies limped to failure: Rollins Chemical Company, Barium Reduction Company, Westvaco, Warner Klipstein Plant, Dunkirk Glass Company, and Hamilton Lumber Company all closed by 1937. Most of these companies would be the sites of Union Carbide. Union Carbide became a wholly owned subsidiary of the Dow Chemical Company on February 6, 2001. Thomas Memorial Hospital was built in the Spring Hill Area as a tribute to Herbert J. Thomas Jr., a Medal of Honor recipient during World War II, in 1946. Both are currently large employers in the Kanawha Valley. South Charleston was incorporated in 1917, and the 1920 census showed 3,650 residents. During the years that followed, with the expansion of Union Carbide, the town grew tremendously, having 19,000 residents at one time.

Interstate 64 opened in 1975, and South Charleston could be reached from the west, north, and south.

Schools in the South Charleston area are Montrose Elementary, Bridgeview Elementary, Richmond Elementary, South Charleston Middle School, South Charleston High School, and Marshall University Graduate School.

South Charleston High School (SCHS) opened in the fall of 1926, and Kathleen Harless Hamilton was the only senior, becoming the first graduate in 1927. Eighty years later, the class of 2006 brought the number of SCHS alumni to more than 18,500. The SCHS Alumni Association is dedicated to keeping those alumni connected to each other and to the community.

One

In the Beginning

The images in this chapter are of a Pow Wow that the South Charleston Museum sponsored in 1990 to honor the area's Native American heritage and to raise funds for the operation of the museum. Native Americans were in this area over 2,000 years ago, and this Pow Wow brought them back to the city. The music and dancing was captivating and hundreds watched and participated in the dances. Each dance has a special meaning. South Charleston participated in the Regatta parade in Charleston and decorated a flatbed truck, which Native Americans rode on with music. There also was a parade in South Charleston, which included an honor guard that marched onto the local football field where the Pow Wow was held. Also included in this chapter are images of volunteers and organizations that have influenced the cultural growth of South Charleston.

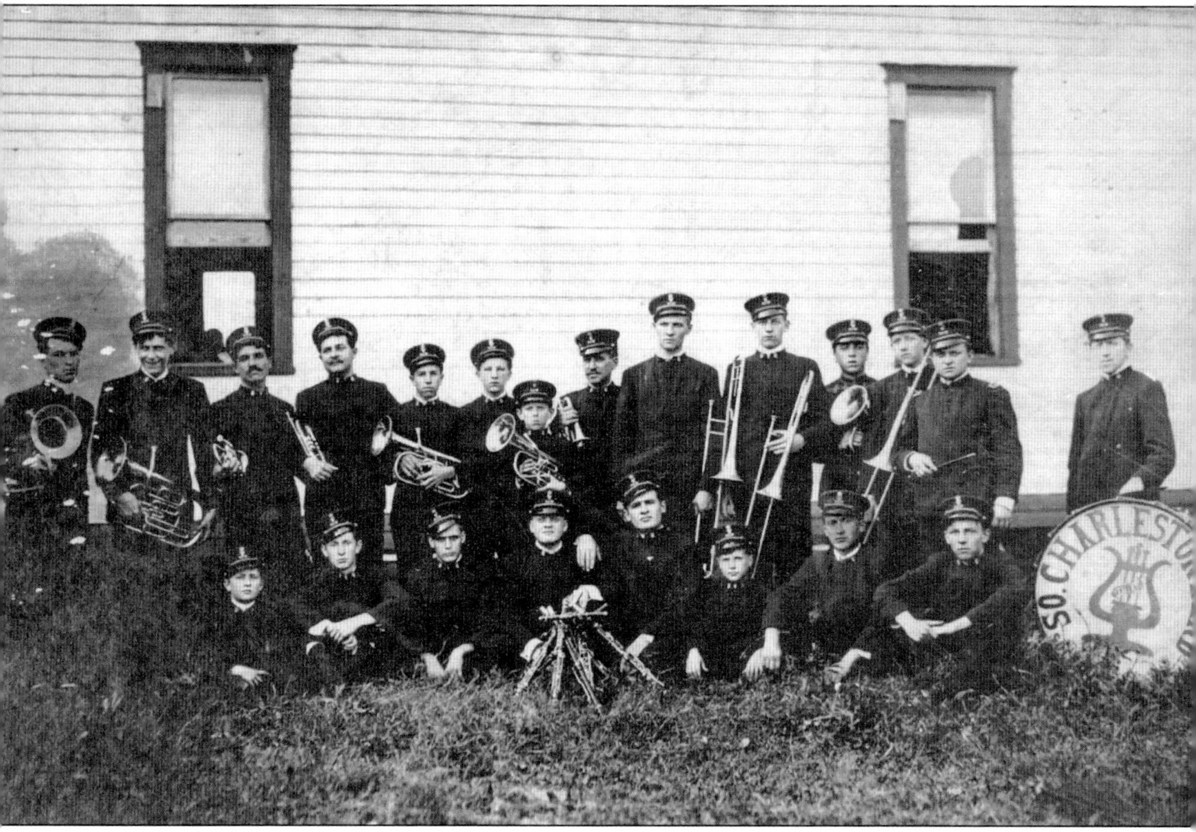

South Charleston's first band was formed by Belgian immigrants who came to South Charleston and established the Banner Plate Glass Window Factory. The band was formed to play at socials, picnics, concerts, and dances. (Courtesy South Charleston Museum.)

In this 1990s picture, Phillis Shawver (with white apron) and others are taking a break after working the concession stand at South Charleston's first American Indian Pow Wow. She was a former Carbide employee, a city councilwoman, and the South Charleston Chamber director. (Courtesy South Charleston Museum.)

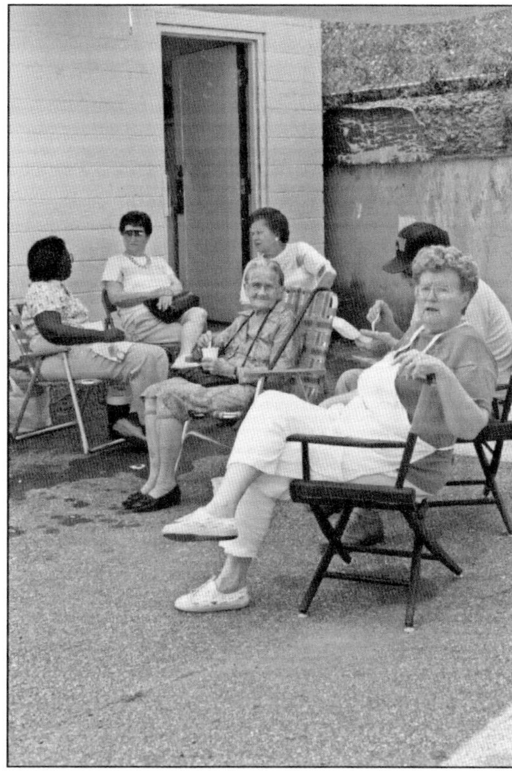

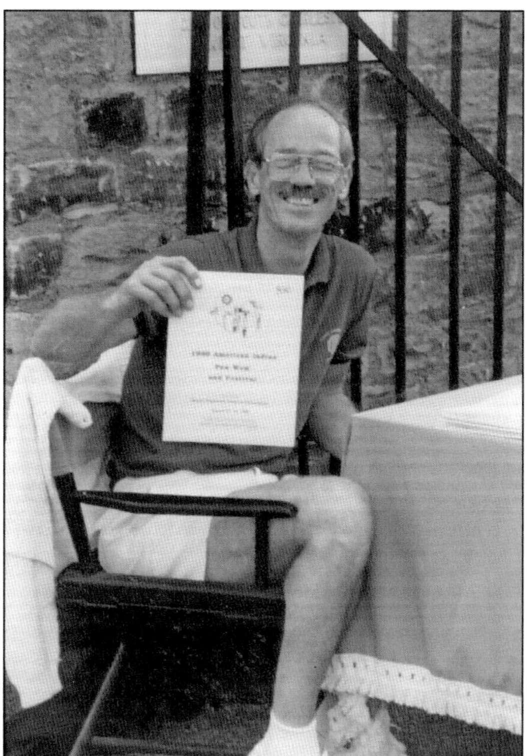

Carless Williams, at the front desk of the Pow Wow, shows the South Charleston Museum's flyer for the event. (Courtesy South Charleston Museum.)

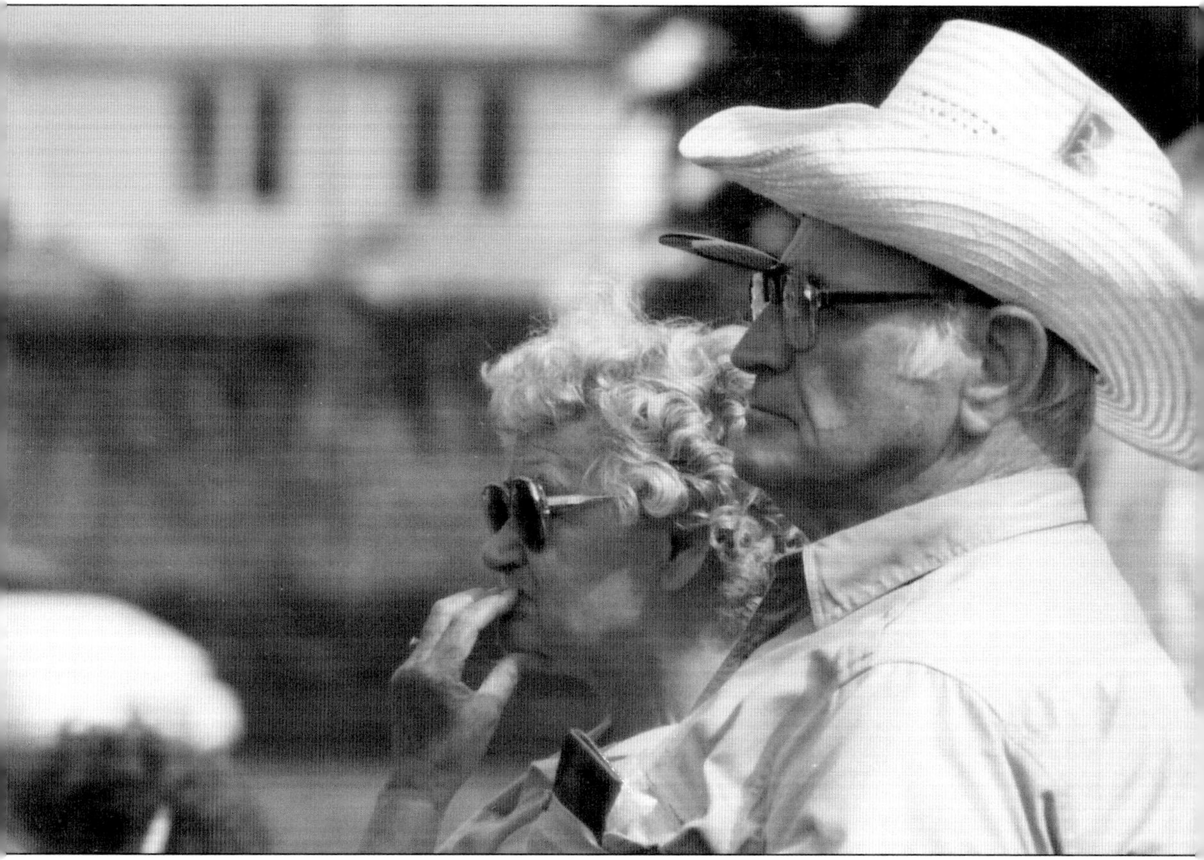

These spectators were watching South Charleston's first Pow Wow. Spectators remarked that it gave them chills to think that over a thousand years ago, Native Americans were probably at this same place. (Courtesy South Charleston Museum.)

The Native American color guard enters South Charleston's Oakes Field for the 1990 Pow Wow. (Courtesy South Charleston Museum.)

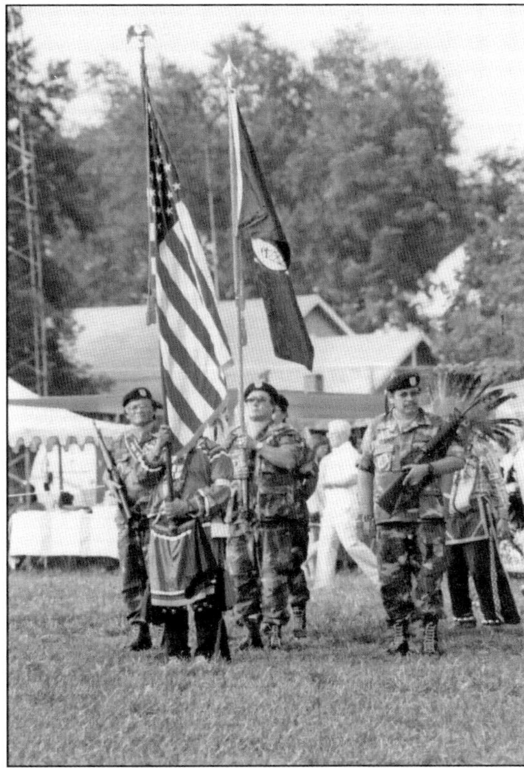

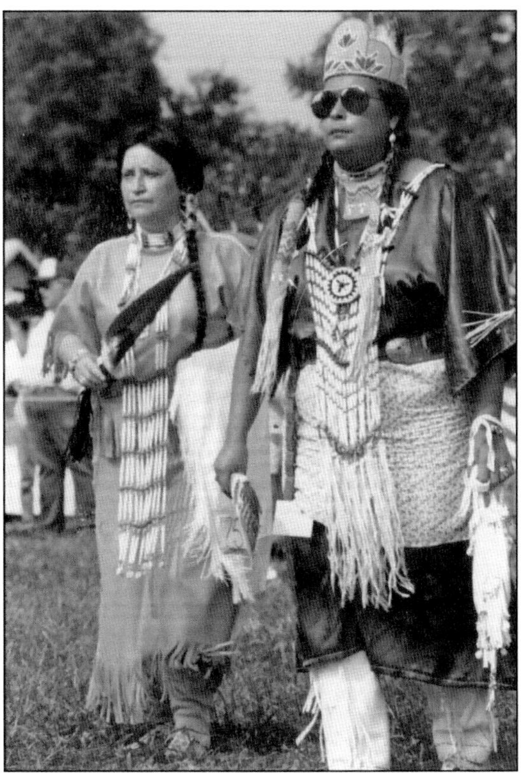

Native American dancers perform at the 1990 Pow Wow. (Courtesy South Charleston Museum.)

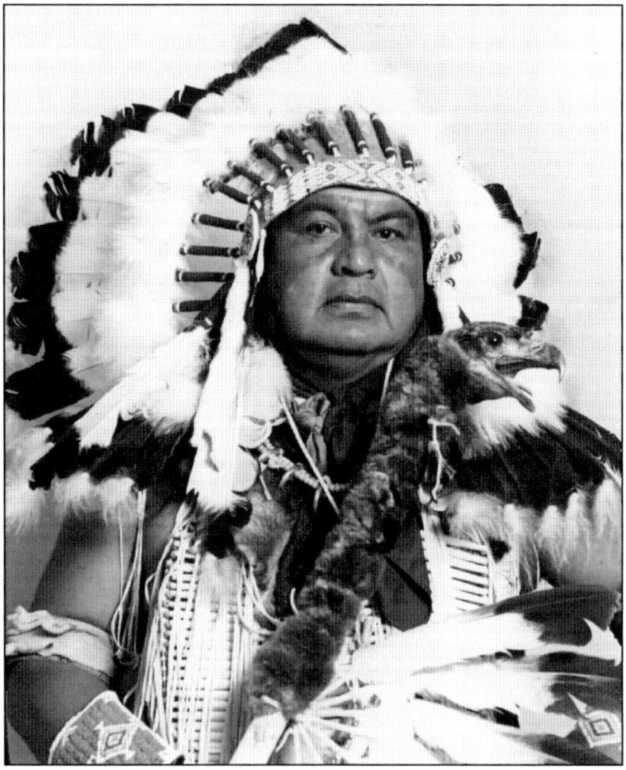

Chief Fred Bushyhead organized the Pow Wow in South Charleston in 1990. (Courtesy South Charleston Museum.)

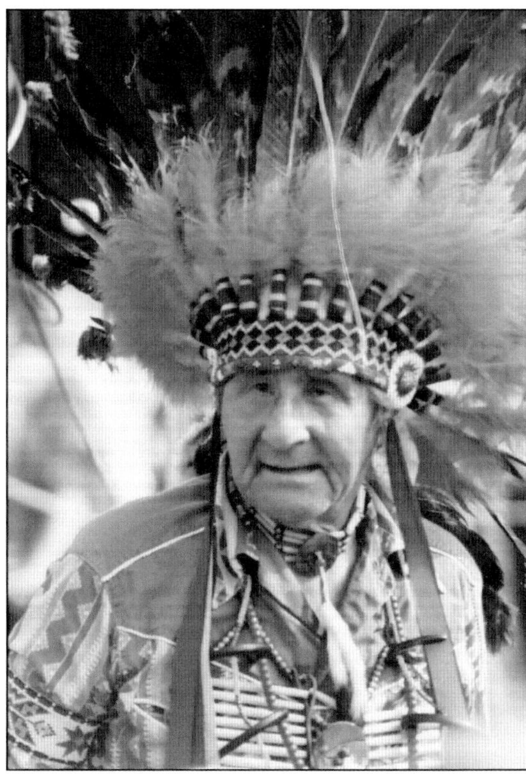

Pictured here is an elderly dancer at the 1990 Pow Wow. (Courtesy South Charleston Museum.)

Children also participated in the competitive dancing at the 1990 Pow Wow. (Courtesy South Charleston Museum.)

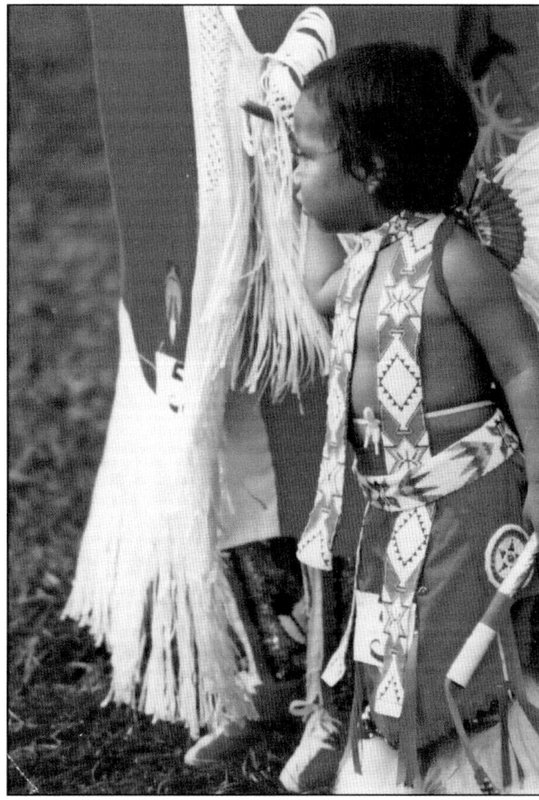

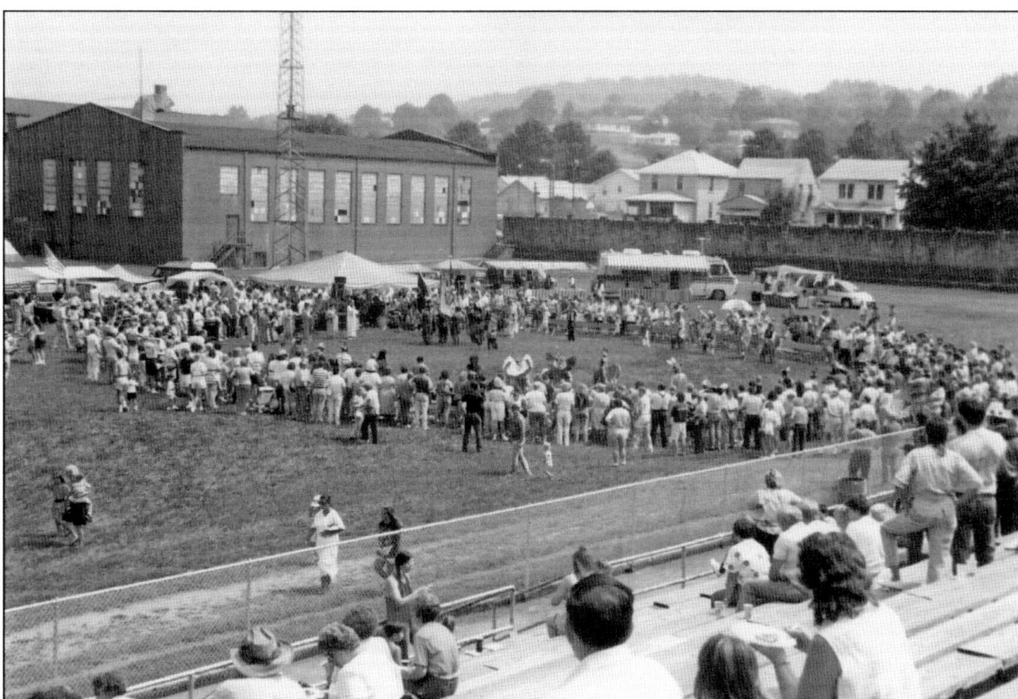

Spectators are viewing the Pow Wow at Oakes Field. (Courtesy South Charleston Museum.)

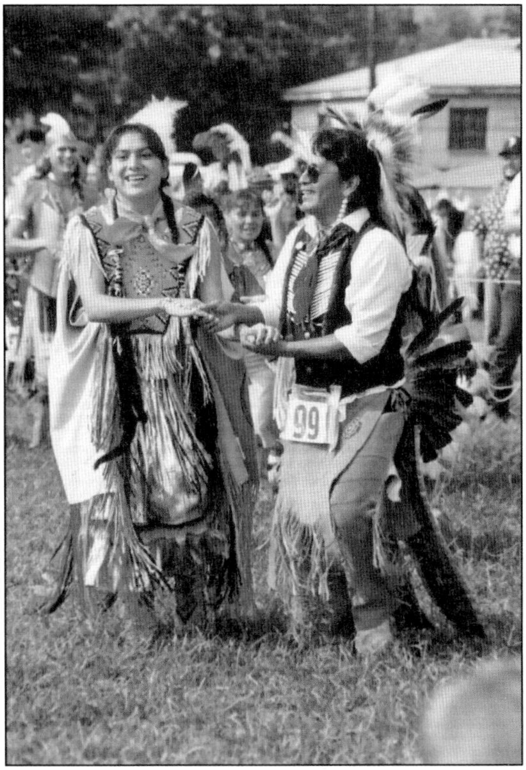

Here dancers compete in a special couples dance at the Pow Wow. (Courtesy South Charleston Museum.)

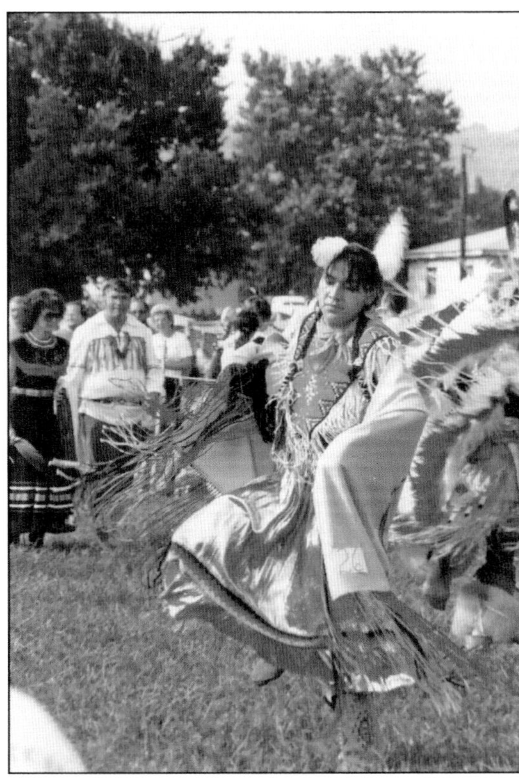

With beautiful regalia, a female dancer competes at the 1990 Pow Wow. (Courtesy South Charleston Museum.)

Two

The Belgian Influence

Belgian families came to South Charleston in the early 1900s and started the Banner Plate Glass Window Factory at 333 MacCorkle Avenue, the present site of the Rite Aid Store. The Belgians organized the city's first band. The cemetery on Glendale Avenue in South Charleston has markers from several of these early immigrants, and it was once known as the Belgian Cemetery. Their tombstones read, "born in Belgium and died in South Charleston." The women wore beautiful dresses and donned Gibson-girl hairdos, and they were noted as great cooks. They would walk to the trestle bridge and cross over to the west side of Charleston to attend St. Anthony's Catholic Church.

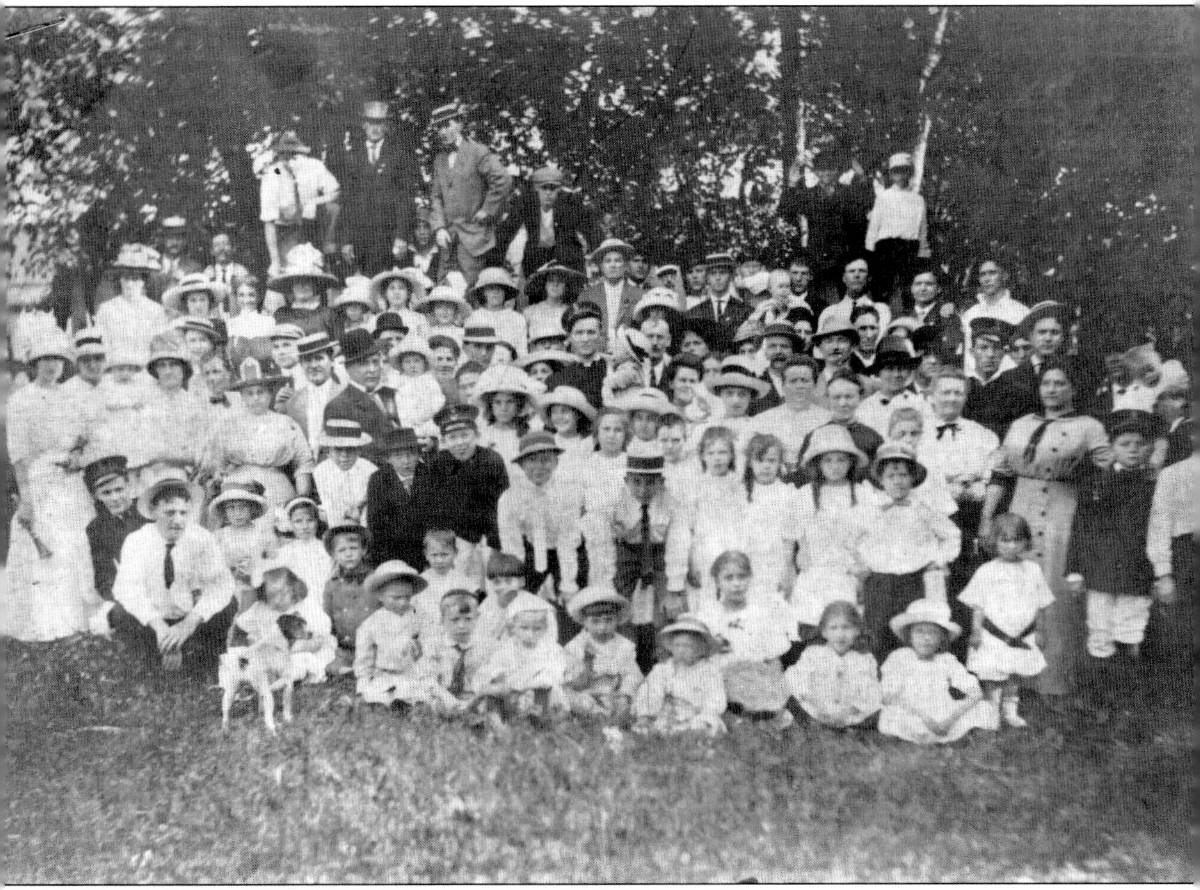

The Belgians came to South Charleston, West Virginia, and established the Banner Plate Glass Window Factory. This c. 1914 photograph was most likely taken during a Belgian carnival, where families gathered for music and socializing. (Courtesy South Charleston Museum.)

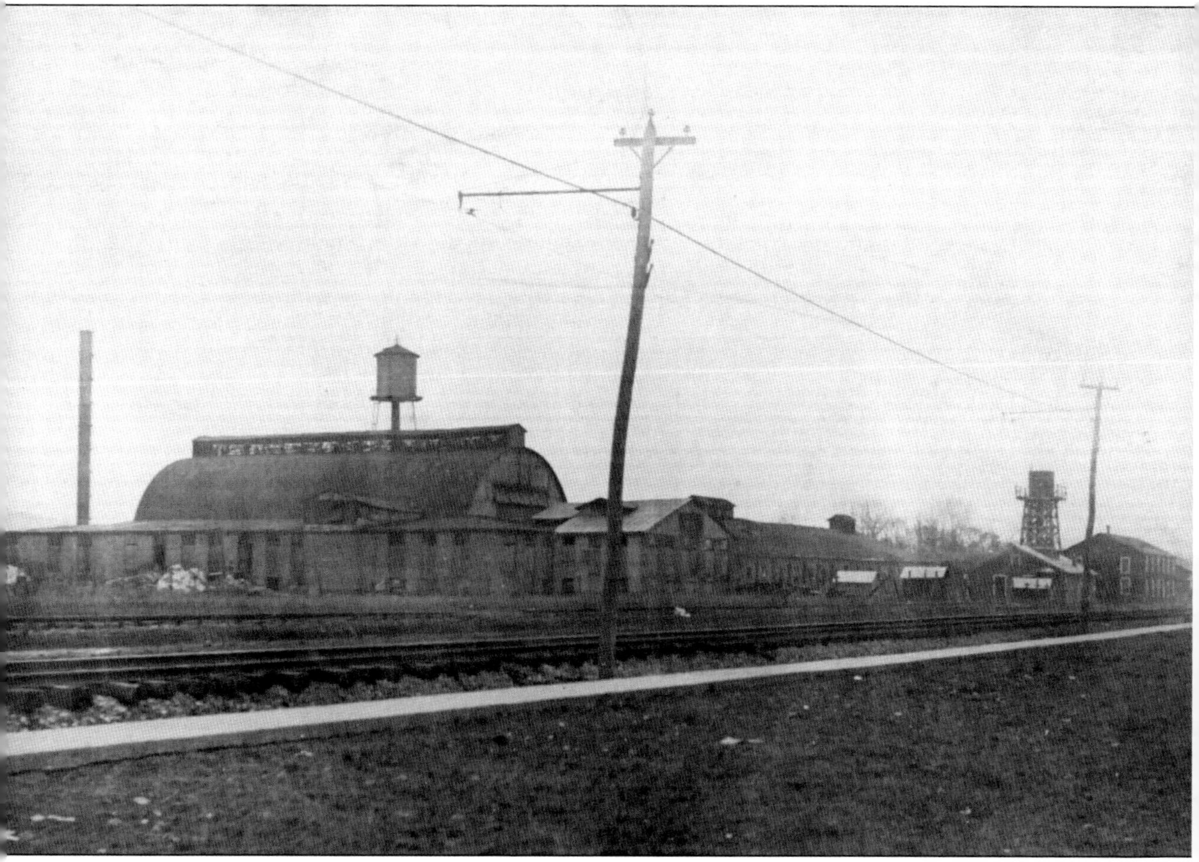

The Dunkirk Window Glass Company was located on MacCorkle Avenue in South Charleston. (Courtesy South Charleston Museum.)

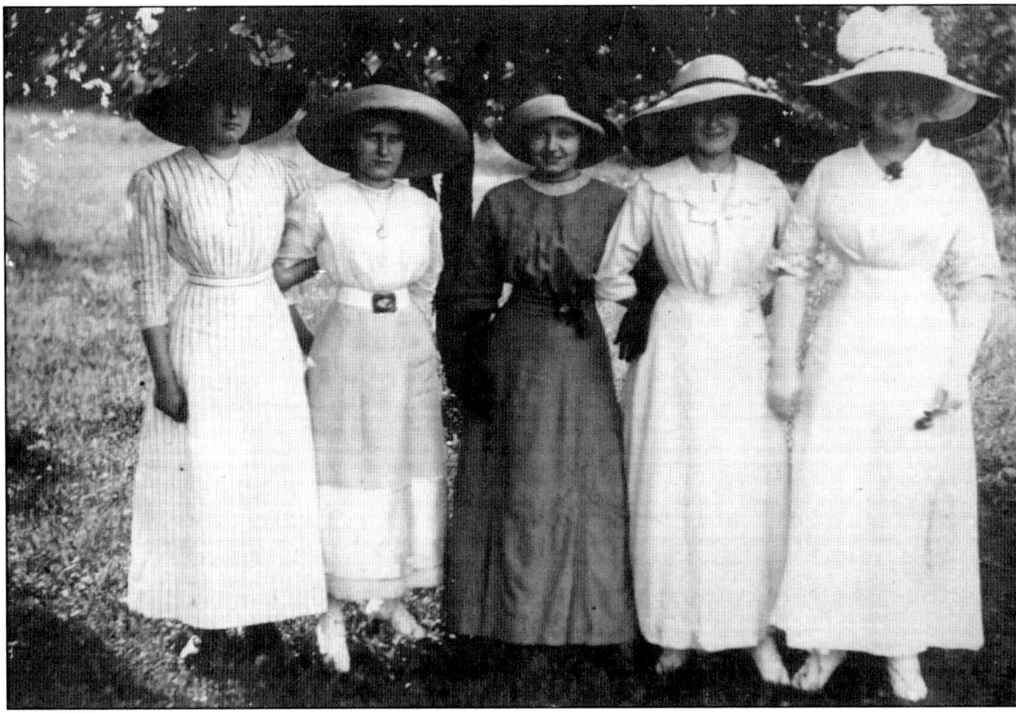

At the turn of the 20th century, South Charleston was known as a Belgian town, where French was more common than English, and the beauty of the Belgian belles was legendary. (Courtesy South Charleston Museum.)

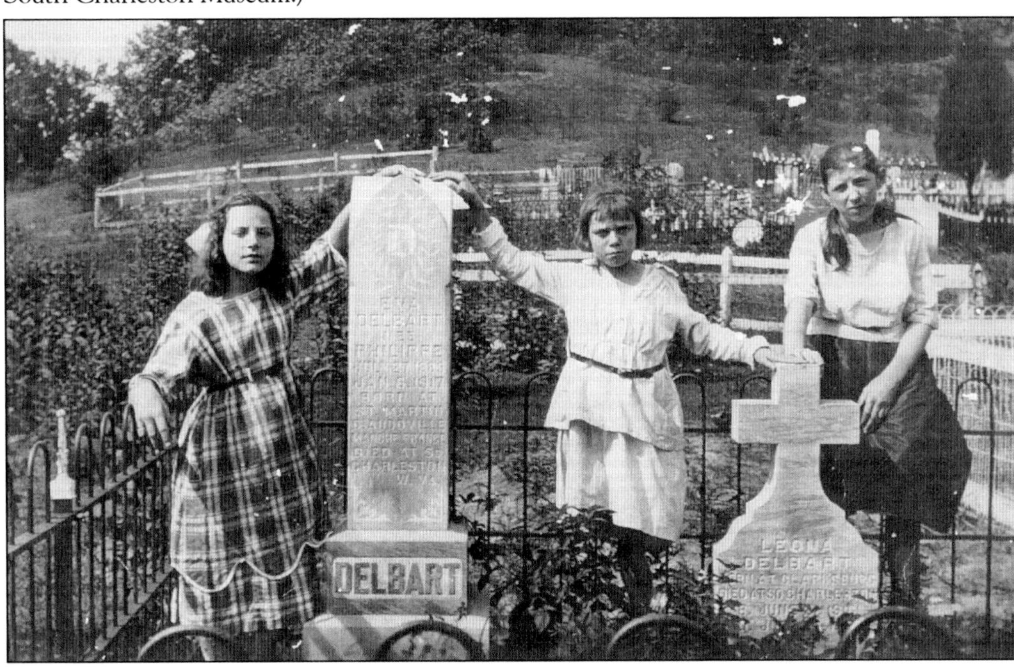

Around 1918, three Belgian girls pose in the Glendale Cemetery in South Charleston. Until recently, the cemetery was known as the Belgian Cemetery. (Courtesy Charles DeHainaut of Galax, Virginia.)

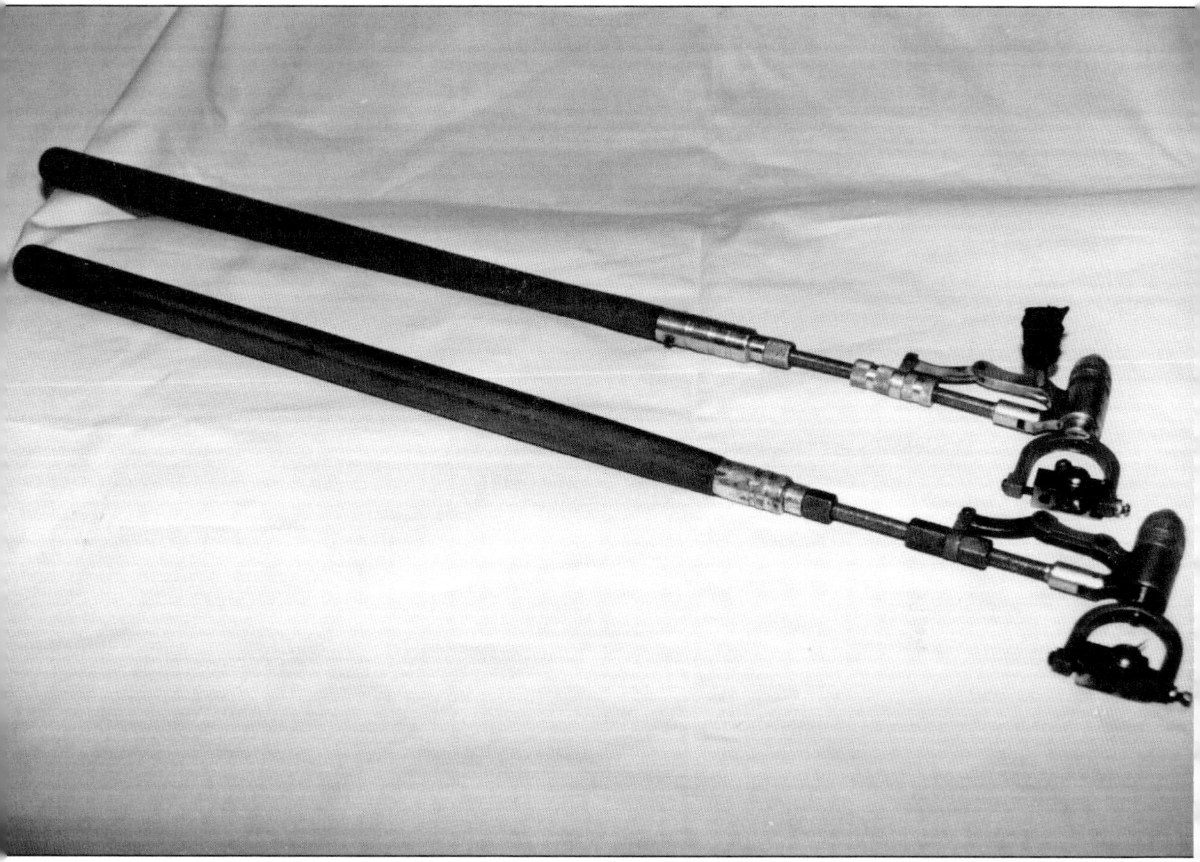

The De Hainaut families donated these glass-cutting tools to the South Charleston Museum. In the early 1900s, the Belgian glassworkers made window glass for homes by hand. Dr. Fred Barkey, a local historian, wrote a book about furnace workers entitled *The Cinderheads in the Hills*. Dr. Barkey said the Belgians came to America for better jobs and wages and because it was difficult for them to obtain coal to fuel their furnaces in Belgium. (Courtesy South Charleston Museum.)

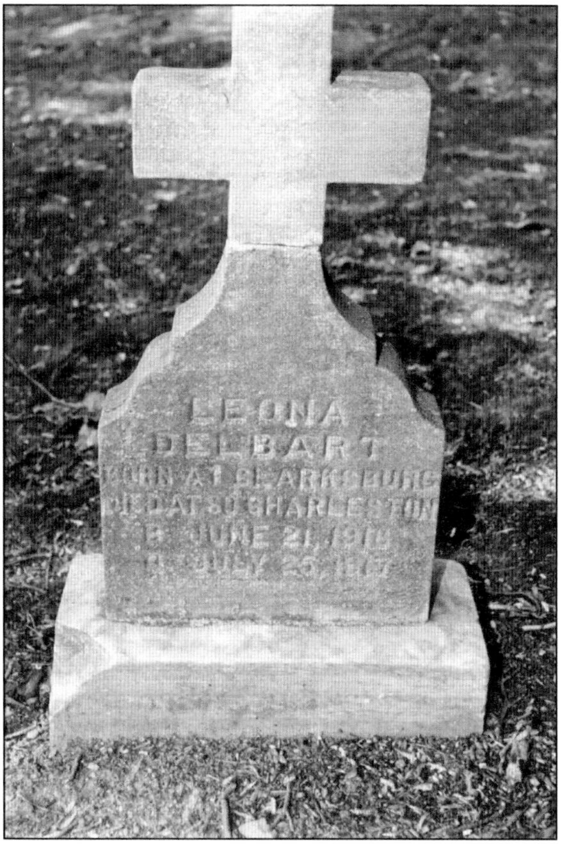

Glendale cemetery on Glendale Avenue was once known as the Belgian Cemetery, and many Belgians were buried there. (Courtesy South Charleston Museum.)

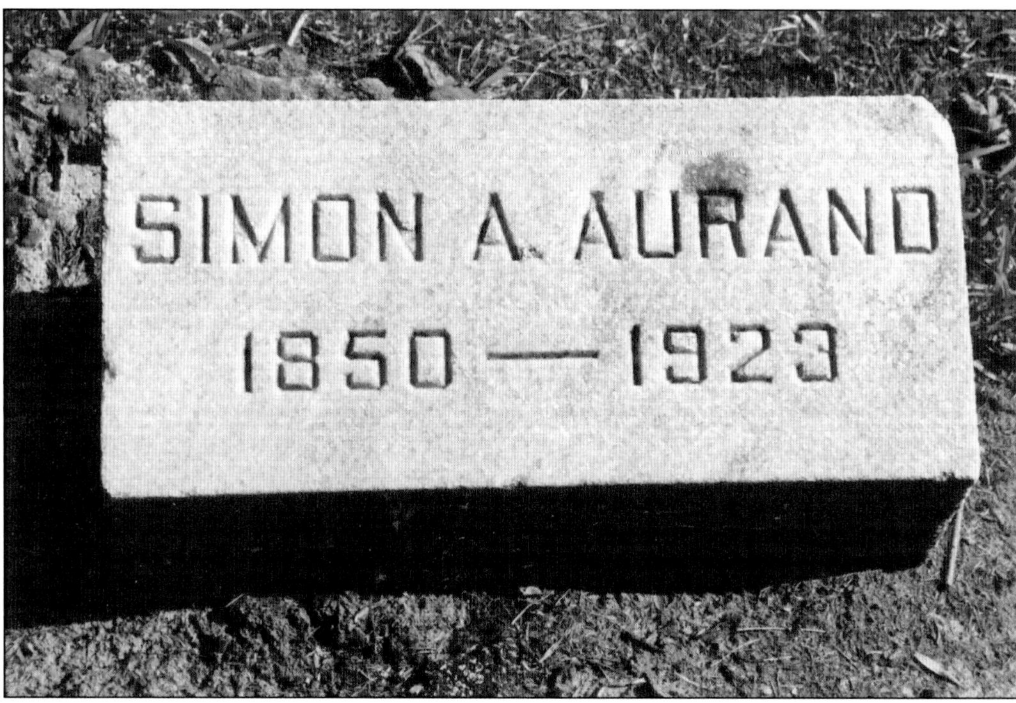

This is the tombstone of Eva Delbart née Philippe, who was born July 27, 1889, in France, and died January 6, 1917, in South Charleston. (Courtesy South Charleston Museum.)

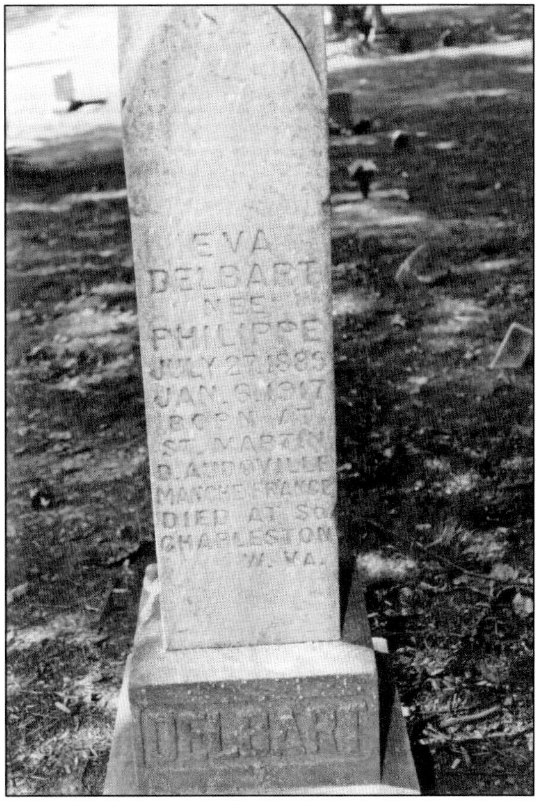

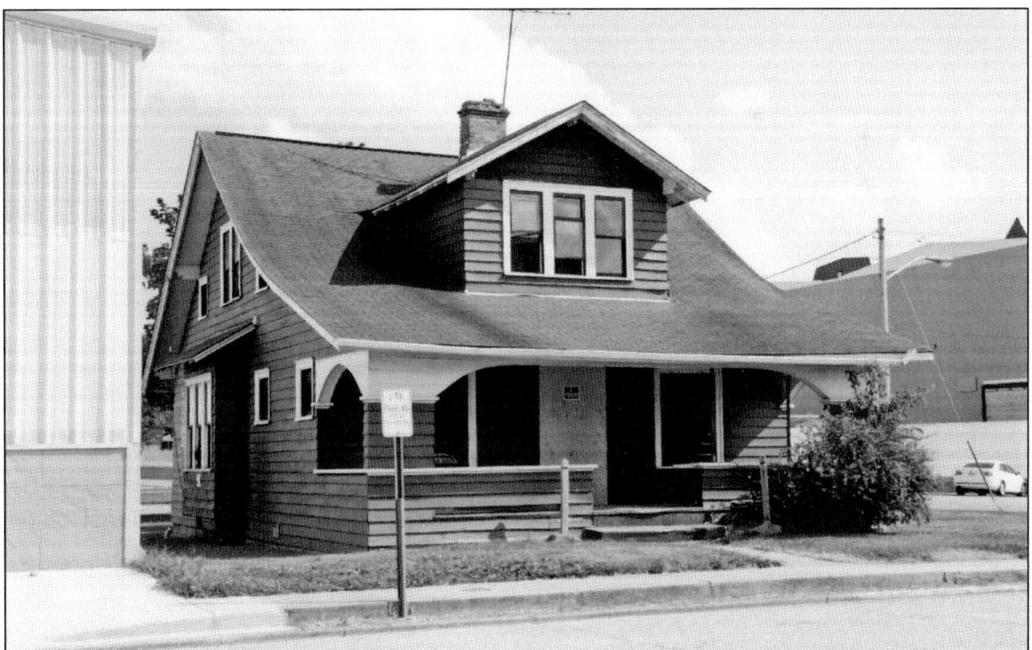

A Belgian family built this home on Seventh Avenue in the early 1900s. The home was demolished in 2009. (Courtesy Linda Weekly.)

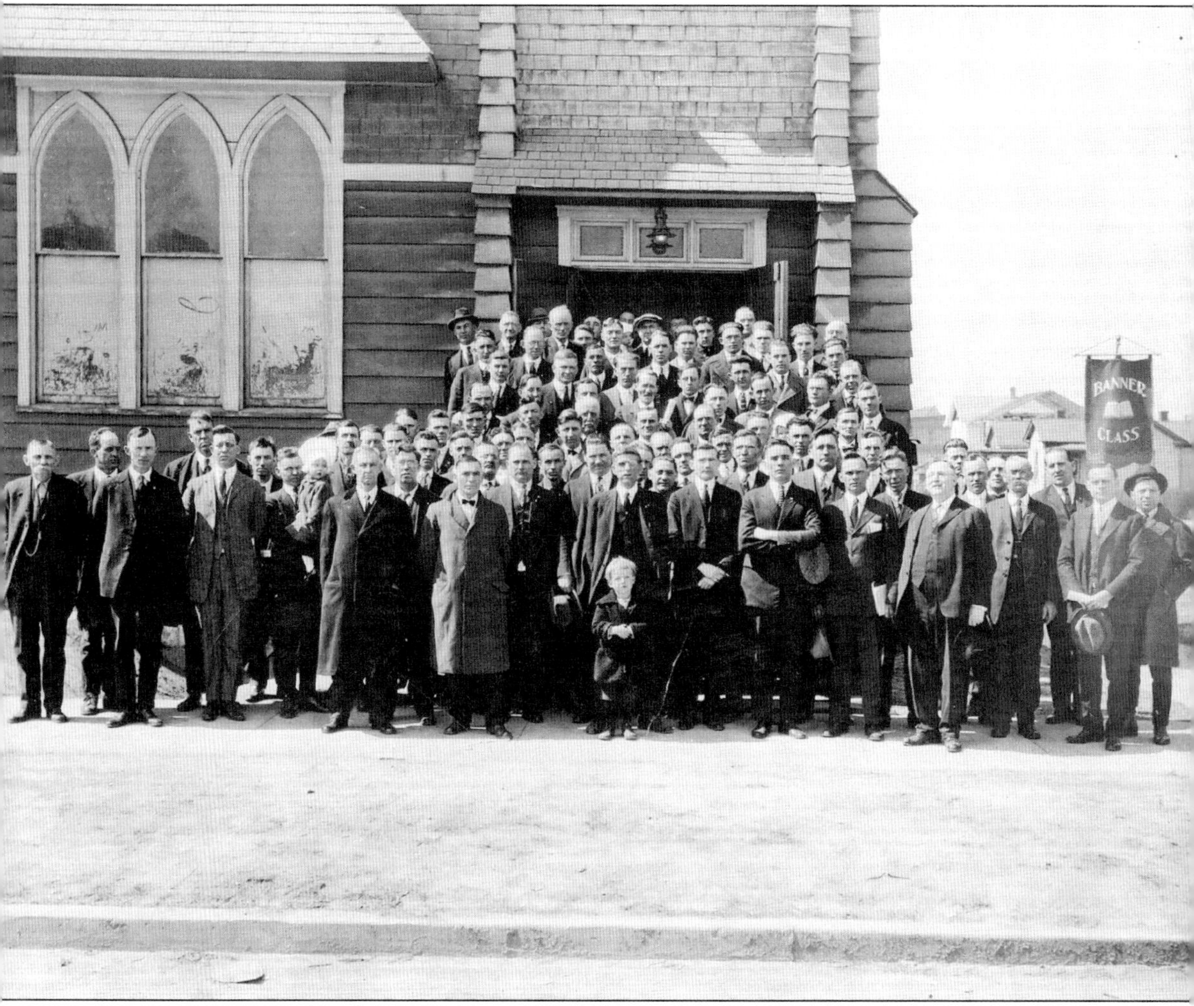

The First Baptist Church is located on D Street in South Charleston. This banner class in front of the church was probably being honored for their large attendance in the early 1900s. (Courtesy South Charleston Museum.)

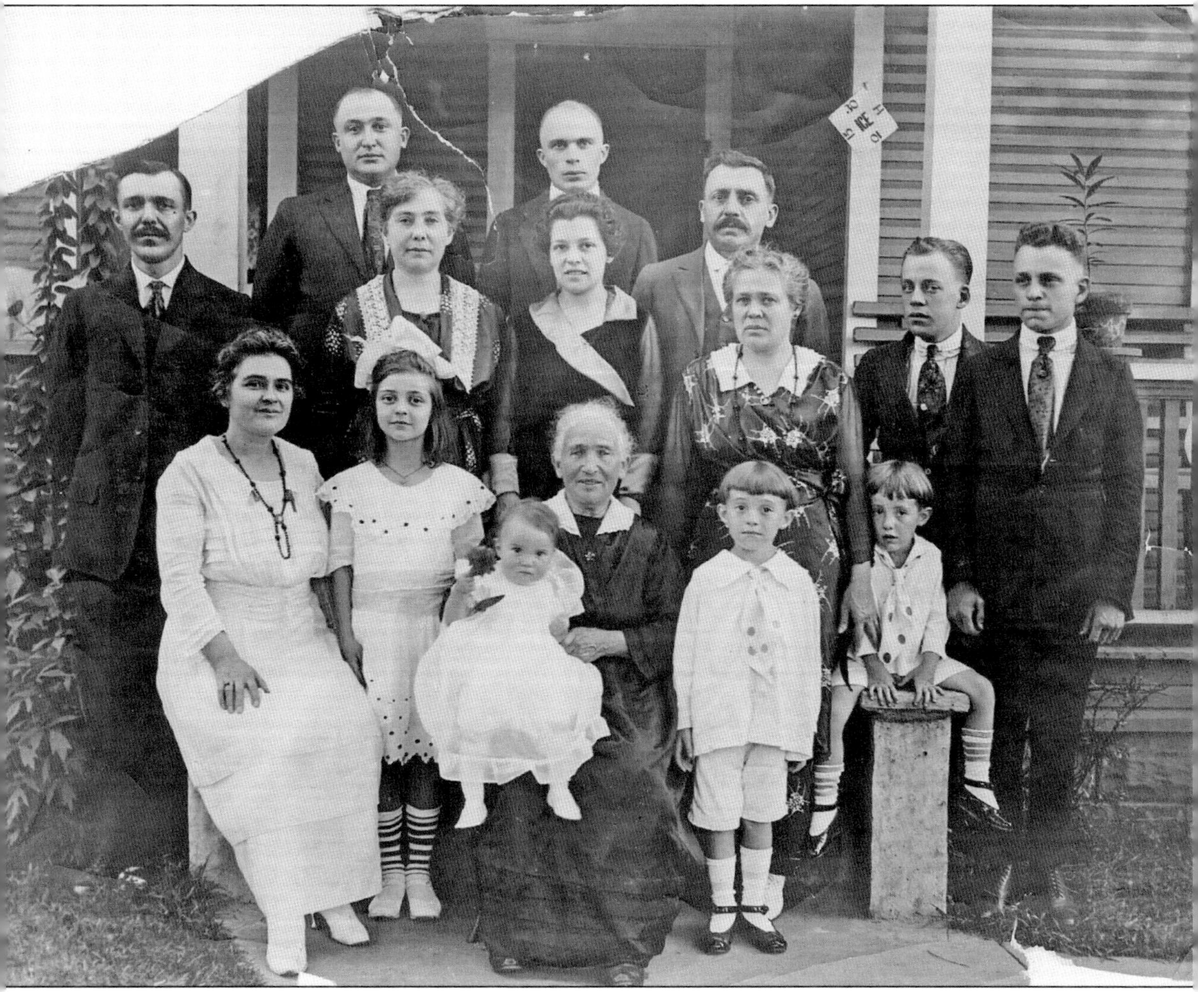

The Belgians pictured here in the 1900s are H. B. Dupriauex, daughter Martha, grandmother Leoni Borreau, baby Margaret Hentaue, aunt Appoire Pacat, Albert Heniereau, Maurice Heniscae, Albert Henisae, Adelina Henisae, Carman Pascat Brigale, Joseph Pascat (his father), Fred Barreat, and Alice Barreat. (Courtesy South Charleston Museum.)

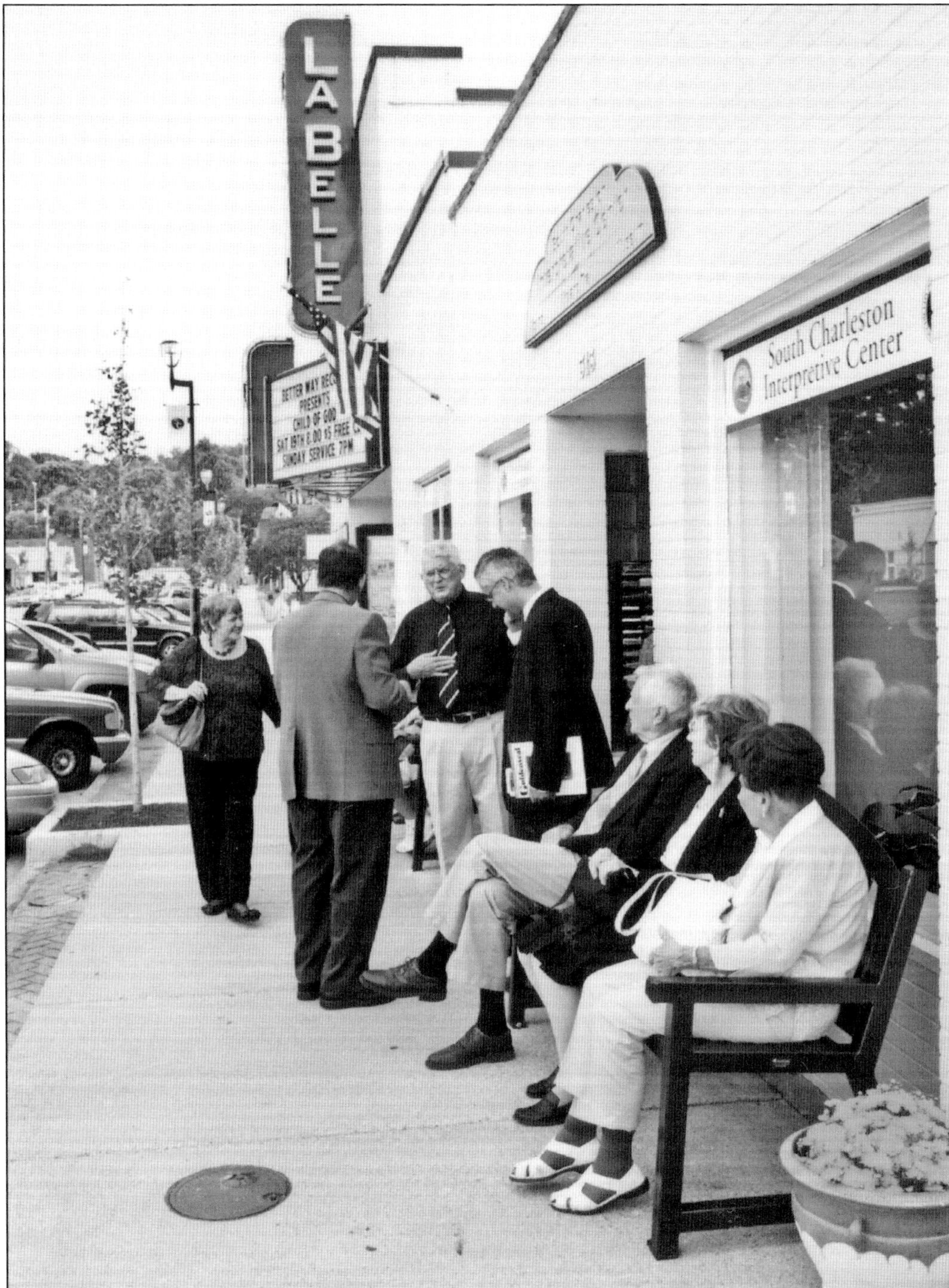

The unveiling of the Belgian display honoring the Belgian legacy in South Charleston was on September 12, 2009. The display is housed at the Interpretive Center located at 313 D Street. Sigurd Schelstraete of the Belgium Embassy in Washington, D.C., is shown talking with Steve Fesenmaier and Dr. Fred Barkey. Schelstraete is holding the notebook. (Courtesy George A. Brown III.)

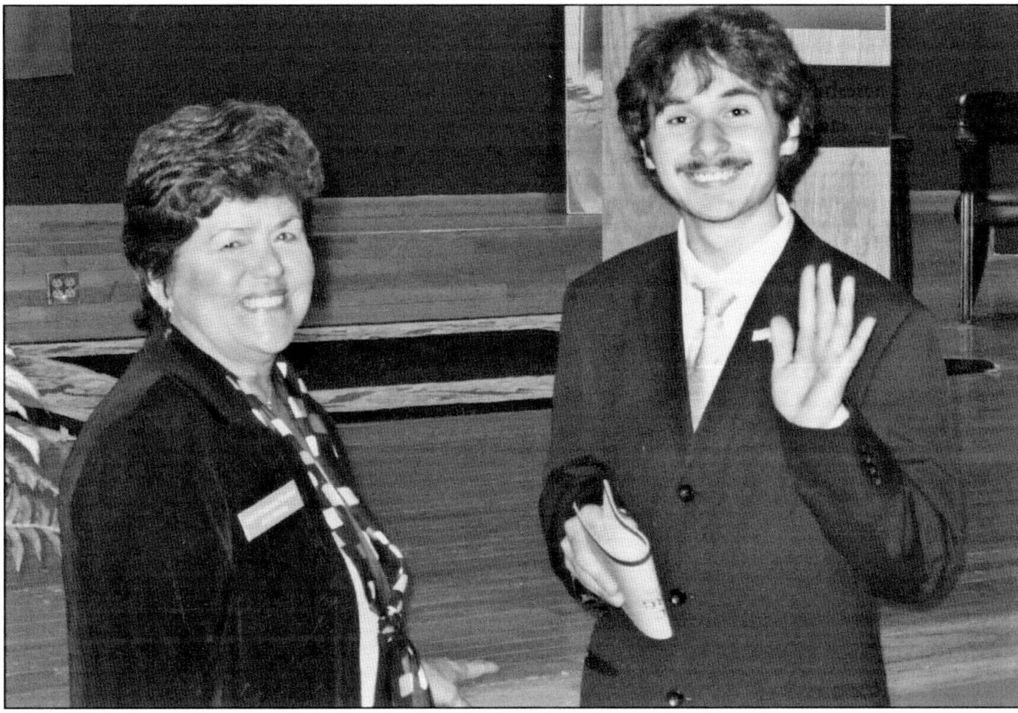

Cody Britton and Judy Romano attended the Belgian reception at the Historic La Belle Theater. (Courtesy George A. Brown III.)

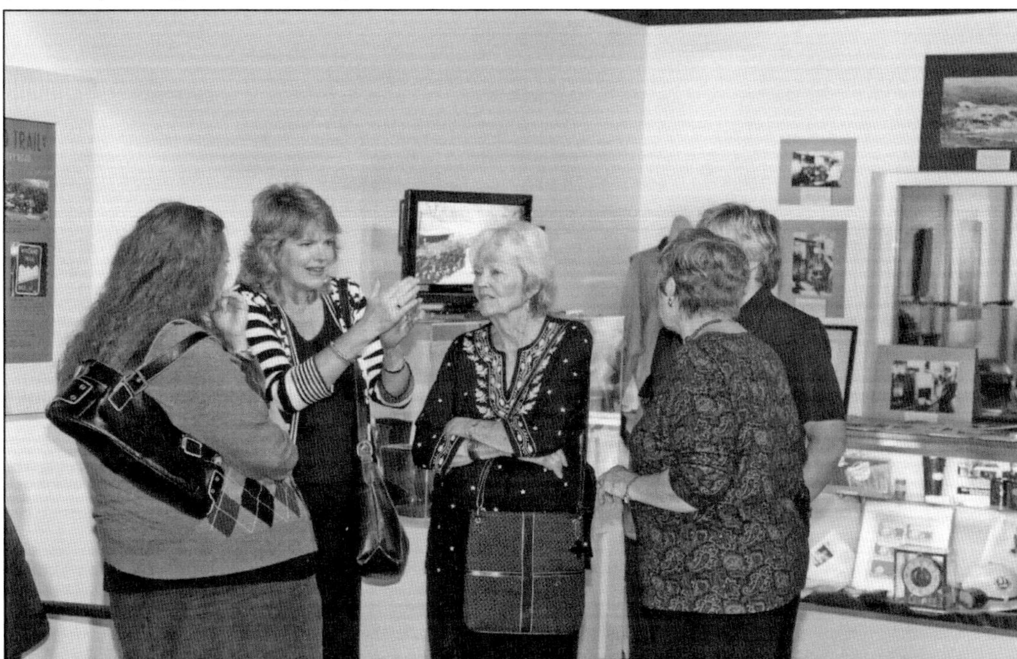

Guests at the grand opening of the Belgian exhibit at the Interpretive Center included the Kiser family. From left to right are Nicole Ernest, Valerie Bone, Jean Kiser, Felicia Patten (Knoxville, TN), and Alice Quick.(Courtesy George A. Brown III.)

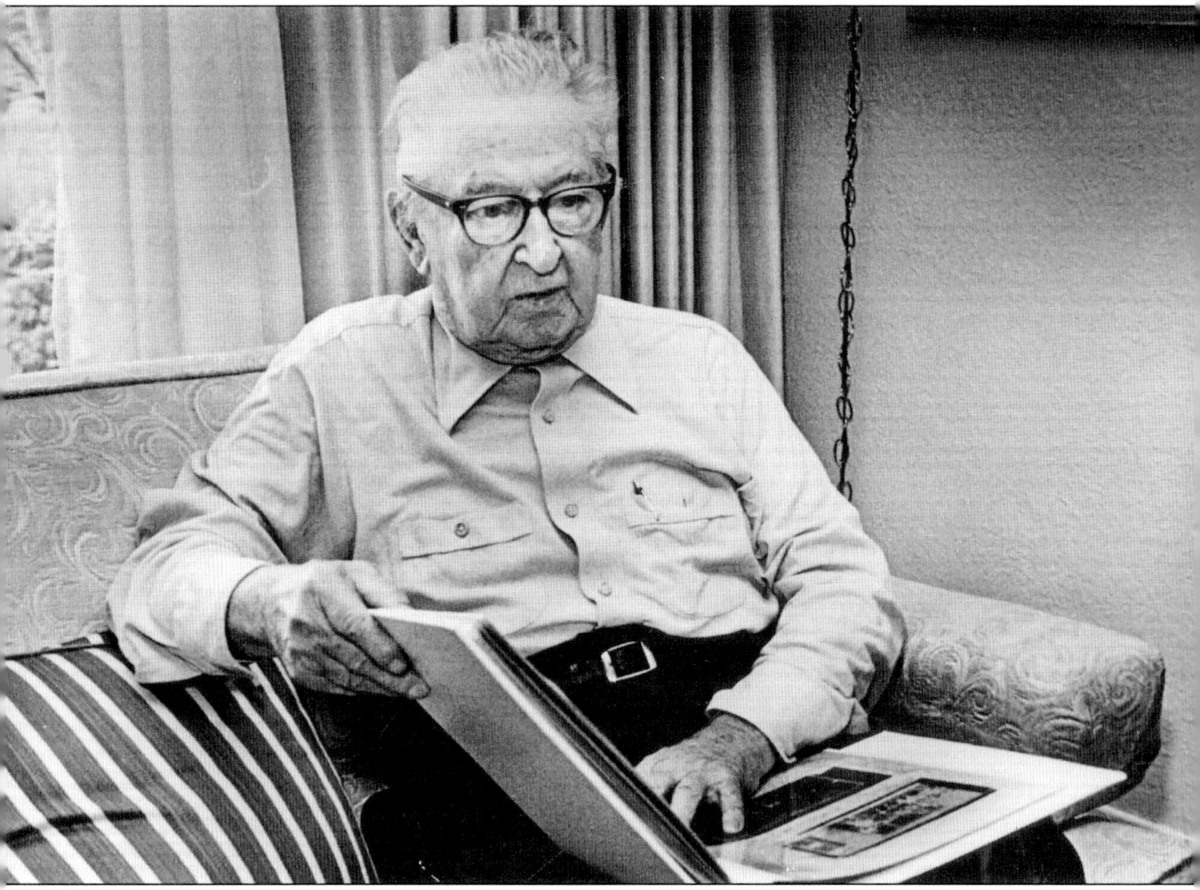

George Del Forge explains that his family came to South Charleston from Belgium and how primitive the area was in the early 1900s. (Courtesy South Charleston Museum.)

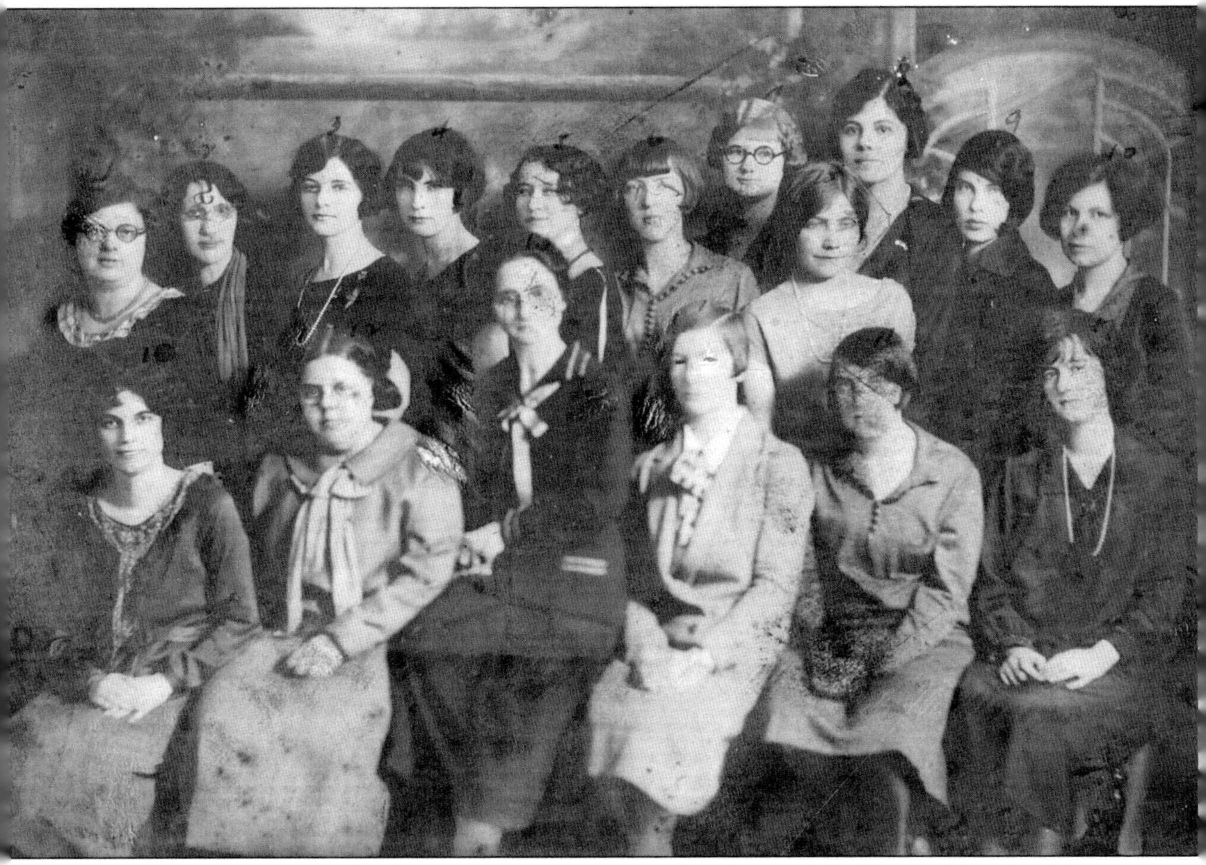

Legible names on the back of this 1900s picture are: Ms. George, Ms. Henry, Minnie Fish, Dorothy, Maureen, Verma Sparkes, Ruth Criniti, Ms. Eggleton, Ms. Hamilton, Eva George, Mrs. Tomlison—superintendent, Virginia Sutherland, Alice Le Fevre, Elizabeth Dundson, and Slack Brotherton. (Courtesy South Charleston Museum.)

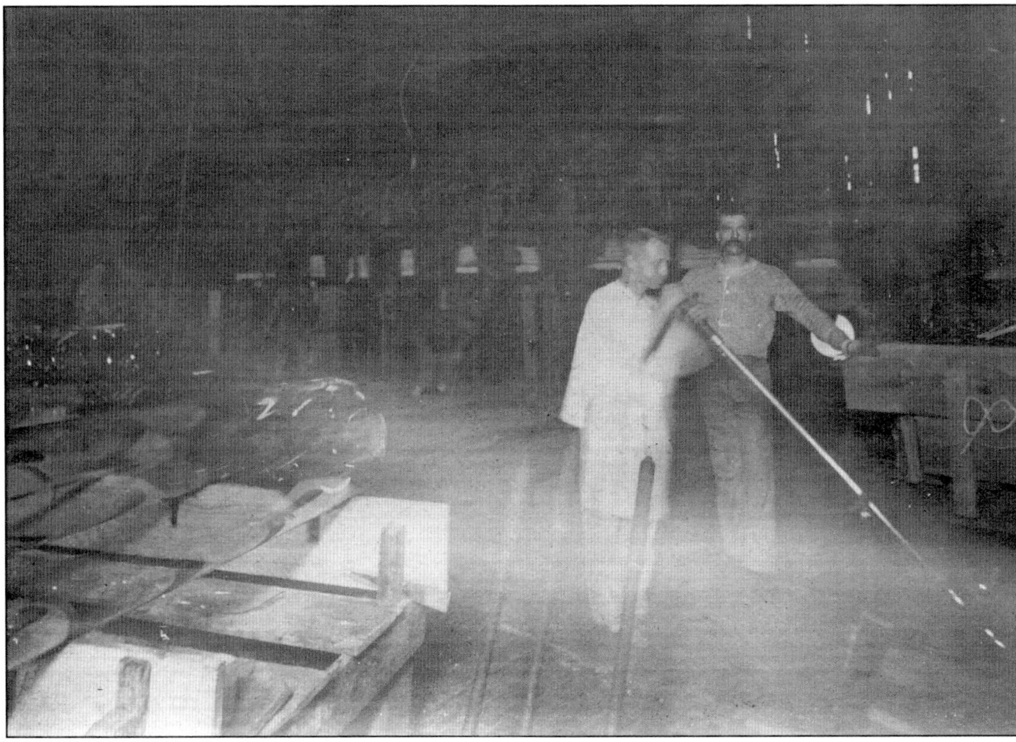

A Belgian laborer is blowing window glass in the early 1900s at the Dunkirk Window Glass Company in South Charleston. Dunkirk was sold to Libbey Owens Glass Company in 1928, and in 1933, the property was sold to Union Carbon Company. (Courtesy South Charleston Museum.)

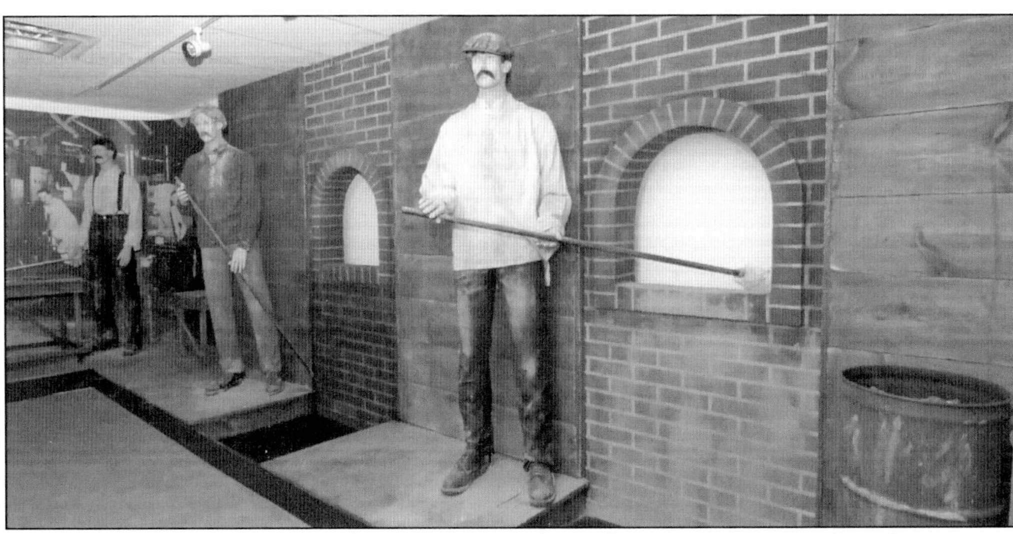

These Belgian displays at the Interpretive Center, located at 313 D Street, explain the process of glassmaking by hand. The exhibit includes several artifacts donated by area descendants of the Belgian families. (Courtesy Tom Hindman, *Charleston Daily Mail*.)

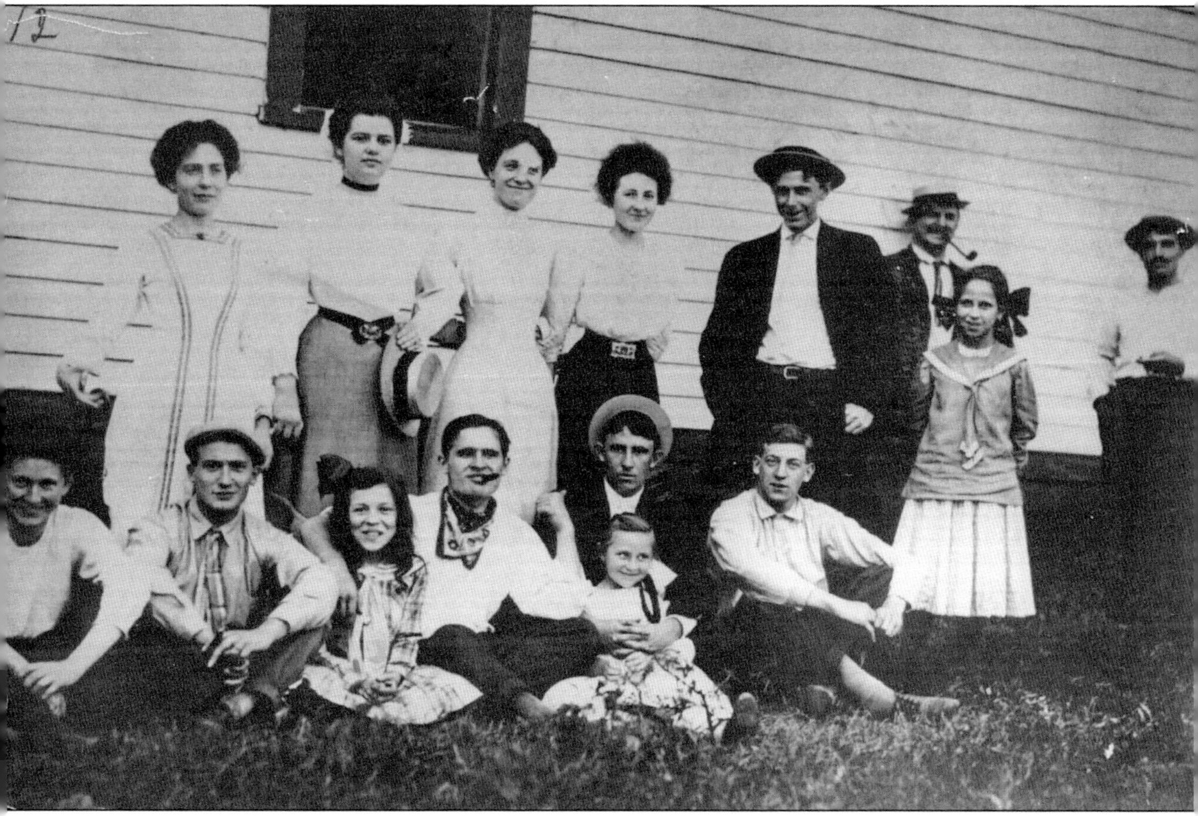

A group of Belgians congregate for a holiday or family event in 1912. The Belgians loved to gather with friends and relatives. (Courtesy South Charleston Museum.)

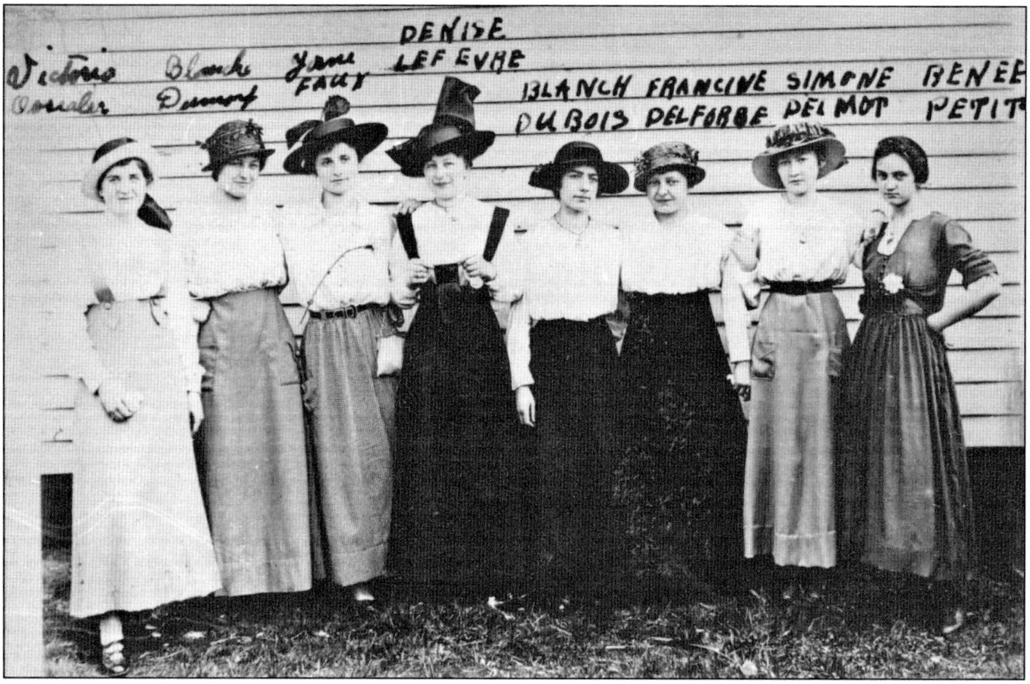

Belgian ladies are pictured here in a 1914 photograph. From left to right are Victoria Oescaler, Blance Dcmouex, Youse Faux, Denise LeFevre, Blanch DuBois, Francine Delforge, Simone Delmot, and Renee Petit. The Belgian families were among South Charleston's first residents. (Courtesy South Charleston Museum.)

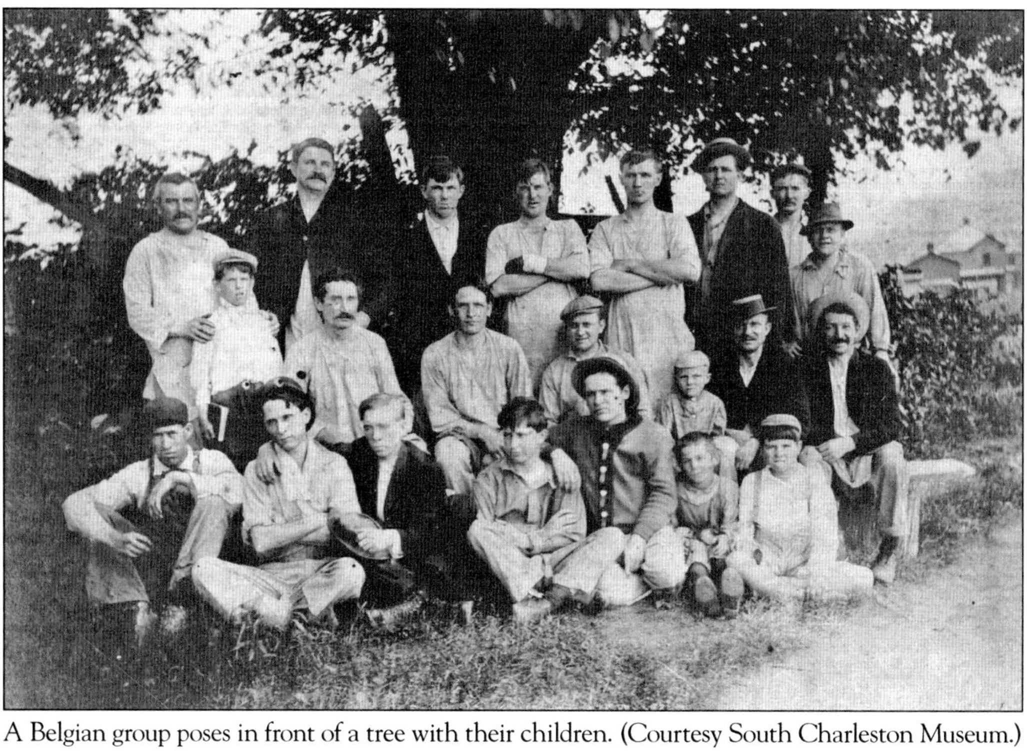

A Belgian group poses in front of a tree with their children. (Courtesy South Charleston Museum.)

Three

HISTORIC STRUCTURES

There are many historic structures in the South Charleston and Spring Hill area. Oakes Field and city hall were built in the early 1940s before World War II by the Works Progress Administration, a federal jobs program initiated by Pres. Franklin Roosevelt. The Criel Mound has been in our city for centuries, and many Belgian homes were built in the early 1900s. Union Carbide and Carbon built facilities here beginning in 1925. Many chemical plants and industrial facilities were built before and during World Wars I and II. The Naval Ordnance facility was built by the federal government in the early 1900s and changed hands to FMC Ordnance in 1962 and then Park Corporation in 1970.

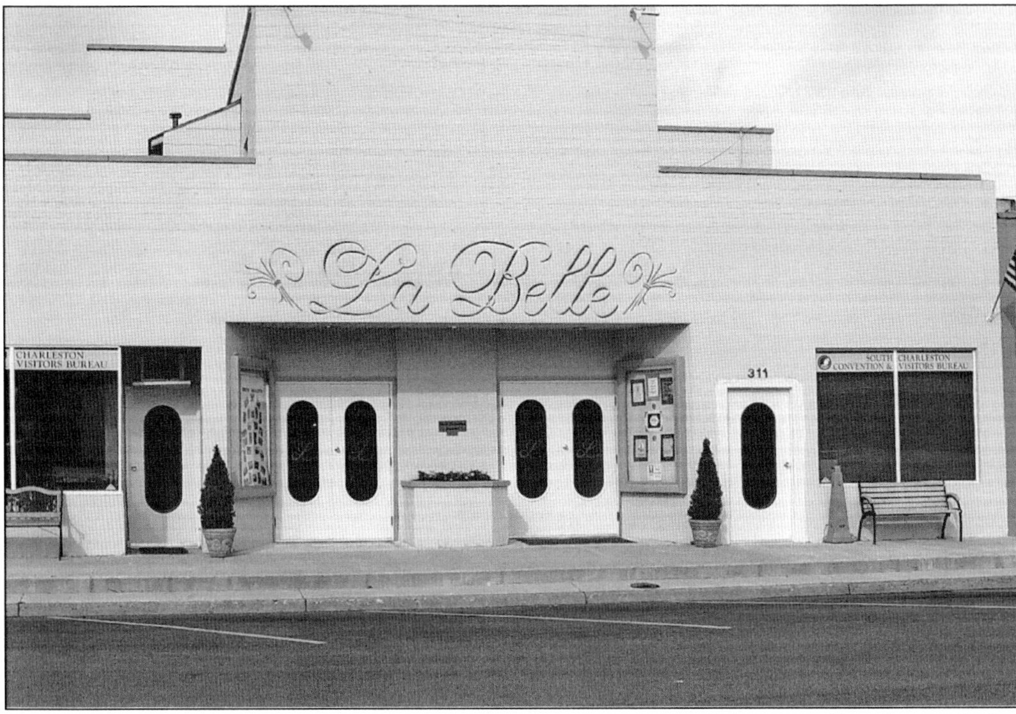

Linda Weekly, an area photographer, took these two pictures of the La Belle Theater before (above) and after (below) renovations in 2003. (Both courtesy Linda Weekly.)

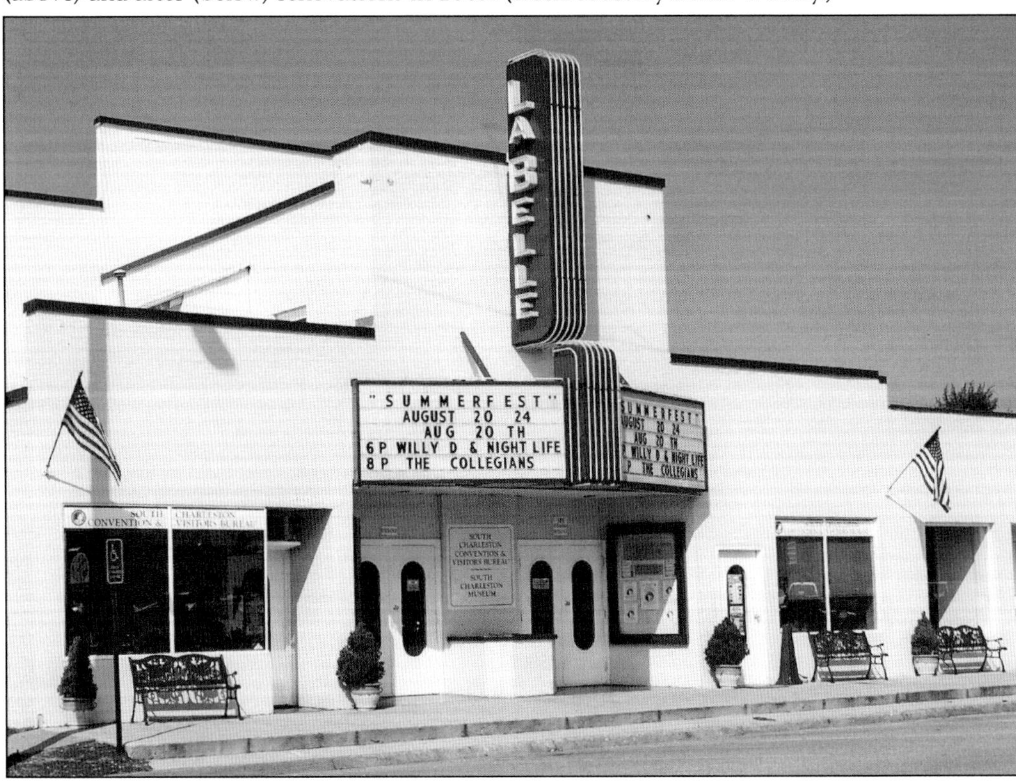

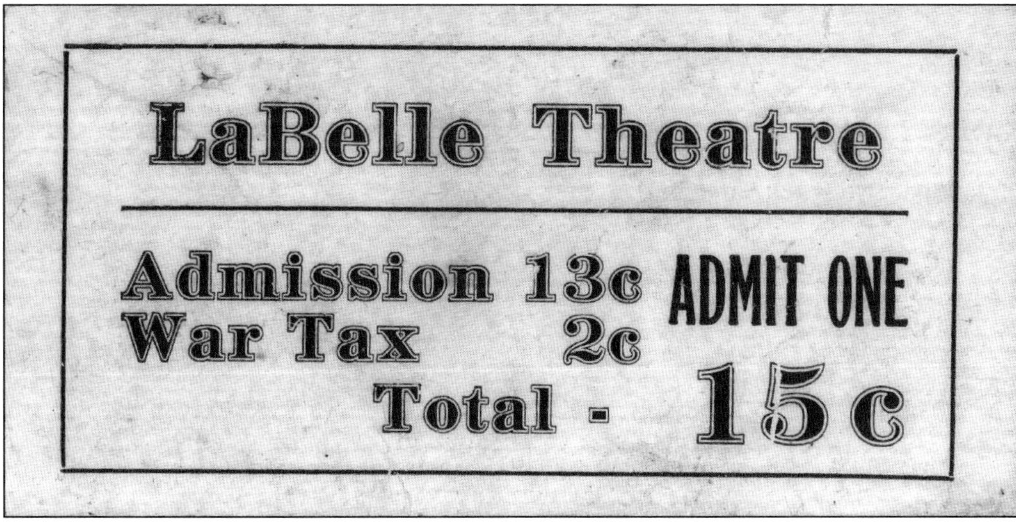

Carl Dolan donated this ticket from the 1930s to the museum; the theater opened in 1938, and the price for entrance was 15¢ with 2¢ going for war tax. (Courtesy Carl Dolan.)

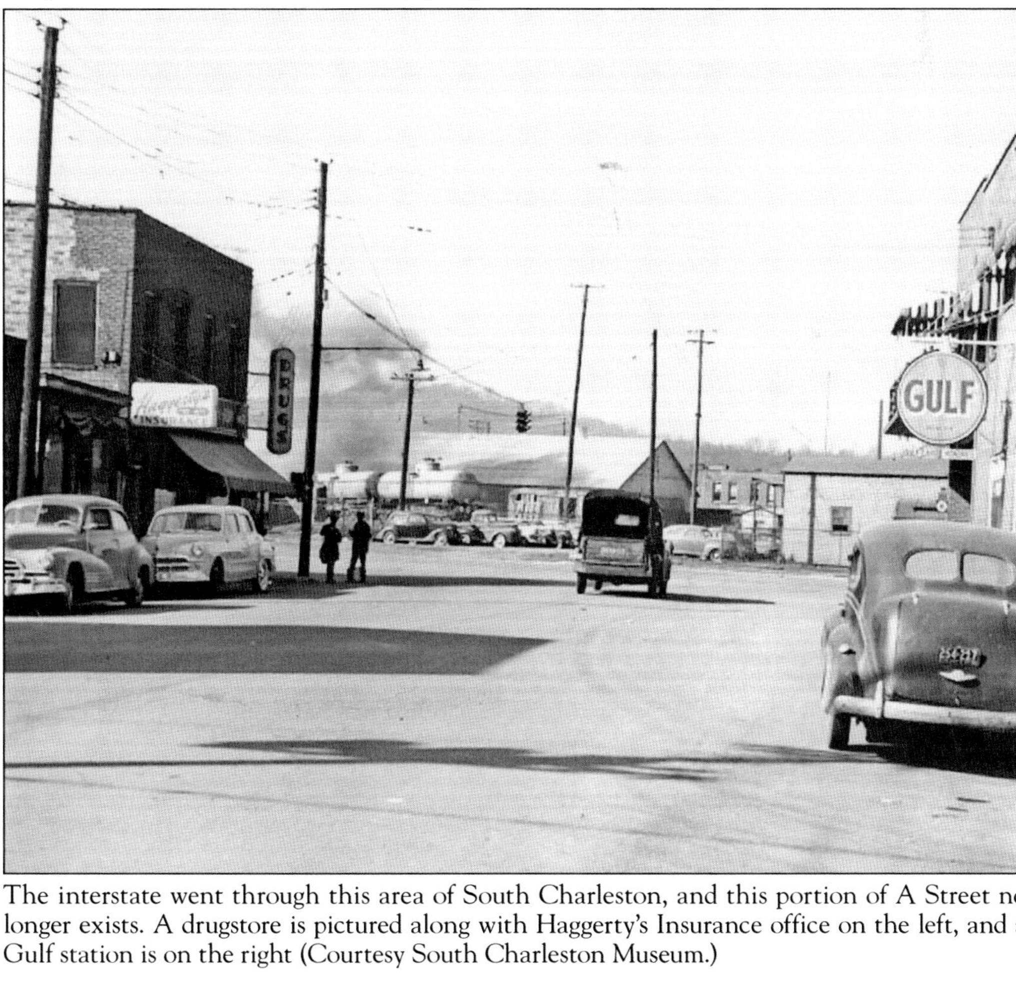

The interstate went through this area of South Charleston, and this portion of A Street no longer exists. A drugstore is pictured along with Haggerty's Insurance office on the left, and a Gulf station is on the right (Courtesy South Charleston Museum.)

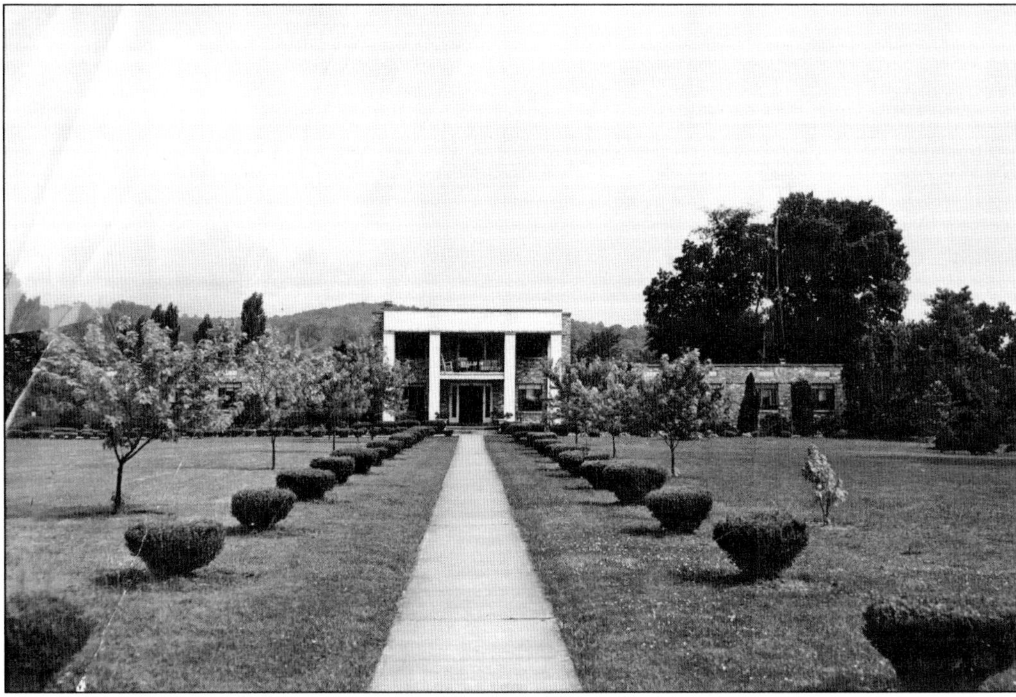

In the 1940s, the Dunn Hospital was on MacCorkle Avenue; today the La-Z-Boy Furniture Store and the Greater Charleston Dialysis Center are located on this property. (Courtesy South Charleston Museum.)

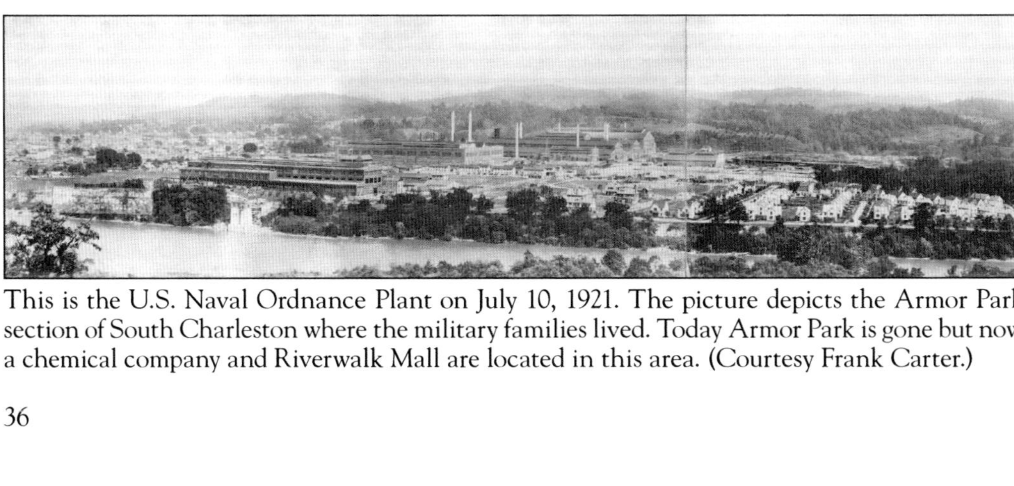

This is the U.S. Naval Ordnance Plant on July 10, 1921. The picture depicts the Armor Park section of South Charleston where the military families lived. Today Armor Park is gone but now a chemical company and Riverwalk Mall are located in this area. (Courtesy Frank Carter.)

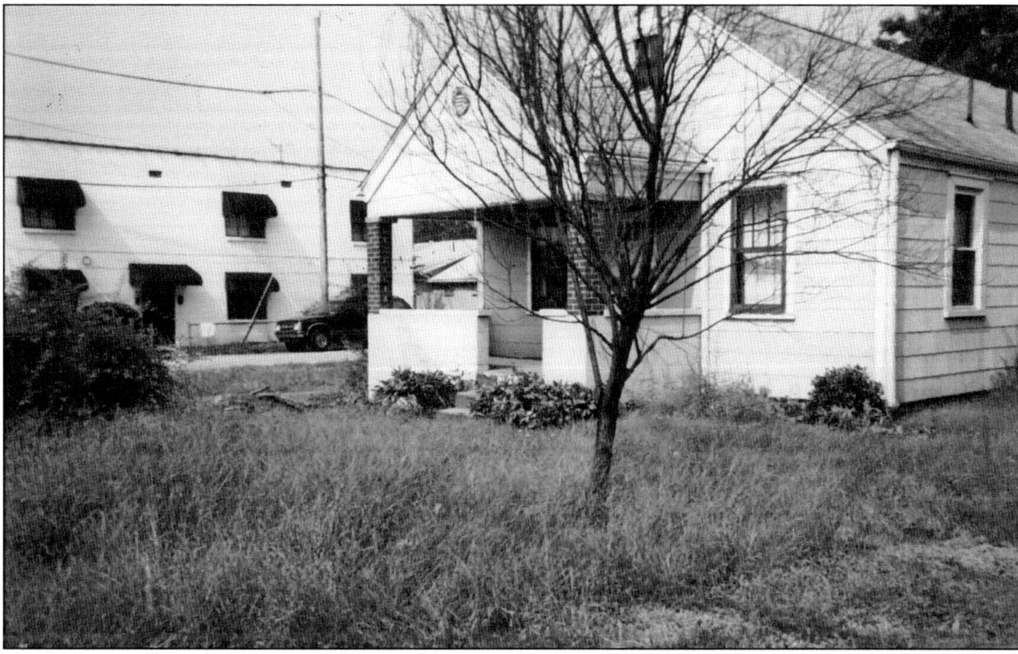

Addie Fleck's home, the old YMCA building, and the Archery building were all demolished to make way for a doctor's office. (Courtesy Judy Romano.)

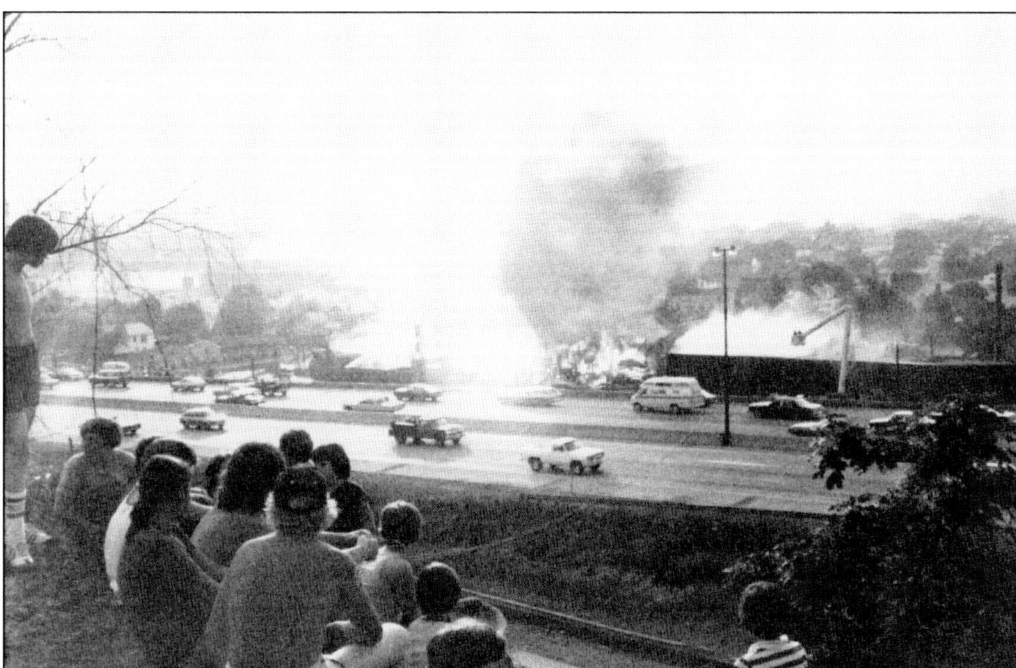

Evans Warehouse on First Avenue caught on fire in May 1977. Interstate 64 is in the foreground, and the Naval Ordnance Center is in the background. People are watching the fire from the hillside above I-64 and the Kanawha Turnpike. (Courtesy South Charleston Museum.)

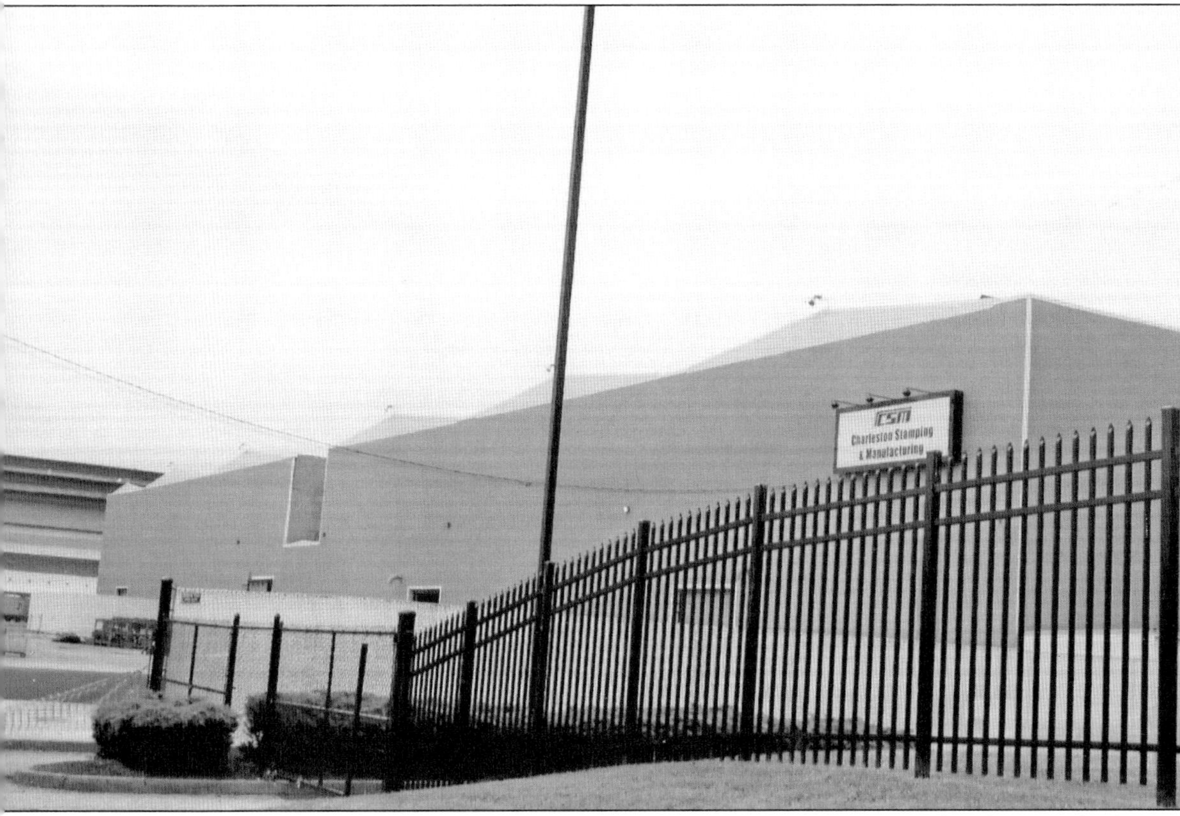

Ray Park, owner of the Park Corporation, bought the Naval Ordnance complex that was built during World War I from FMC Ordnance in 1970. (Courtesy Dan Blue.)

The 1,200-passenger *West Virginia Belle* was docked in South Charleston in the late 1980s and early 1990s. The *Belle* was sold and turned into a floating casino. (Courtesy South Charleston Museum.)

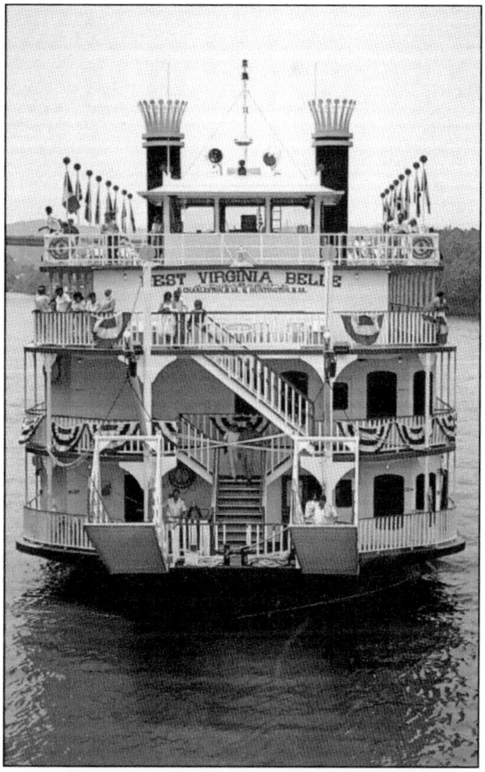

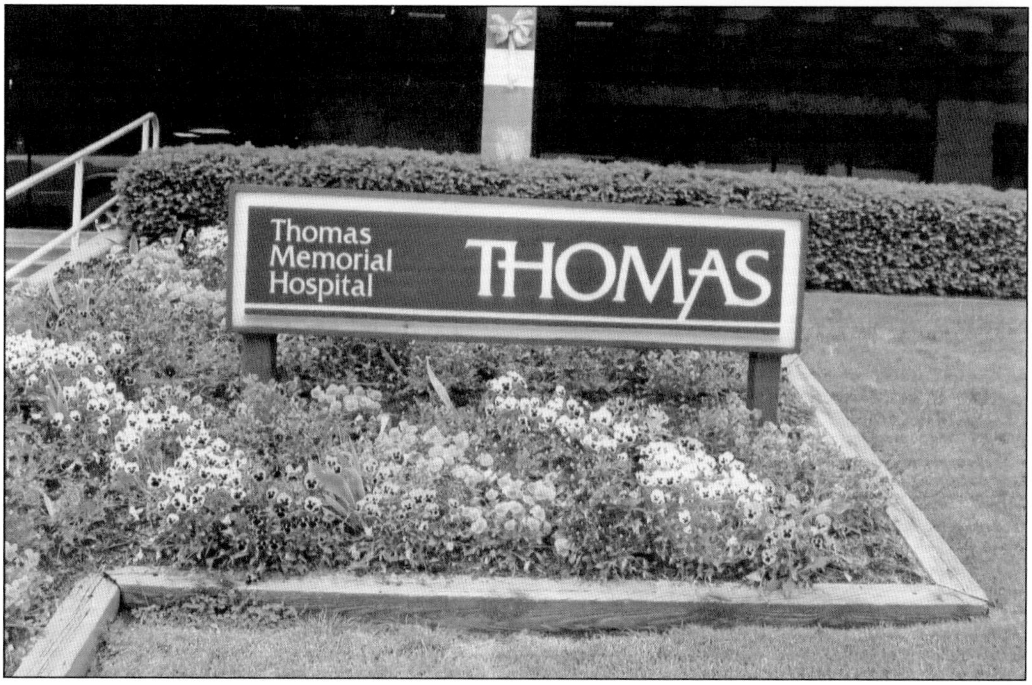

The hospital was originally named the Herbert J. Thomas Memorial Hospital in the 1940s. Herbert J. Thomas gave his life to save his platoon in World War II, and earned a Medal of Honor for his deeds. (Courtesy South Charleston Museum.)

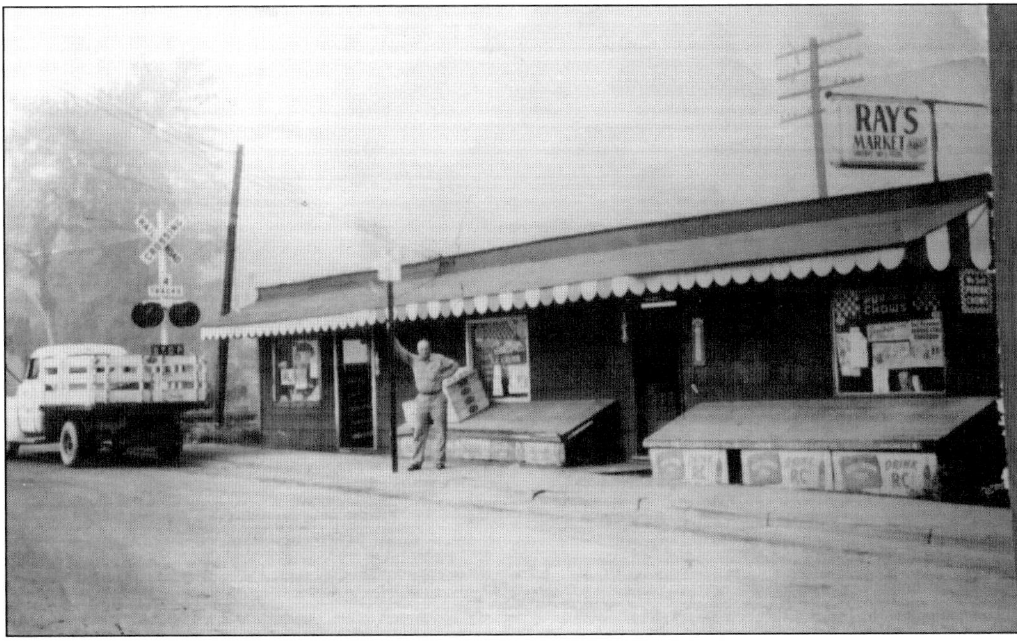

Ray's Market was a grocery store located in the Spring Hill area of South Charleston from 1950 to 1966. (Courtesy Lucky Ray.)

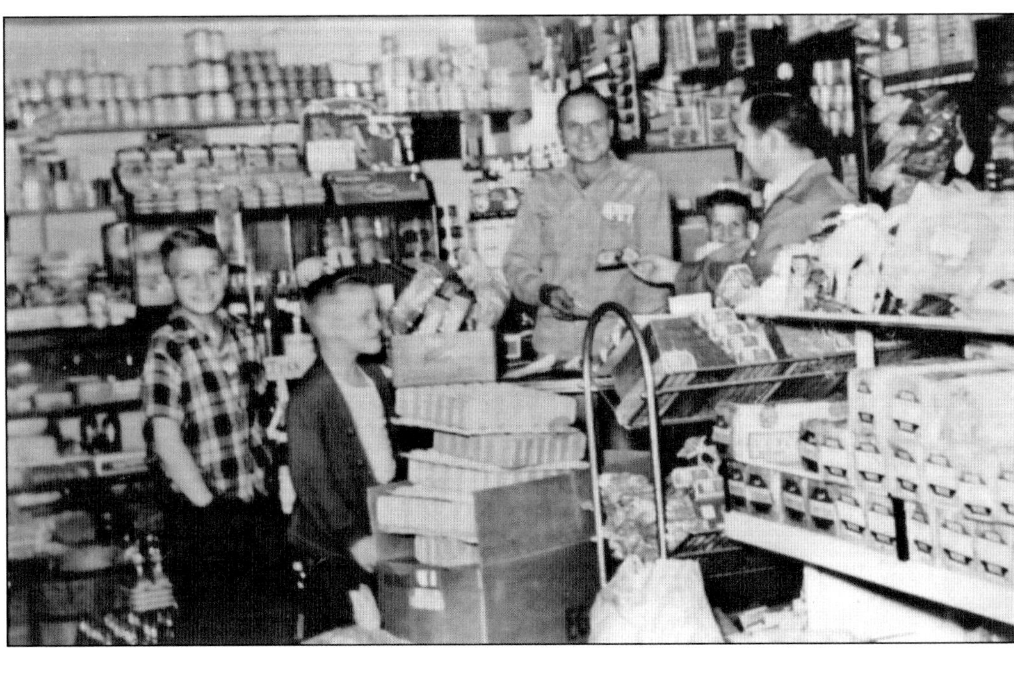

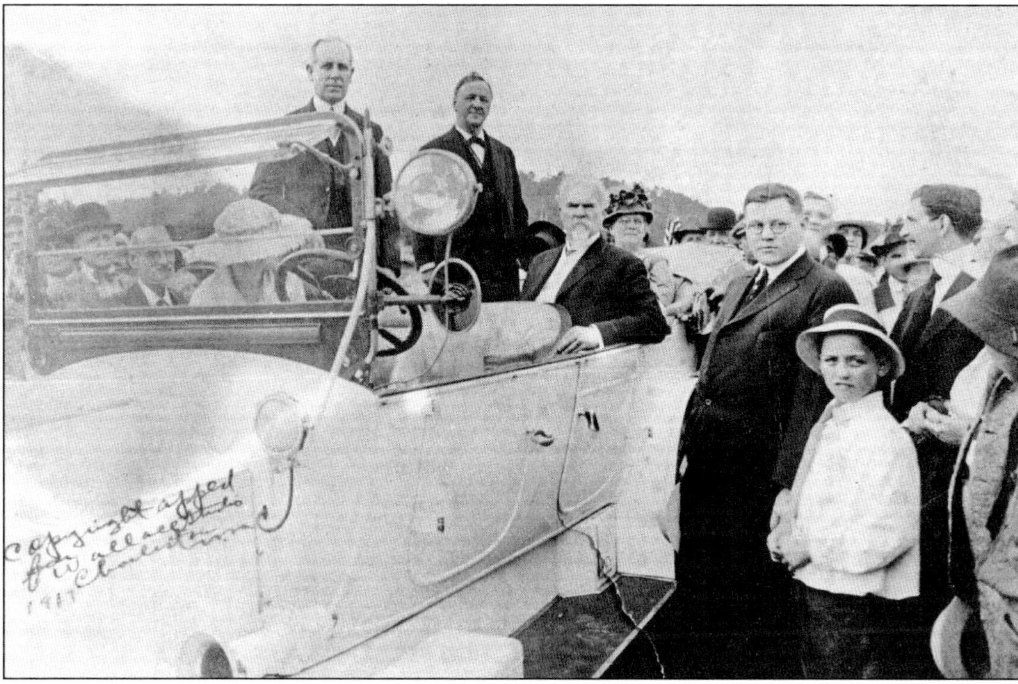

Several dignitaries visited the Naval Ordnance Center in 1917. This picture shows Gov. William A. MacCorkle in his automobile with other unidentified people at the opening of the Ordnance facility. (Courtesy South Charleston Museum.)

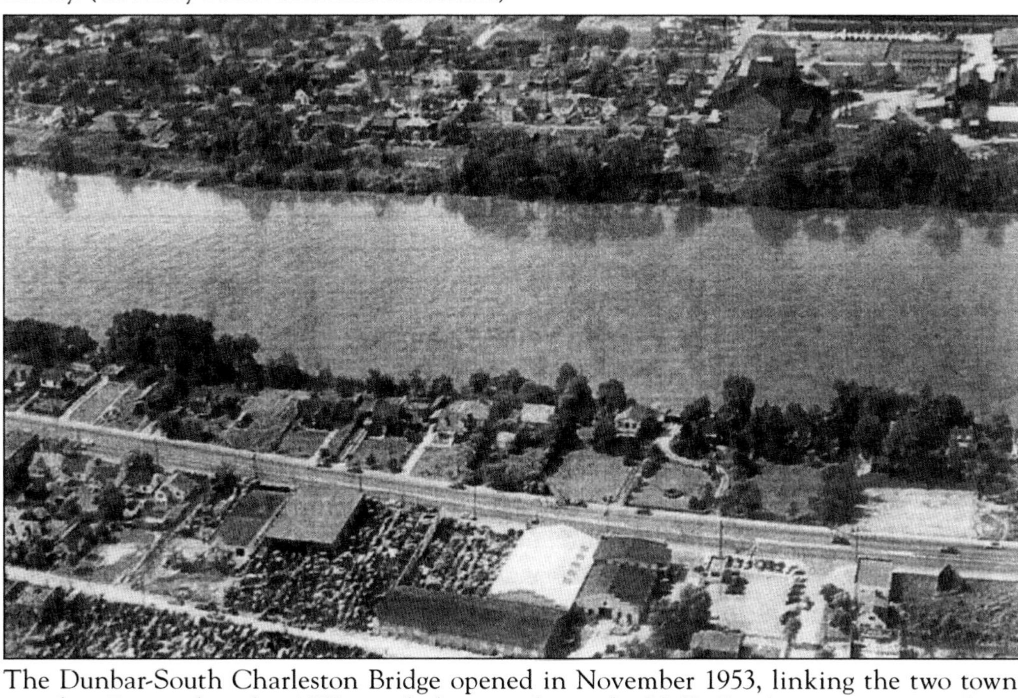

The Dunbar-South Charleston Bridge opened in November 1953, linking the two towns together. Pictured in this 1952 aerial photograph are the H. D. Sparks automotive junkyard and the Fletcher Enamel Company of Dunbar, which made kitchen utensils. (Courtesy South Charleston Museum.)

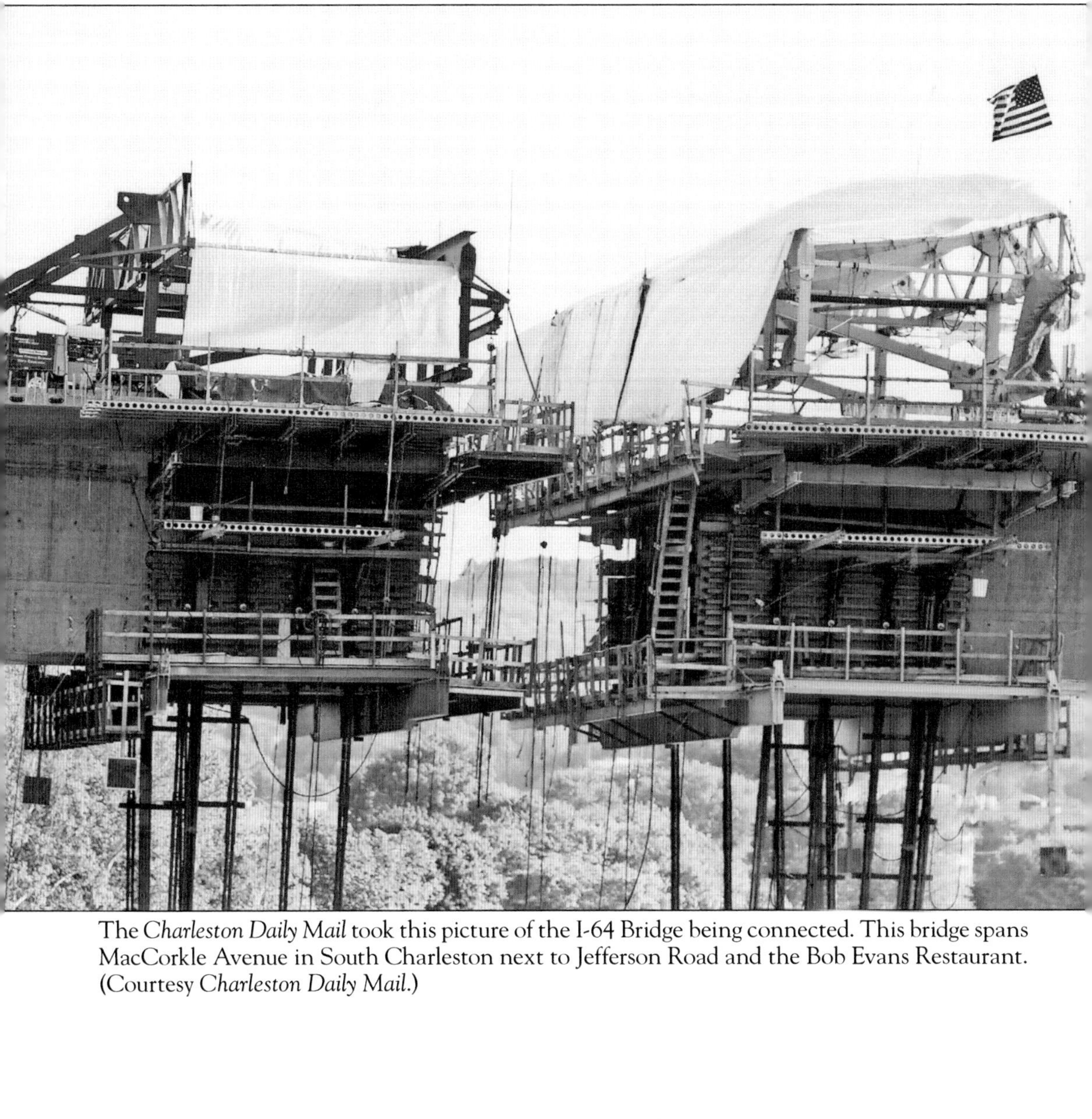

The *Charleston Daily Mail* took this picture of the I-64 Bridge being connected. This bridge spans MacCorkle Avenue in South Charleston next to Jefferson Road and the Bob Evans Restaurant. (Courtesy *Charleston Daily Mail.*)

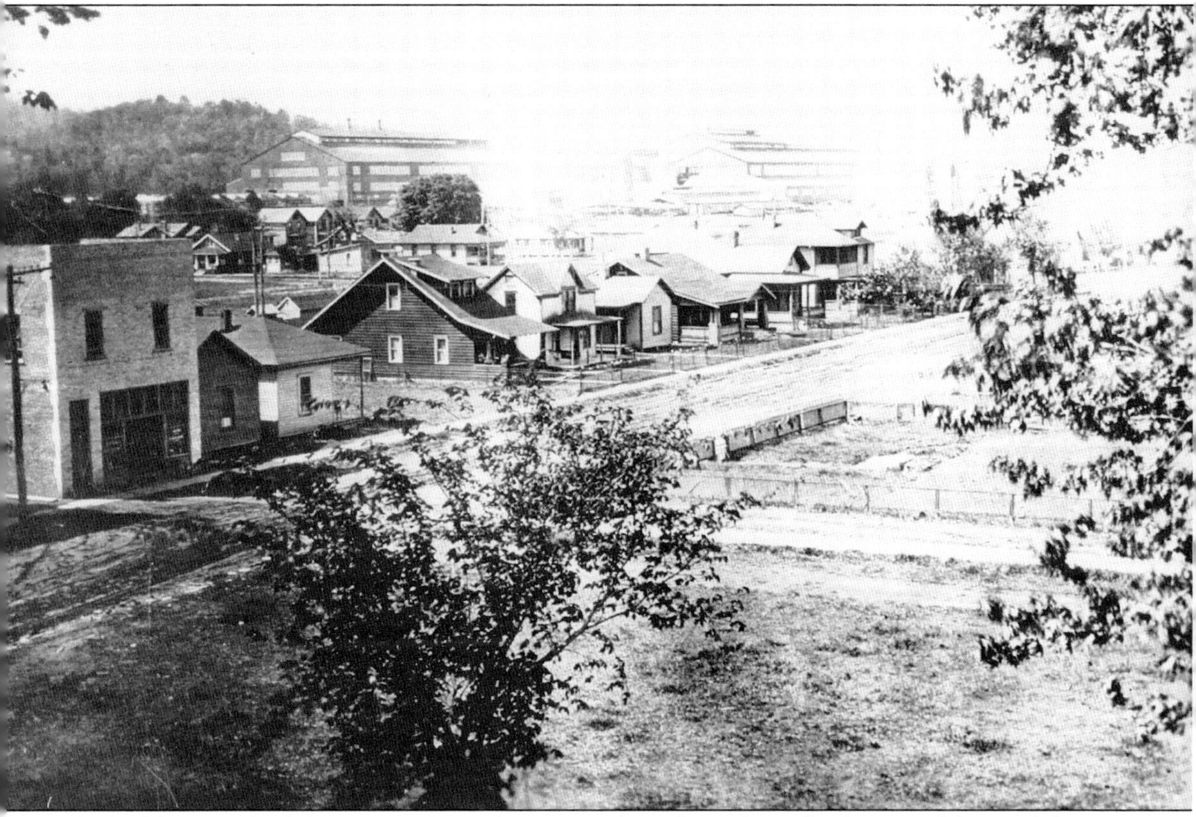

The building on the left is Vogue Dry Cleaners, and on the right is the front yard fence of the Salamie residence. There are no homes left on this 200 block of Seventh Avenue, only businesses. (Courtesy Salamie family.)

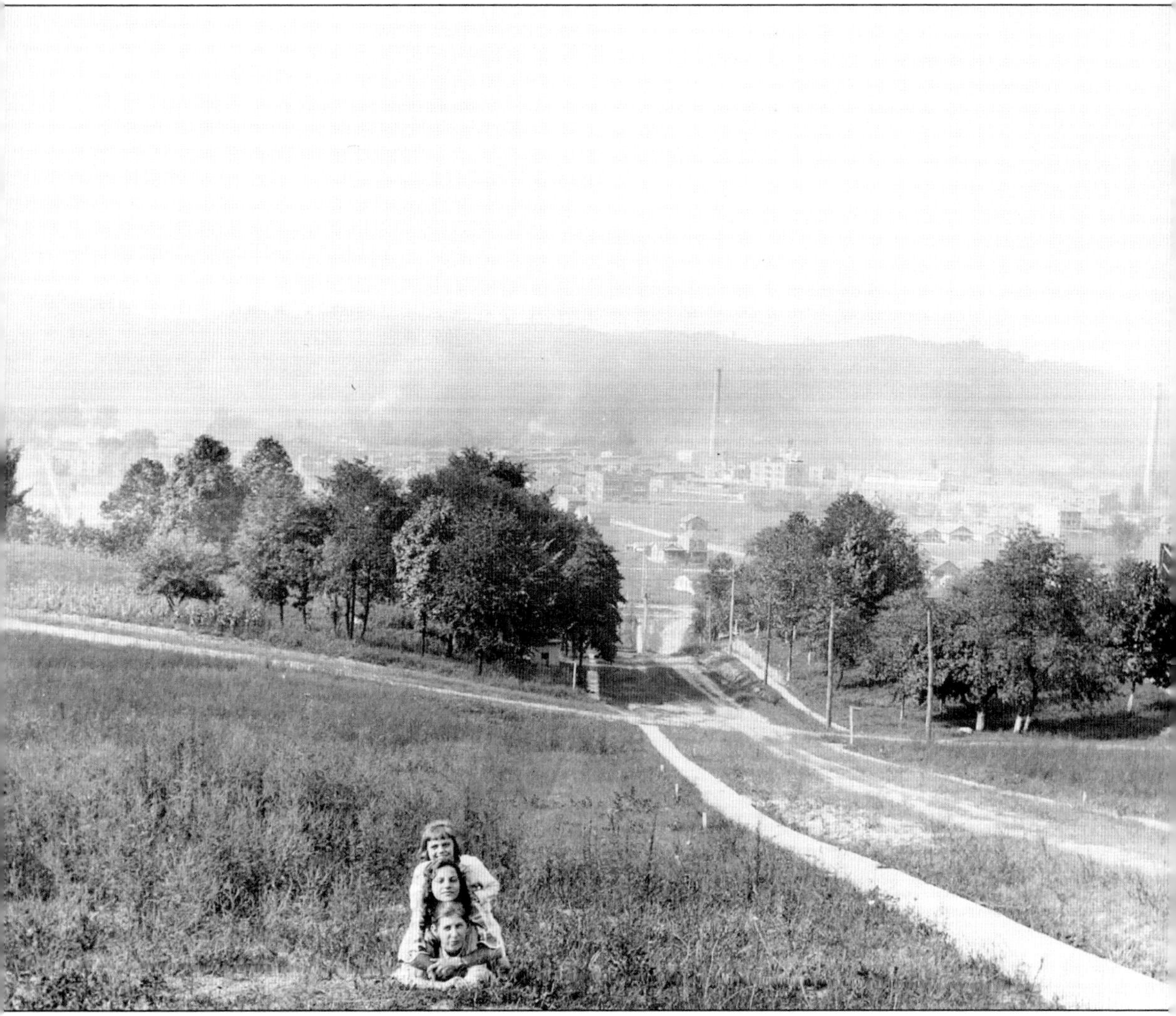

These three children posed on the Montrose Drive hillside before homes were built there. Today homes are on both sides of the road. (Courtesy Diana Salamie.)

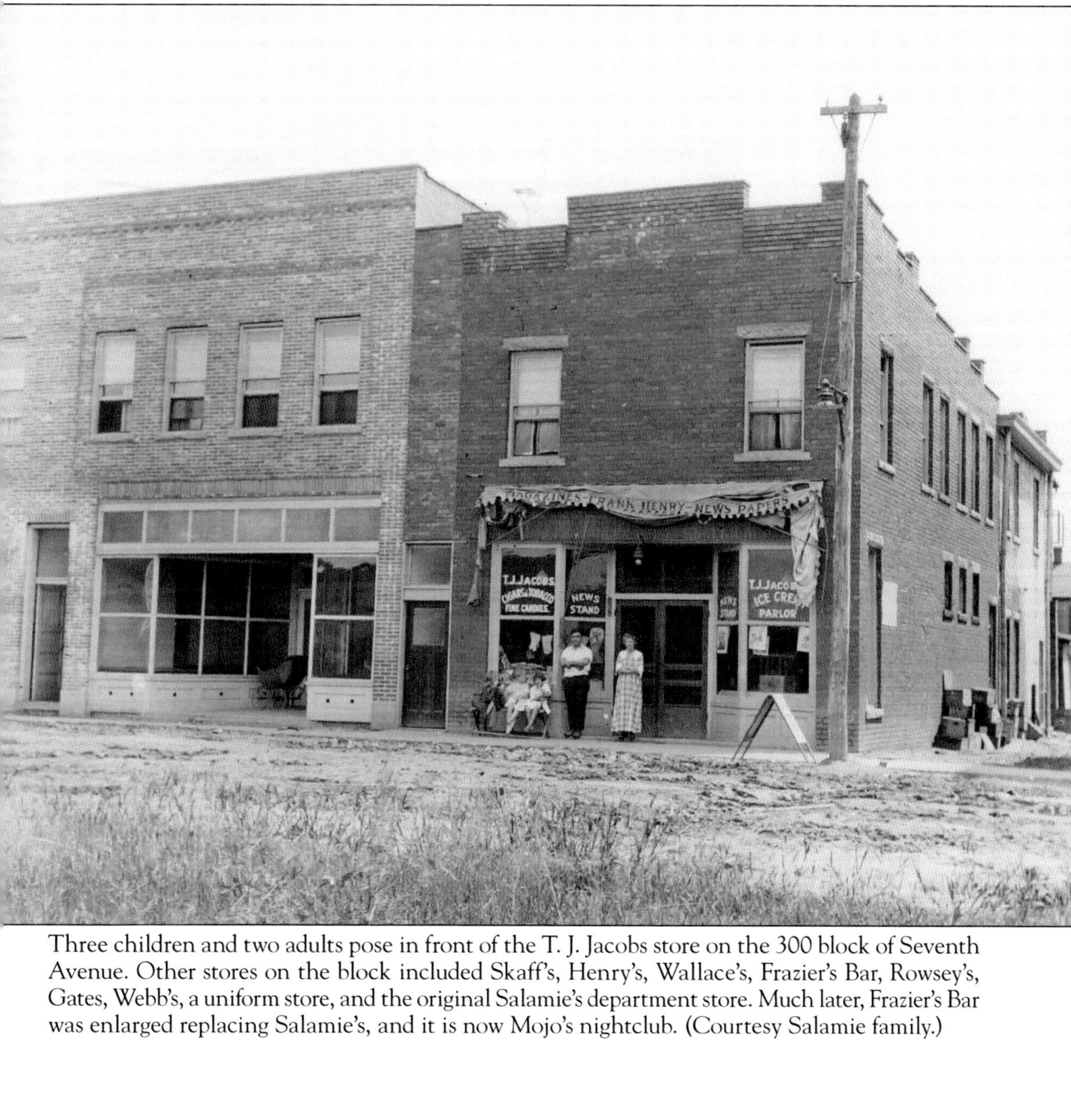

Three children and two adults pose in front of the T. J. Jacobs store on the 300 block of Seventh Avenue. Other stores on the block included Skaff's, Henry's, Wallace's, Frazier's Bar, Rowsey's, Gates, Webb's, a uniform store, and the original Salamie's department store. Much later, Frazier's Bar was enlarged replacing Salamie's, and it is now Mojo's nightclub. (Courtesy Salamie family.)

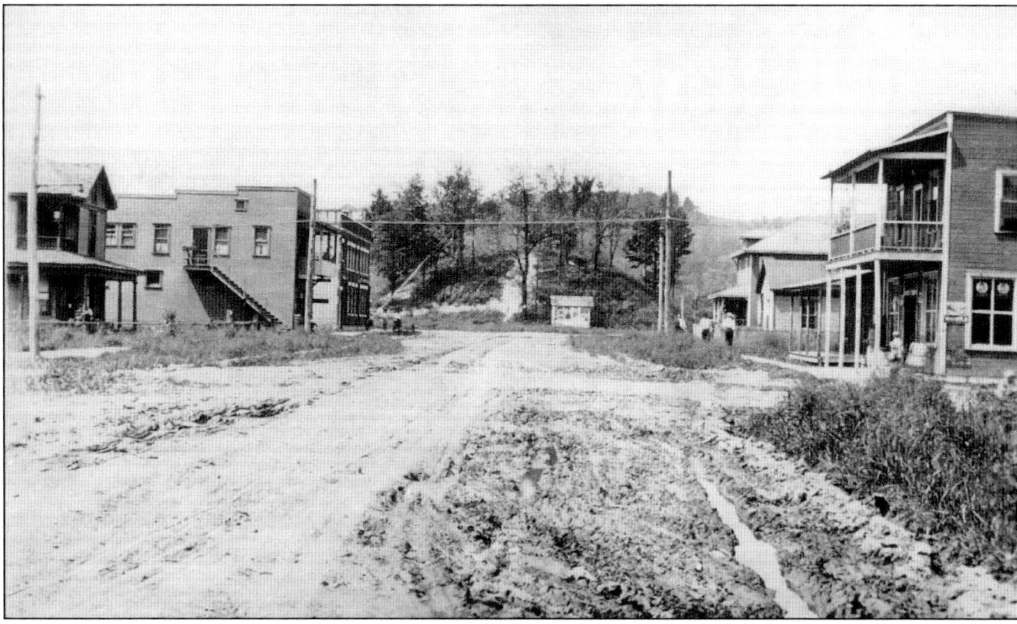

Today the blocks of 500 and 600 D Street are paved with businesses on both sides of the street. This area had the new home of Salamie's, a small mall, and G. C. Murphy's store. Today these buildings are replaced by Happy Day's Café and the former Beau Tea Full Moments Tea Room, Family Dollar, and Komax. The Salamie family changed the look of South Charleston by constructing many modern buildings on Third, Fourth, Fifth, Sixth, and Seventh Avenues and on D and E Streets. (Courtesy Diana Salamie.)

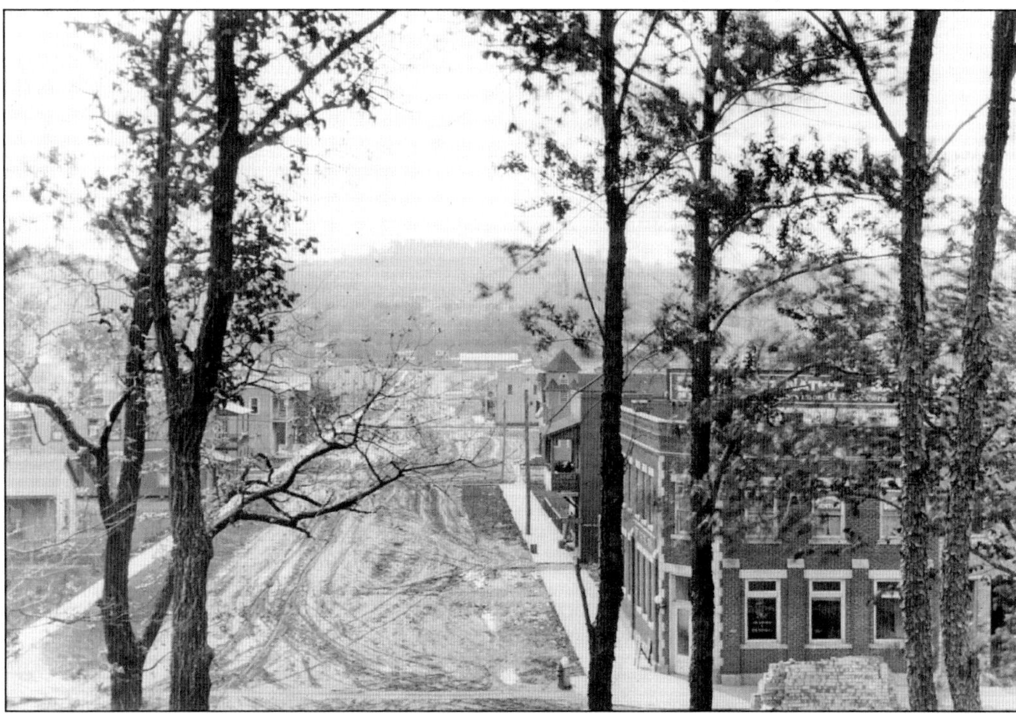

The First National Bank of South Charleston can be seen in this picture, taken from the top of the Criel Mound looking south down D Street. (Courtesy Salamie family.)

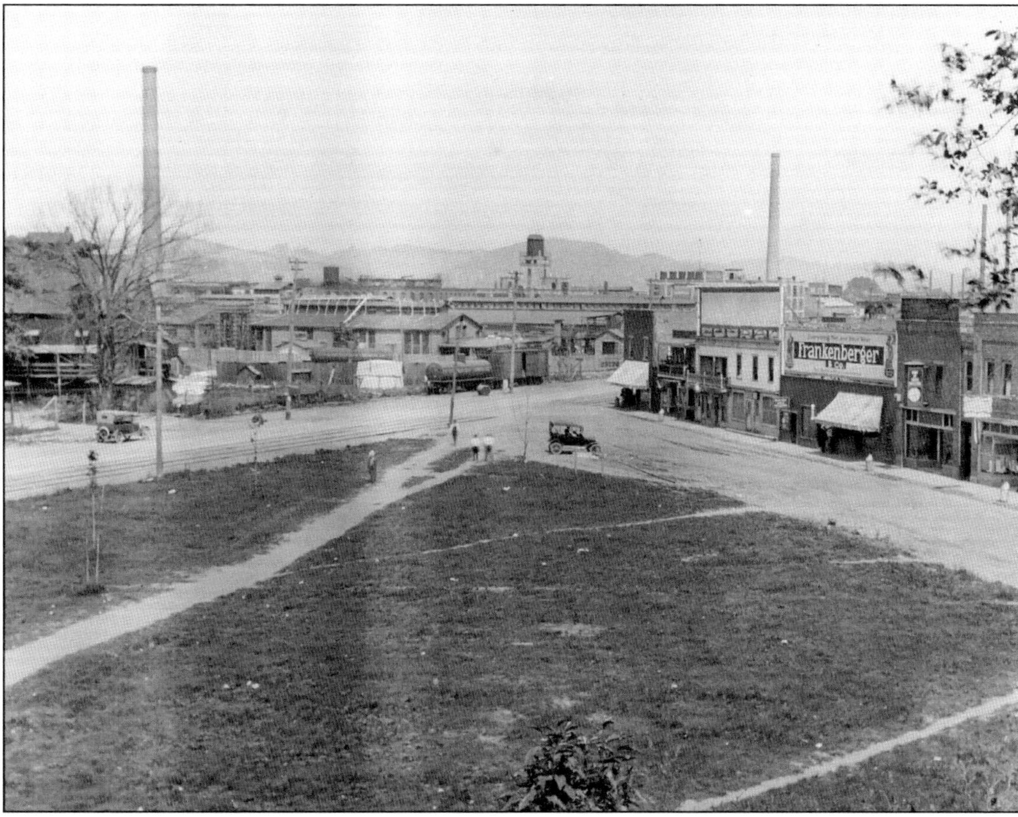

Banner Plate Glass Window Factory can be seen on the left side of this picture, and George Salamie stands in front of the building to the far right. (Courtesy Salamie family.)

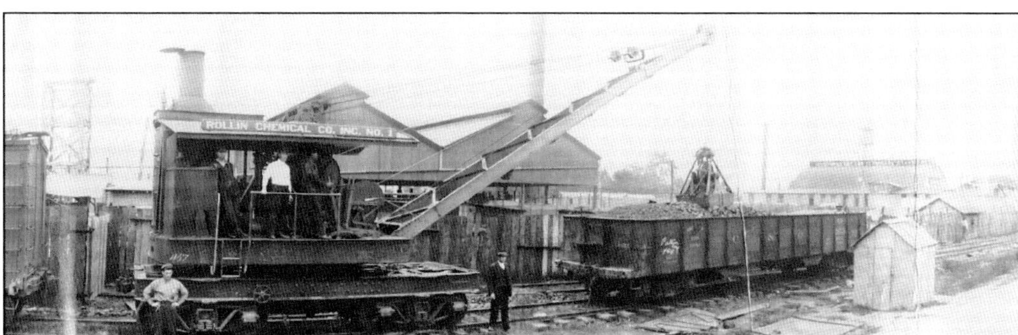

World War I brought many chemical plants to the South Charleston area, the first being Rollins Chemical Company and then Warner Klipstein built the first unit of a plant to produce chlorine. The government built the Naval Ordnance plant in South Charleston in 1917, and it was followed by Carbide, Westvaco (then FMC), Barium, and others. Dunkirk Glass Company can be seen in the background. (Courtesy South Charleston Museum.)

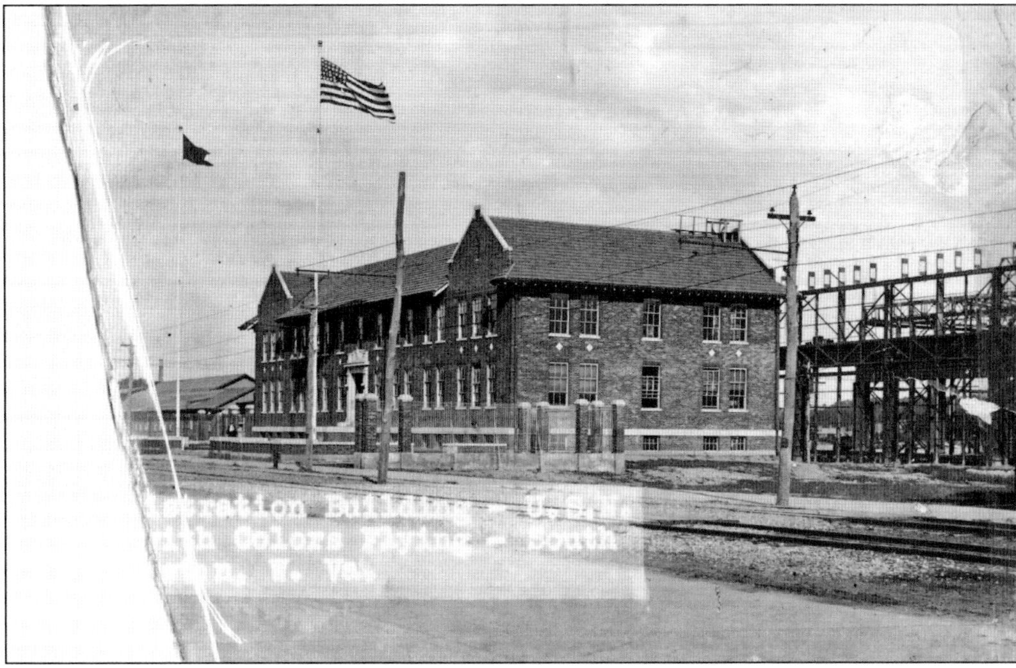

The Naval Ordnance Center was built in 1917, but did not begin production until after World War I ended. The plant was put into action but closed as a government operation in 1922, when it was leased to the Carnegie Illinois Steel Company. In 1940, the plant again went into government hands, producing armor plate, gun barrels, air-to-ground rockets, and torpedo flasks, and boasted the largest machine shop in the world. FMC Ordnance bought the facility in 1962 and made tracked vehicles for the government. In 1970, Ray Park bought the facility. (Courtesy South Charleston Museum.)

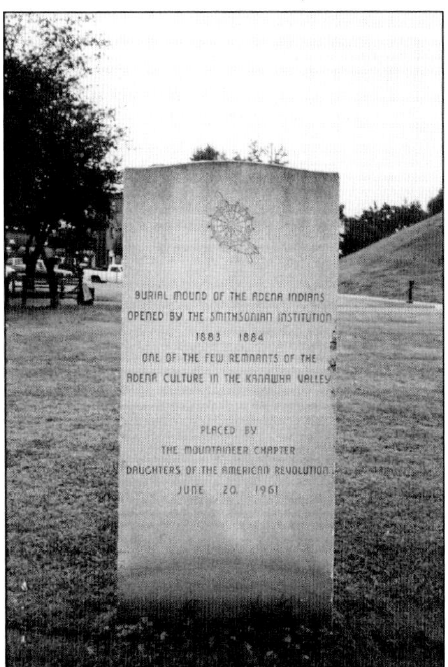

This stone marker is located at the Criel Mound in South Charleston. The Mountaineer Chapter of the Daughters of the American Revolution placed this marker at the mound on June 20, 1961. (Courtesy South Charleston Museum.)

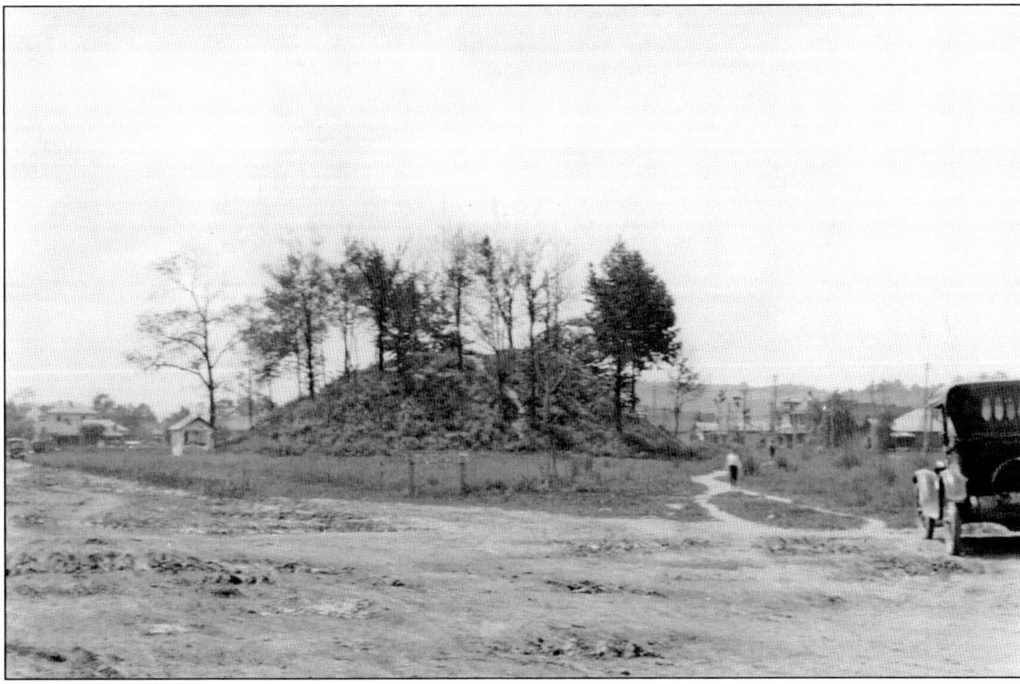

The South Charleston Mound, or Criel Mound, shown here *c.* 1920, is the second largest mound in West Virginia and is located in South Charleston. The Smithsonian Institution excavated the mound in 1883–1884. (Courtesy South Charleston Museum.)

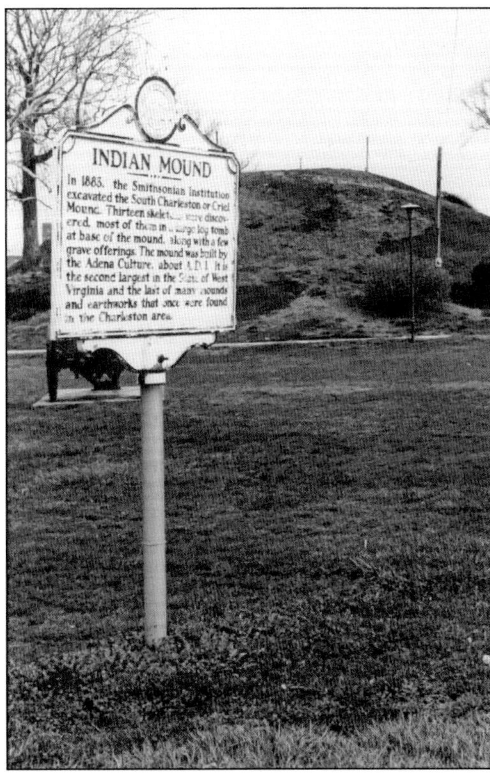

This is a historic marker placed at the Criel Mound by the state of West Virginia. The marker faces MacCorkle Avenue and describes how the mound was built and excavated. (Courtesy South Charleston Museum.)

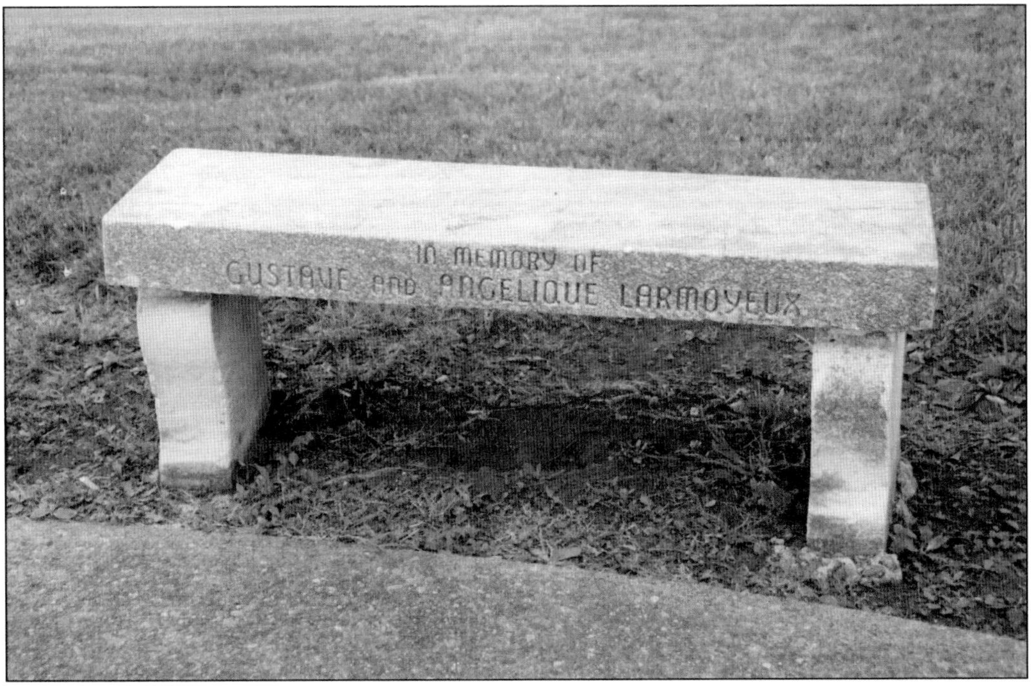

In honor of their parents, the Larmoyeaux family donated this bench. They were early inhabitants of South Charleston. (Courtesy South Charleston Museum.)

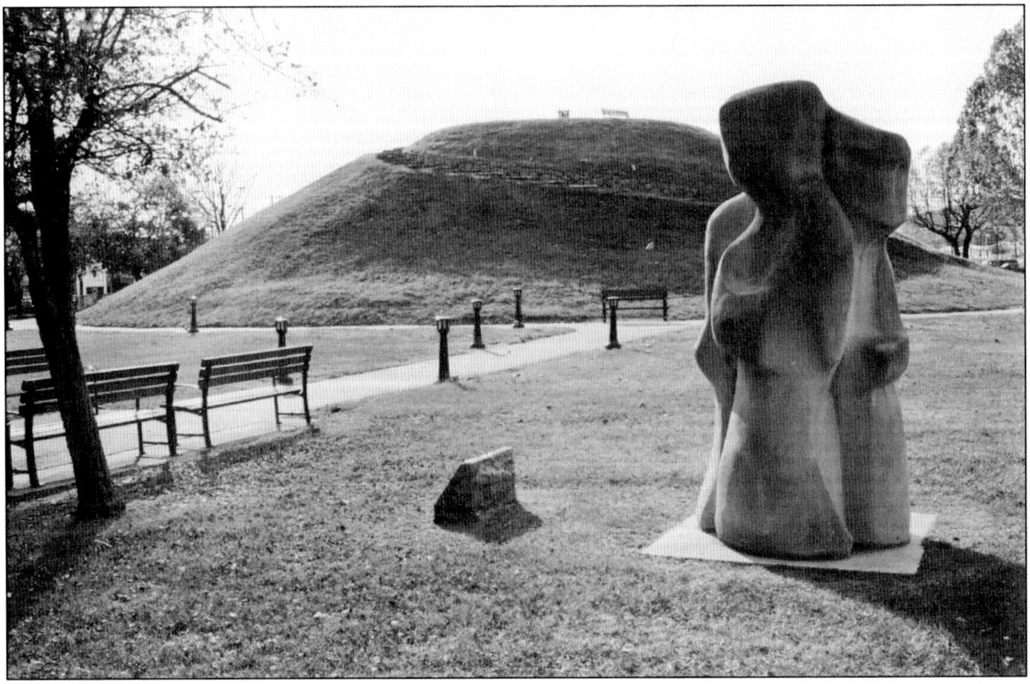

The South Charleston Mound, or Criel Mound, is one of 50 conical mounds of the Adena culture that once existed in the area. This picture shows the sculpture *The Keeper of the Mound*. (Courtesy South Charleston Museum.)

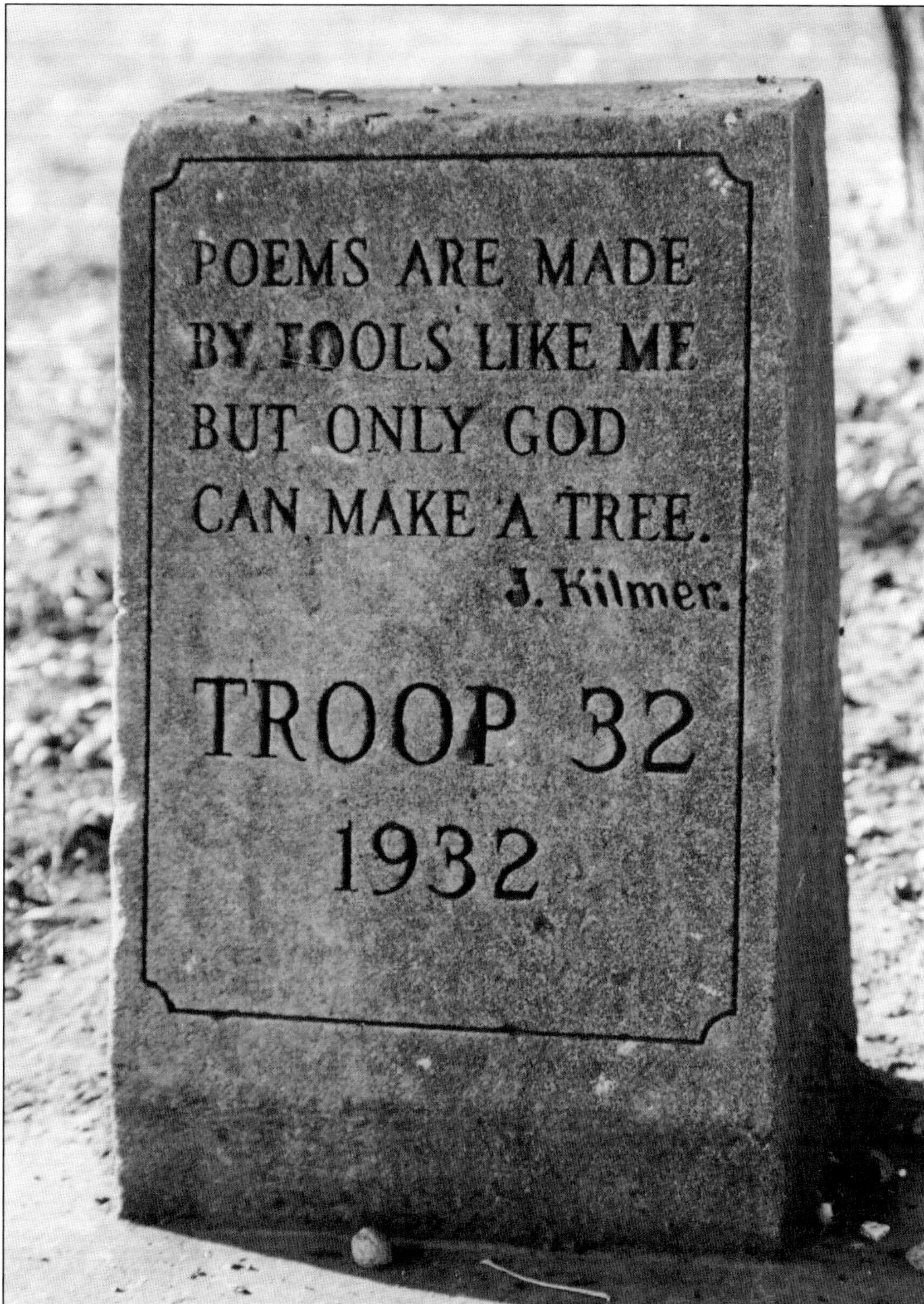

A marker placed by Boy Scout Troop 32 in 1932 reads, "Poems are made by fools like me but only God can make a tree." It is possible the Boy Scouts also planted a tree, but no documentation has been found to support this. (Courtesy South Charleston Museum.)

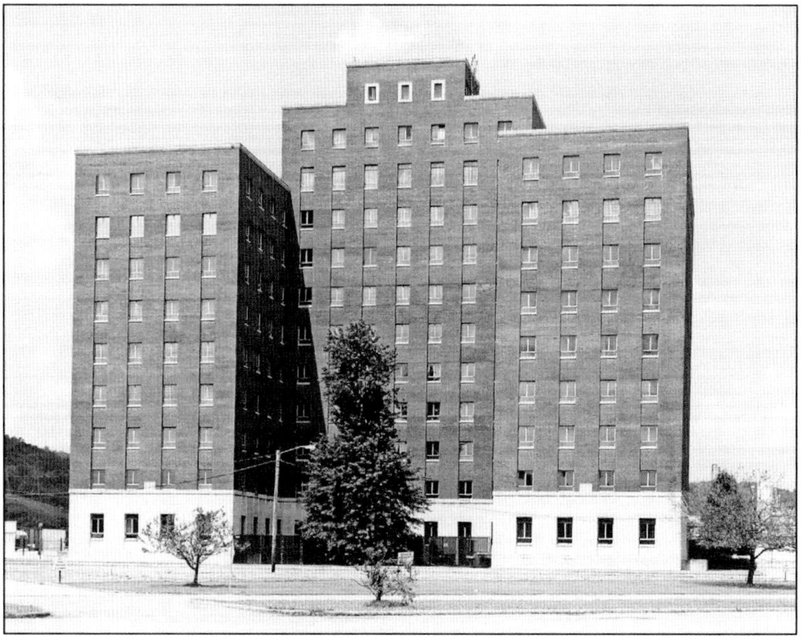

The Dow Chemical Building 82 was donated to the University of Charleston. Chances were sold to push the button that imploded the building on March 28, 2009. (Courtesy Linda Weekly.)

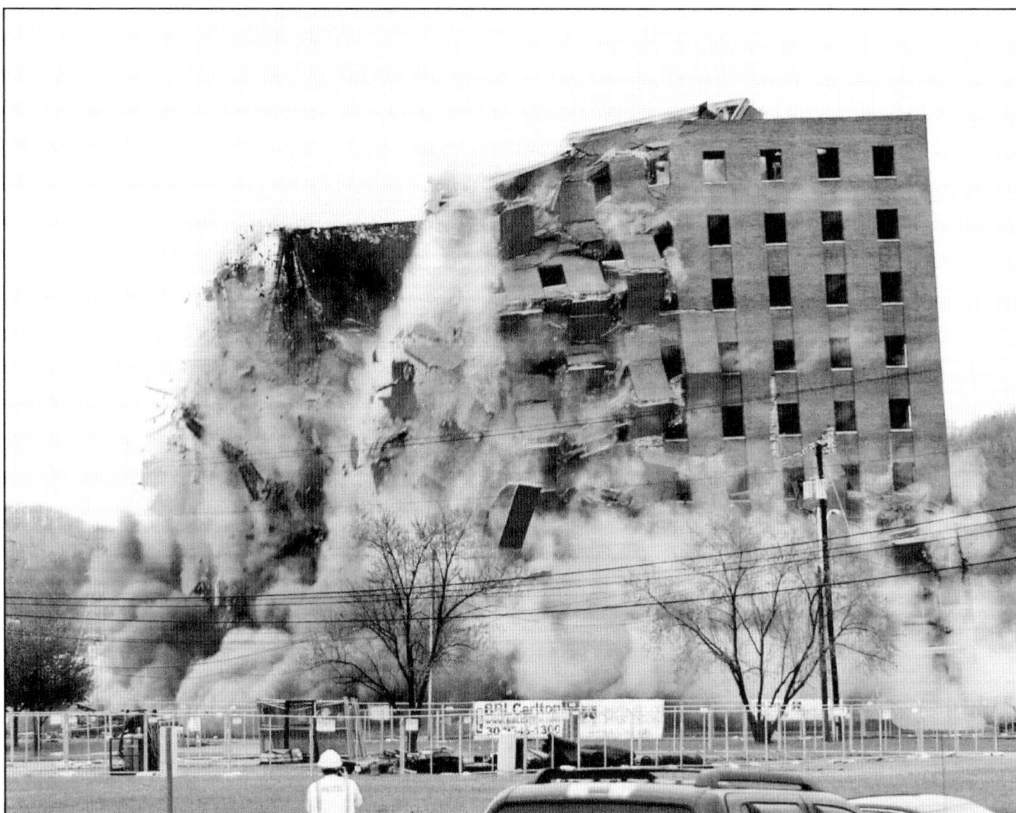

On March 28, 2009, the Dow Chemical Building 82 structure was imploded. Many residents lined the streets and watched the implosion. (Courtesy Linda Weekly.)

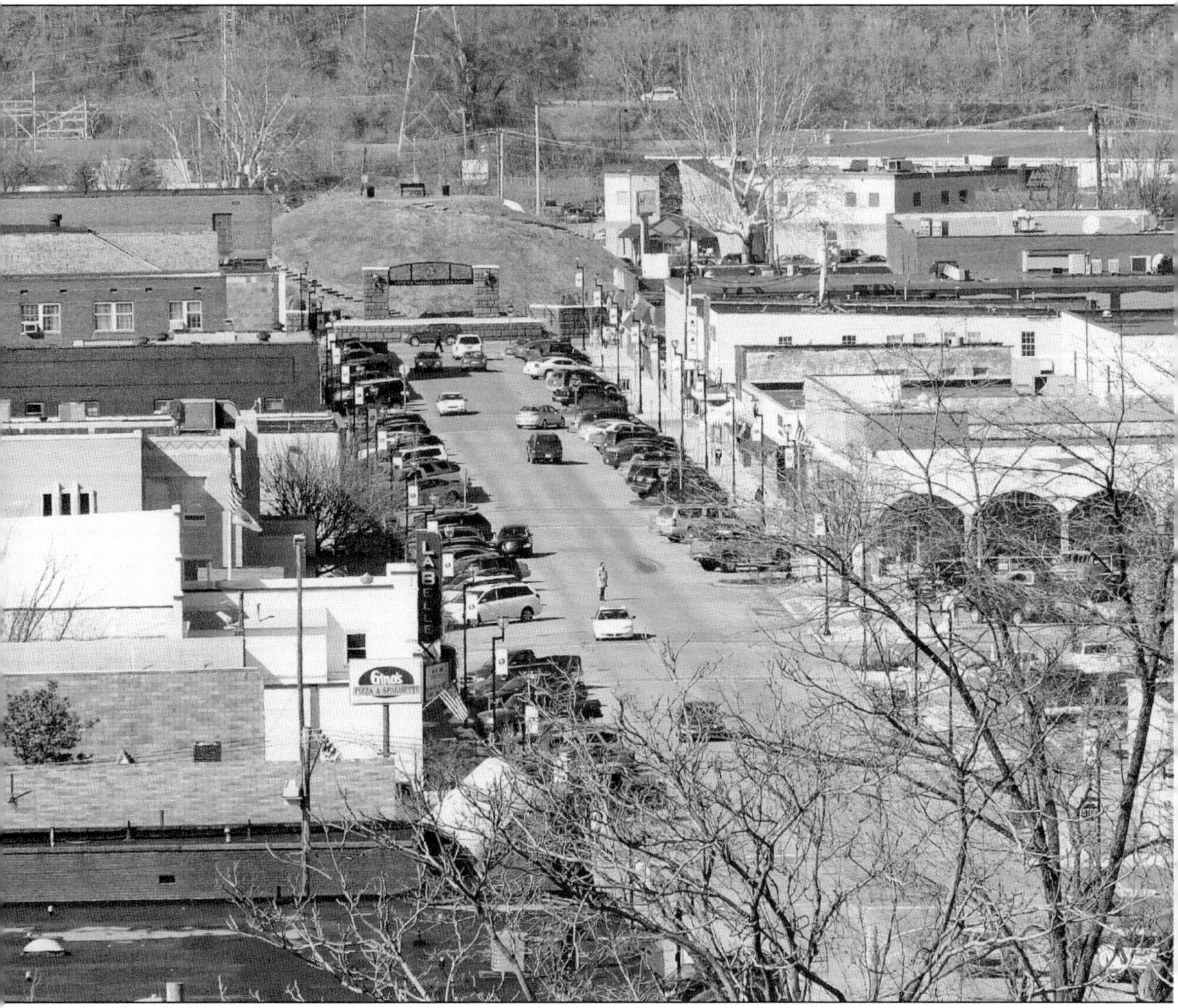

D Street in South Charleston is home to city hall, numerous shops, restaurants, a theater, and several businesses. (Courtesy South Charleston Museum.)

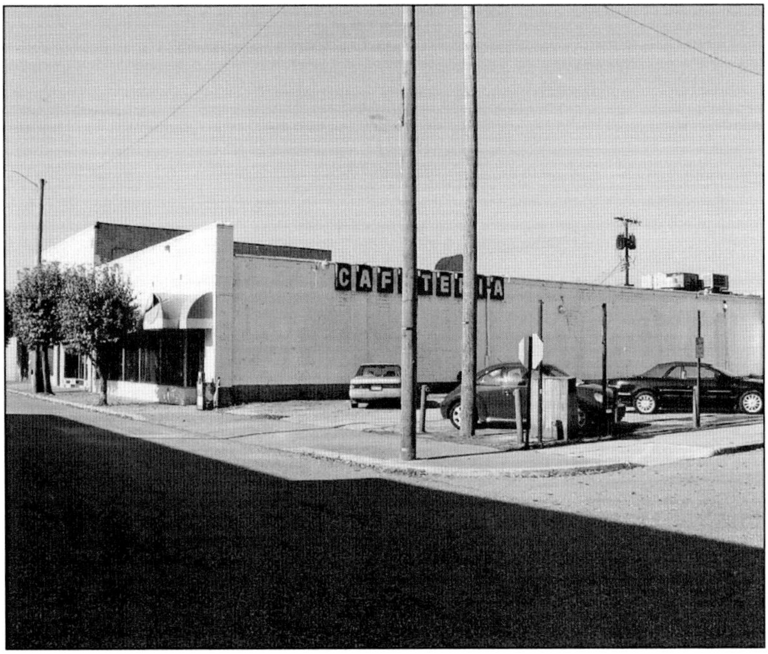

Seventh Avenue in South Charleston was an area where the Belgians lived in the early 1900s. The Salamie family lived on this particular corner in the 1920s. The property was later occupied by a health studio and then the Rose City Cafeteria. (Courtesy Linda Weekly.)

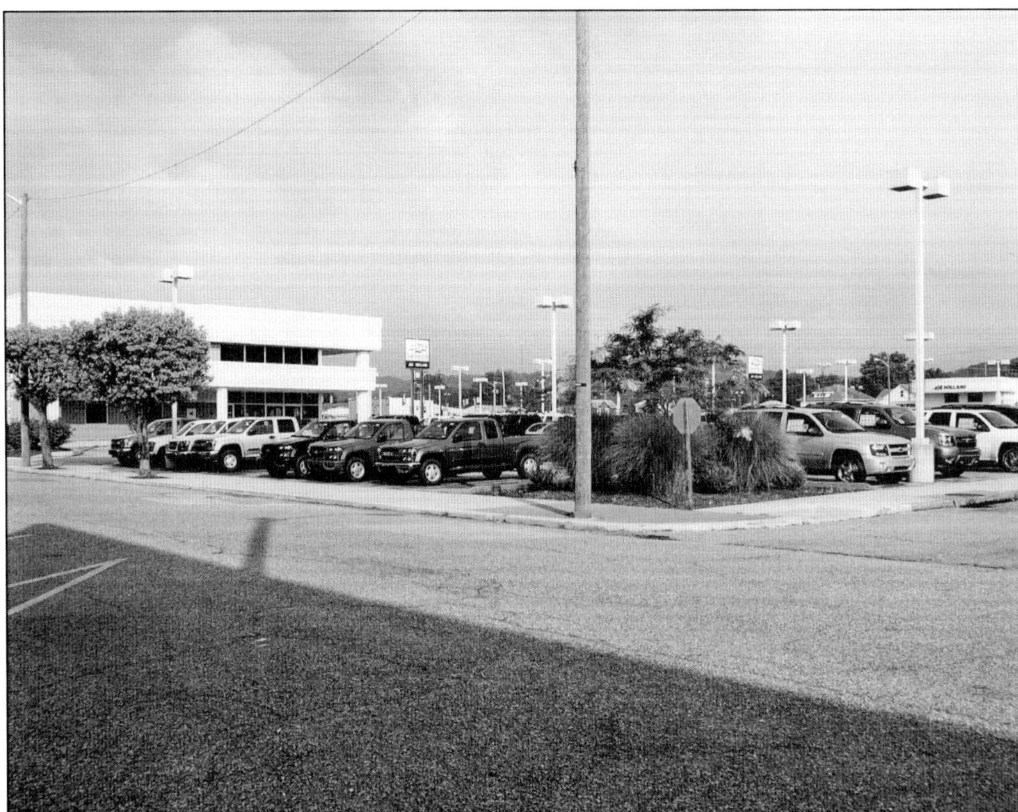

Joe Holland Chevrolet is bordered by Seventh Avenue, Oakes Street, and MacCorkle Avenue. (Courtesy Linda Weekly.)

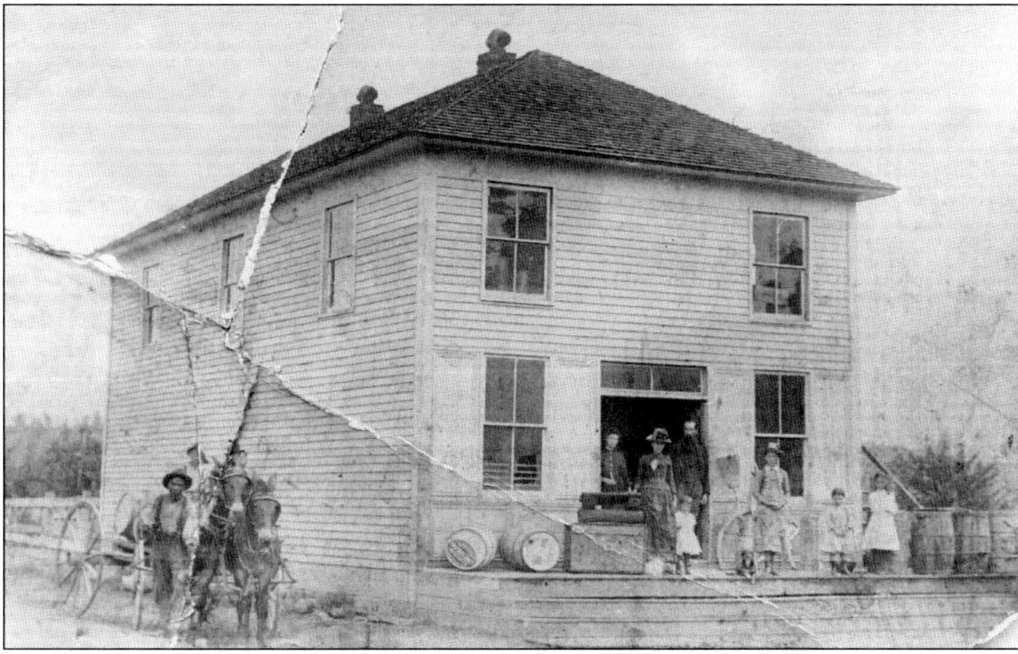

In 1883, A. W. Fox built this store building on the corner of Kanawha Turnpike and Chestnut Street in the Spring Hill section of South Charleston. This was his first store building and served as a general store and post office; an Odd Fellows Lodge occupied the second floor. The building burned in the late 1890s, and Fox constructed a second store from stone on the same site in 1899. (Courtesy Ray O. Pauley II, great-grandson of A. W. Fox.)

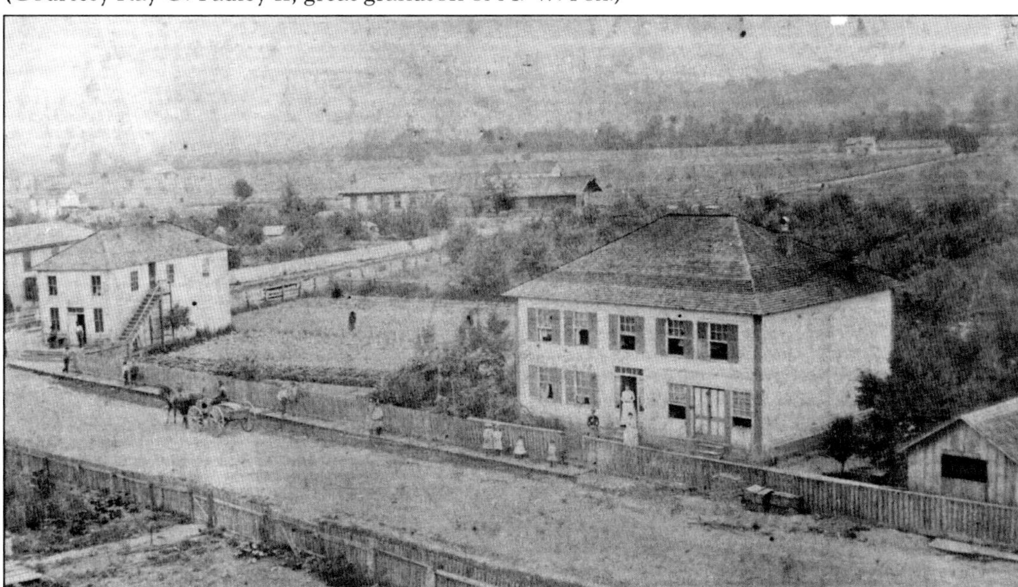

This photograph of the Spring Hill section of South Charleston was taken about 1892 and shows the James River and Kanawha Turnpike. A. W. Fox's general store and post office is located in the right corner, and in the center of the photograph is the Fox home. A large two-story frame building constructed in the 1880s, the home also served as a hotel for travelers on the turnpike. (Courtesy Ray O. Pauley II, great-grandson of A. W. Fox.)

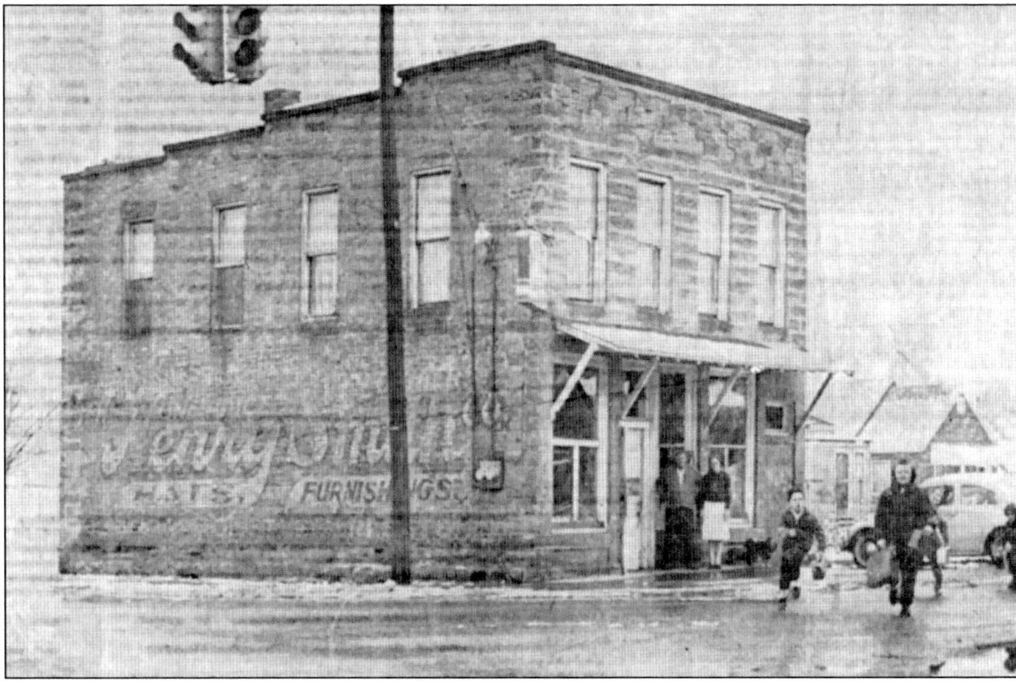

This old stone and brick building has stood at the corner of Chestnut Street and Kanawha Turnpike in the Spring Hill section of South Charleston since 1899. Bill and Antonette Newcomer bought it from the Fox family in 1914. (Courtesy *Charleston Daily Mail*; article by Richard Grimes.)

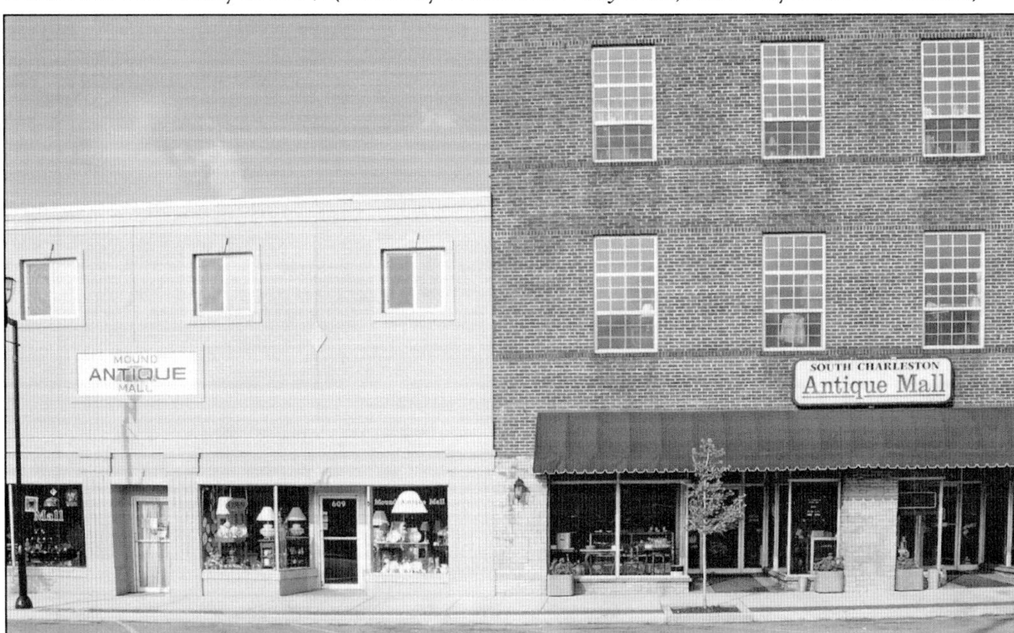

D Street today features two antique shops: the Mound Antique Mall and the South Charleston Antique Mall. These buildings were formerly Mullins Hardware, McClung and Morgan Furniture Store, and Williams Kiddies' Shop. (Courtesy Linda Weekly.)

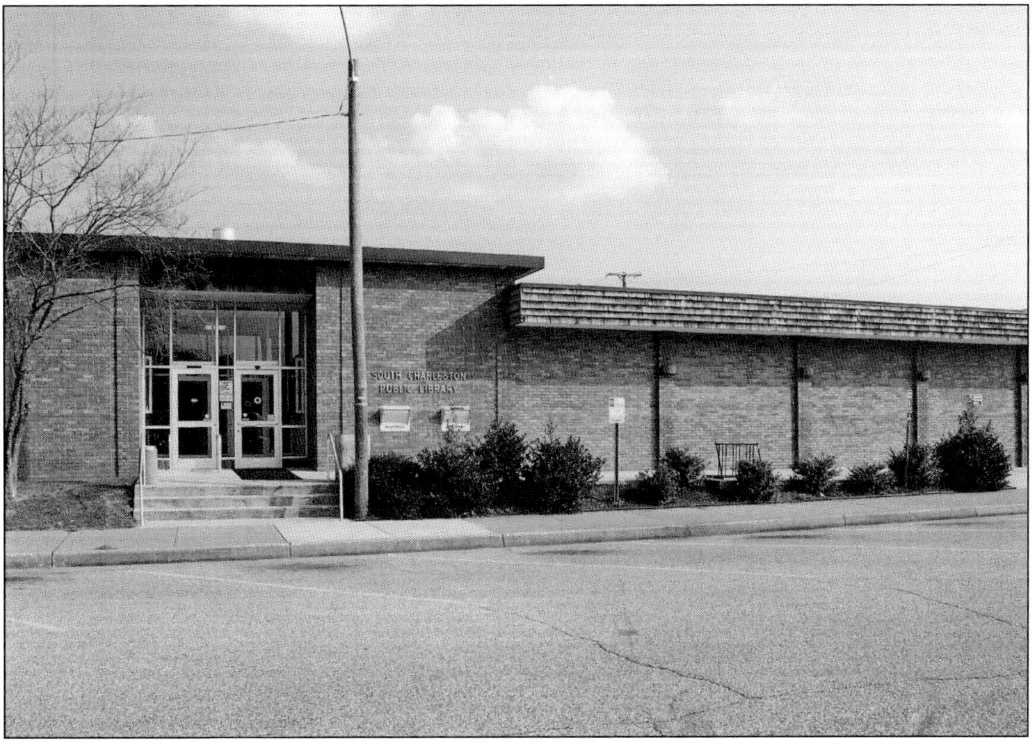

Built in 1968, the South Charleston Public Library is on Fourth Avenue. (Courtesy Linda Weekly.)

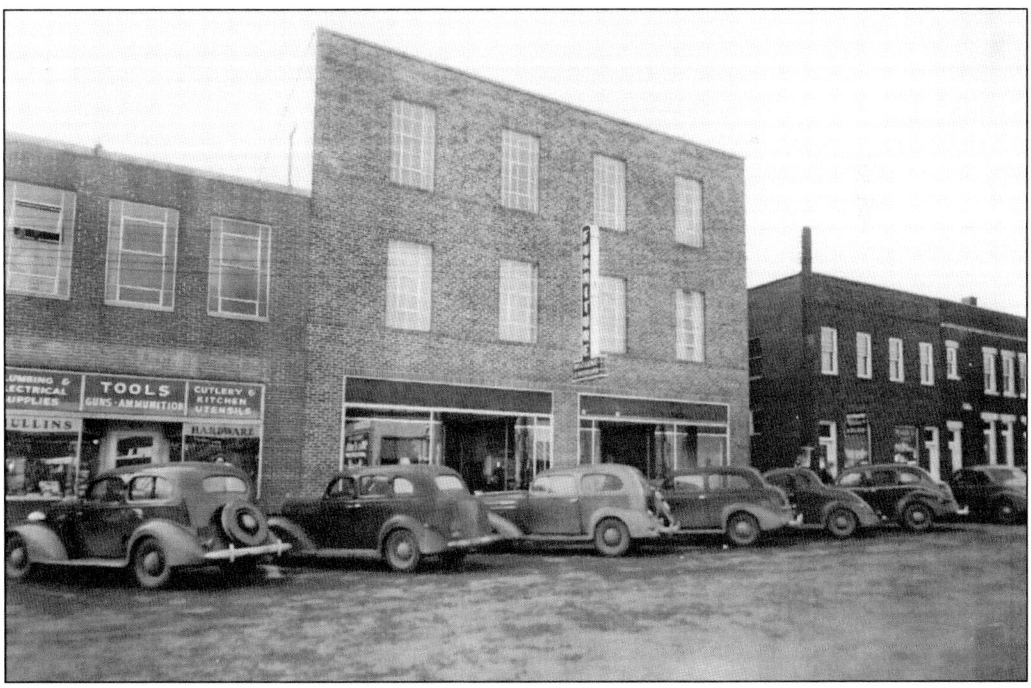

Mullins Hardware Store and McClung and Morgan Furniture Store are shown on D Street in the 1940s. The McClung and Morgan store sold clothing, furniture, drapes, and appliances. (Courtesy Salamie family.)

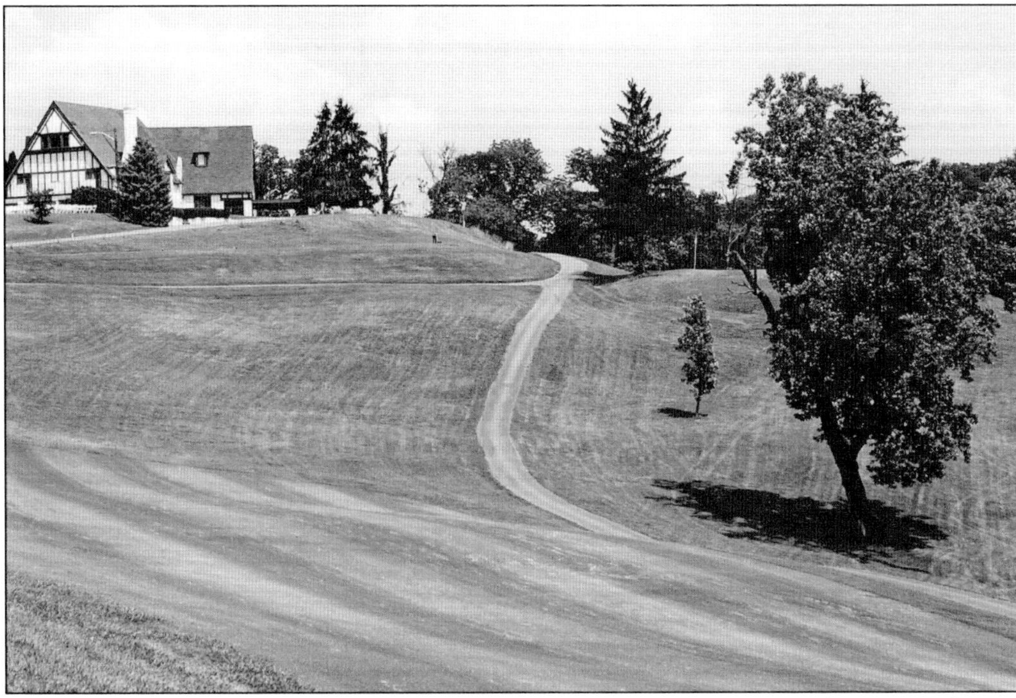

Little Creek Golf Course, located off Spring Hill Avenue in the Spring Hill section of South Charleston, is the oldest country club in the Kanawha Valley. (Courtesy Dan Blue.)

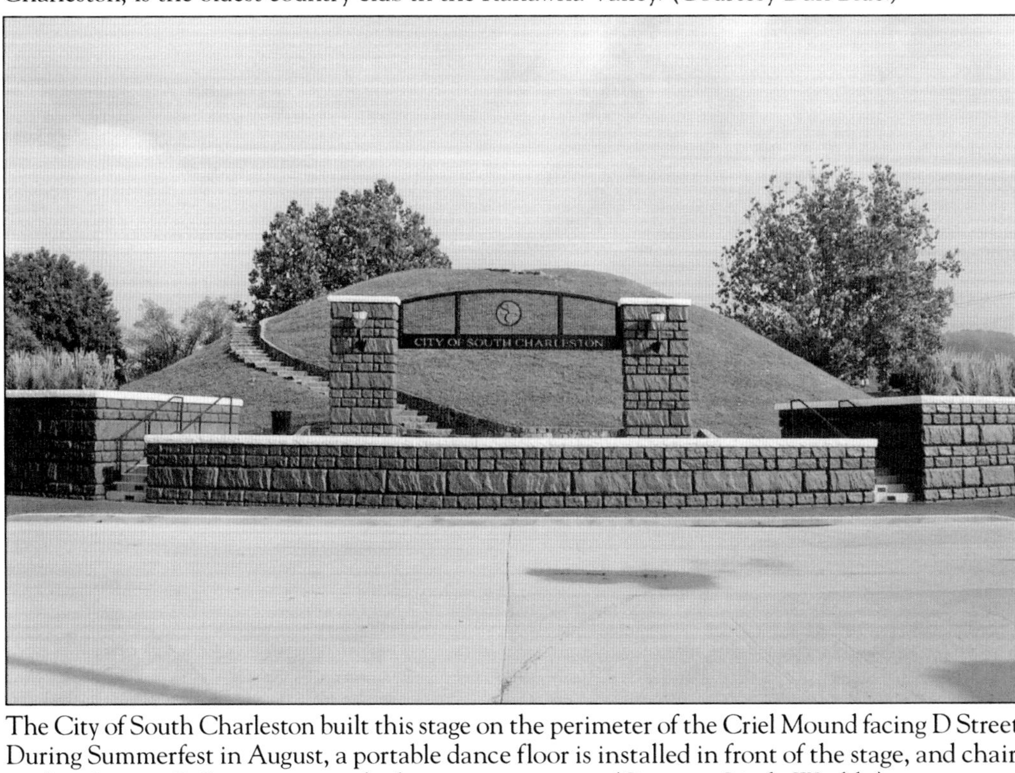

The City of South Charleston built this stage on the perimeter of the Criel Mound facing D Street. During Summerfest in August, a portable dance floor is installed in front of the stage, and chairs are lined up on D Street to view the live entertainment. (Courtesy Linda Weekly.)

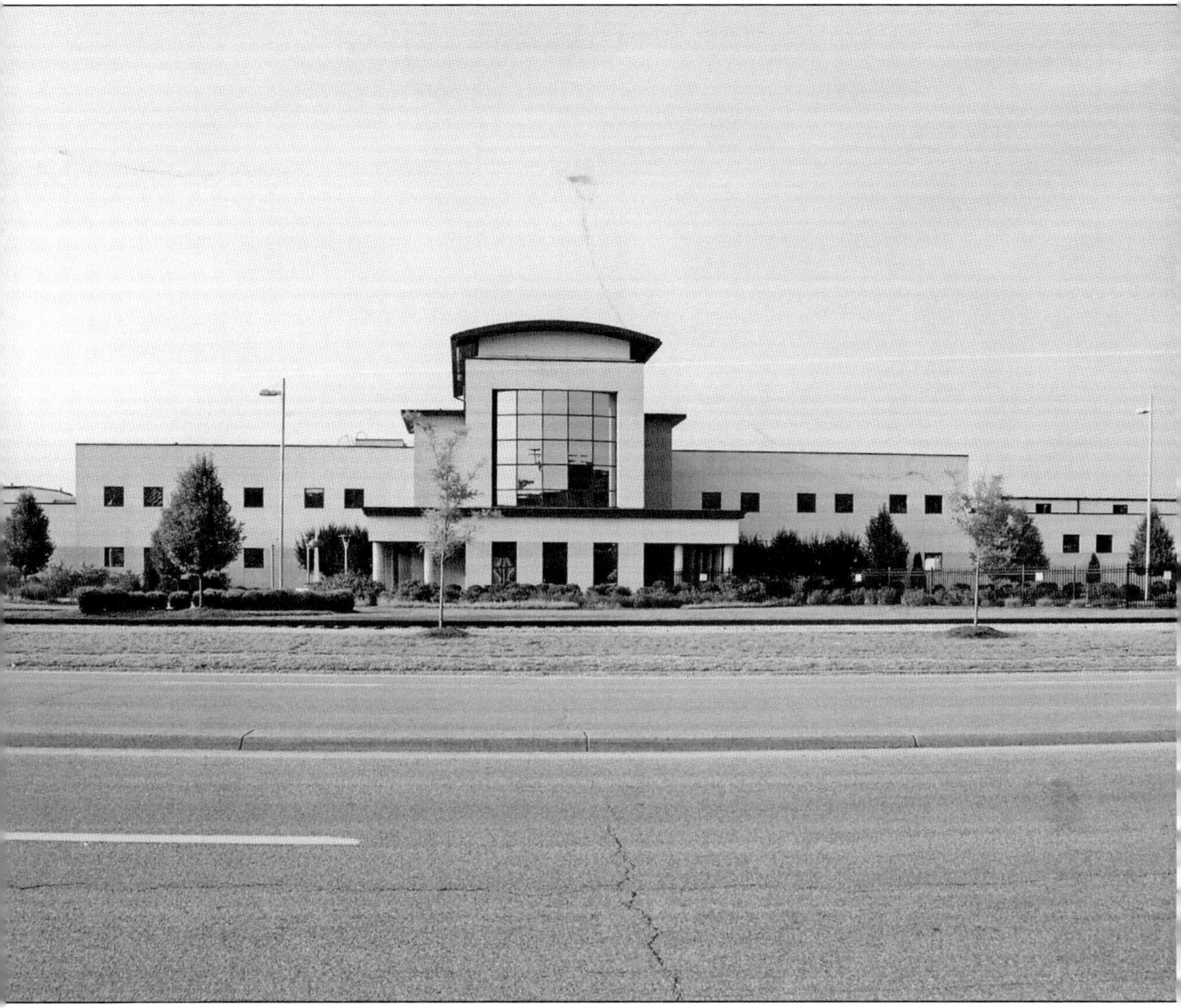

Dow Chemical Company bought the Union Carbide Corporation in 2001 and made many improvements. Older buildings were demolished and a new office complex was constructed. (Courtesy Linda Weekly.)

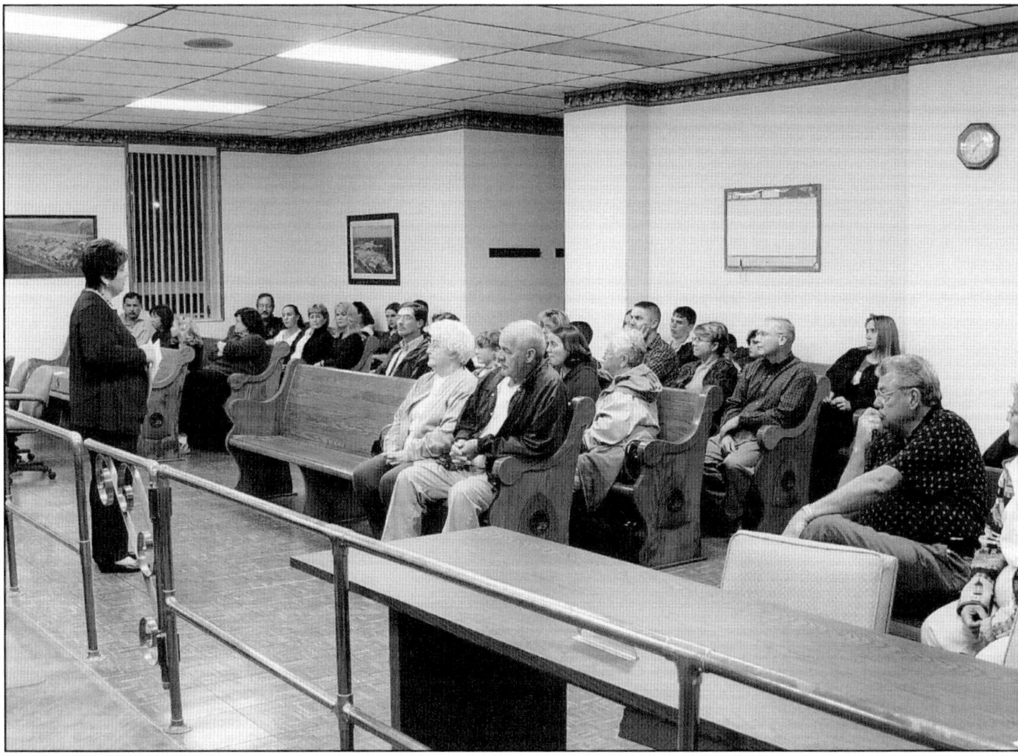

Shown here are the city council chambers in 2003 before the remodeling (above) and after in 2008 (below). (Both courtesy Linda Weekly.)

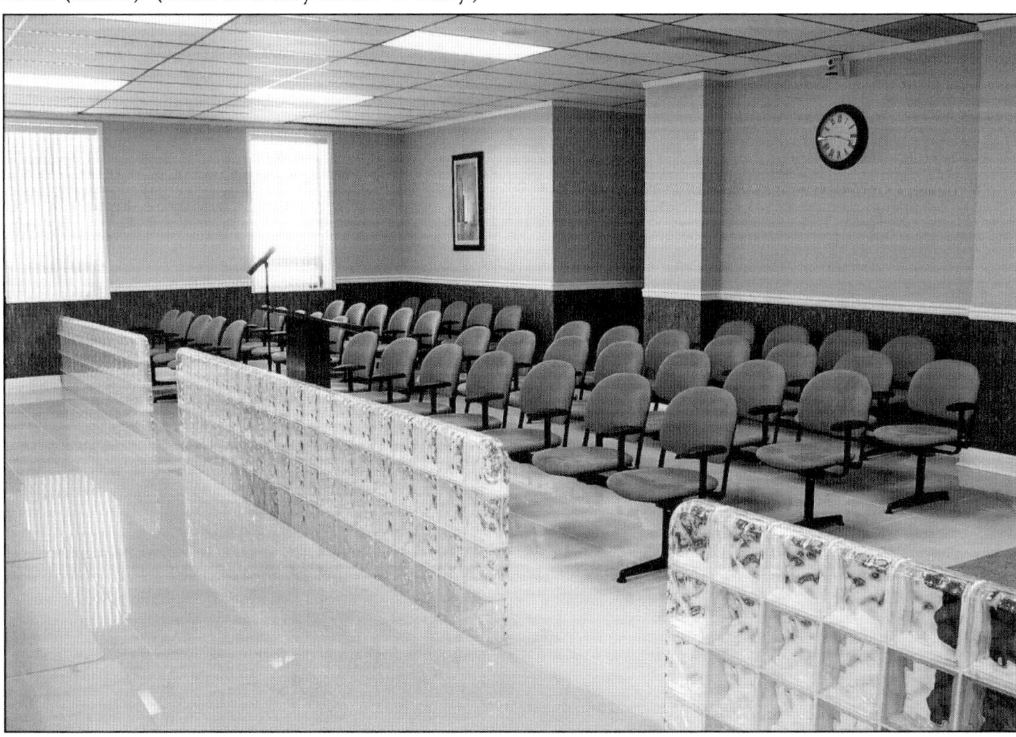

Four

SOUTH CHARLESTON'S PEOPLE

South Charleston is a small town southwest of Charleston. At one time, when the chemical plants were in their heyday and it was known as "the chemical city," the population exceeded 19,000. South Charleston has a mayoral government, city council, and city clerk. The council meetings are viewable on the Internet. The people of South Charleston are very civic-minded and support the organizations, schools, and their projects. This chapter covers some well-known South Charleston people.

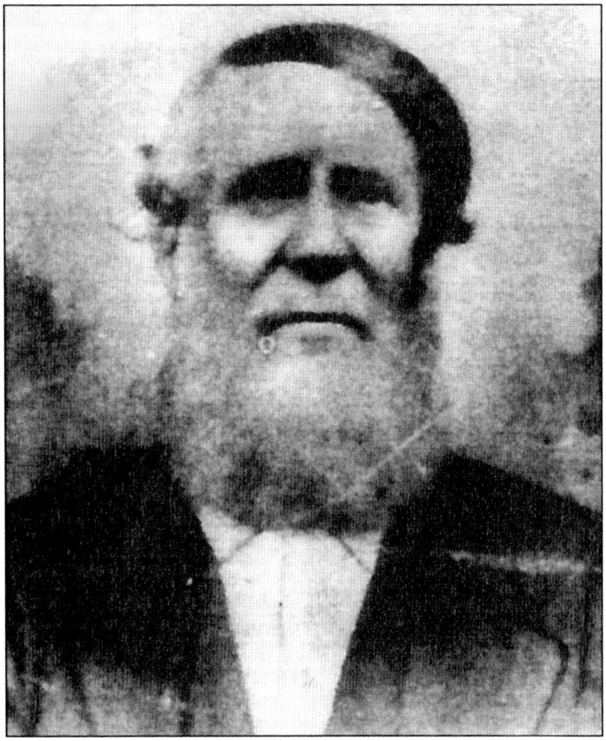

Fleming Cobb and his uncle Thomas Upton were the first two white settlers of present-day South Charleston. Cobb built a log cabin just 75 yards east of the present Davis Creek Bridge. Today Cobb rests in the family cemetery on the edge of the Little Creek Golf Course grounds. He once owned Blaine Island and traded it for a muzzle-loading rifle. (Courtesy Dennis Deitz.)

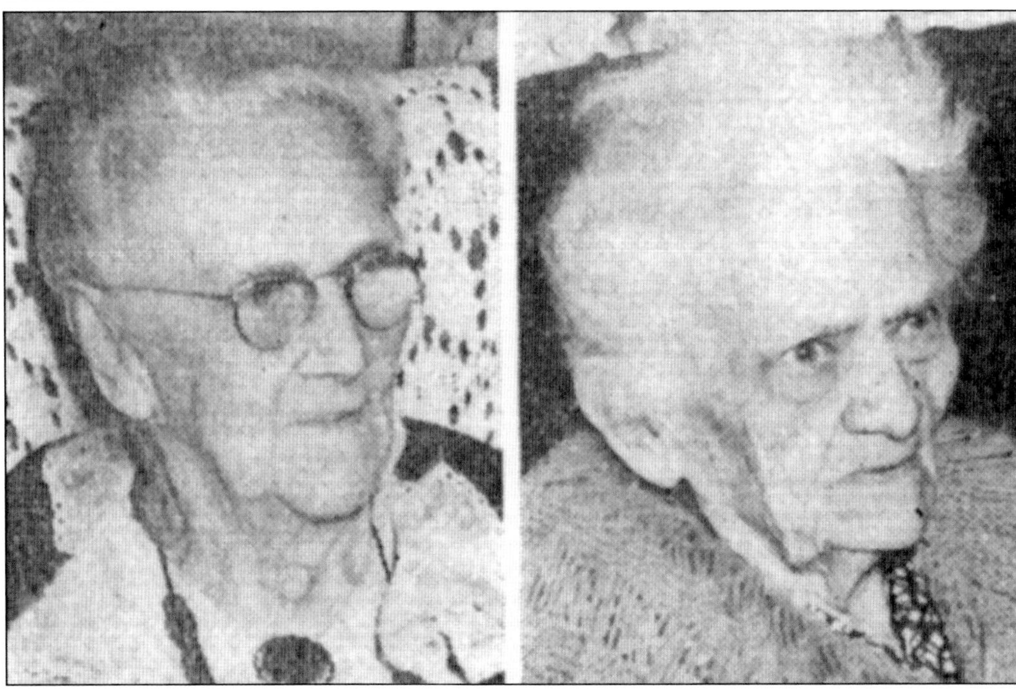

The Sunday, April 10, 1949, *Charleston Gazette* article recognized three sisters, Annie L. Thomas (left), Laura Richmond (right), and Virginia Oakes (not pictured) as the earliest residents of Spring Hill. The three women came to the Kanawha Valley in 1870 and settled on a farm in Spring Hill in 1872. (Courtesy *Charleston Gazette*.)

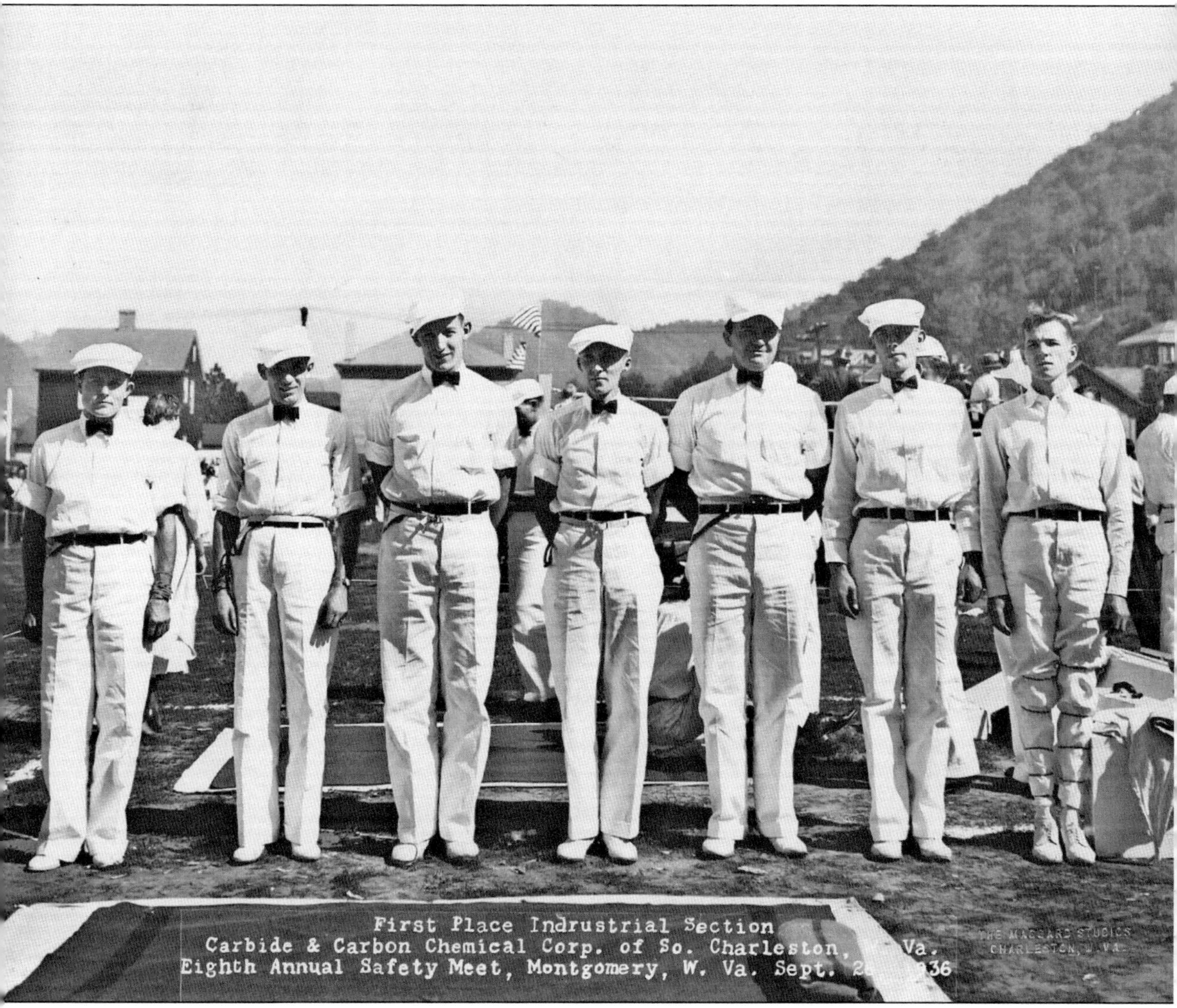

Carbide and Carbon Chemical Corporation took first place in the industrial section of the eighth annual safety meet held in Montgomery, West Virginia, in 1936. (Courtesy South Charleston Museum.)

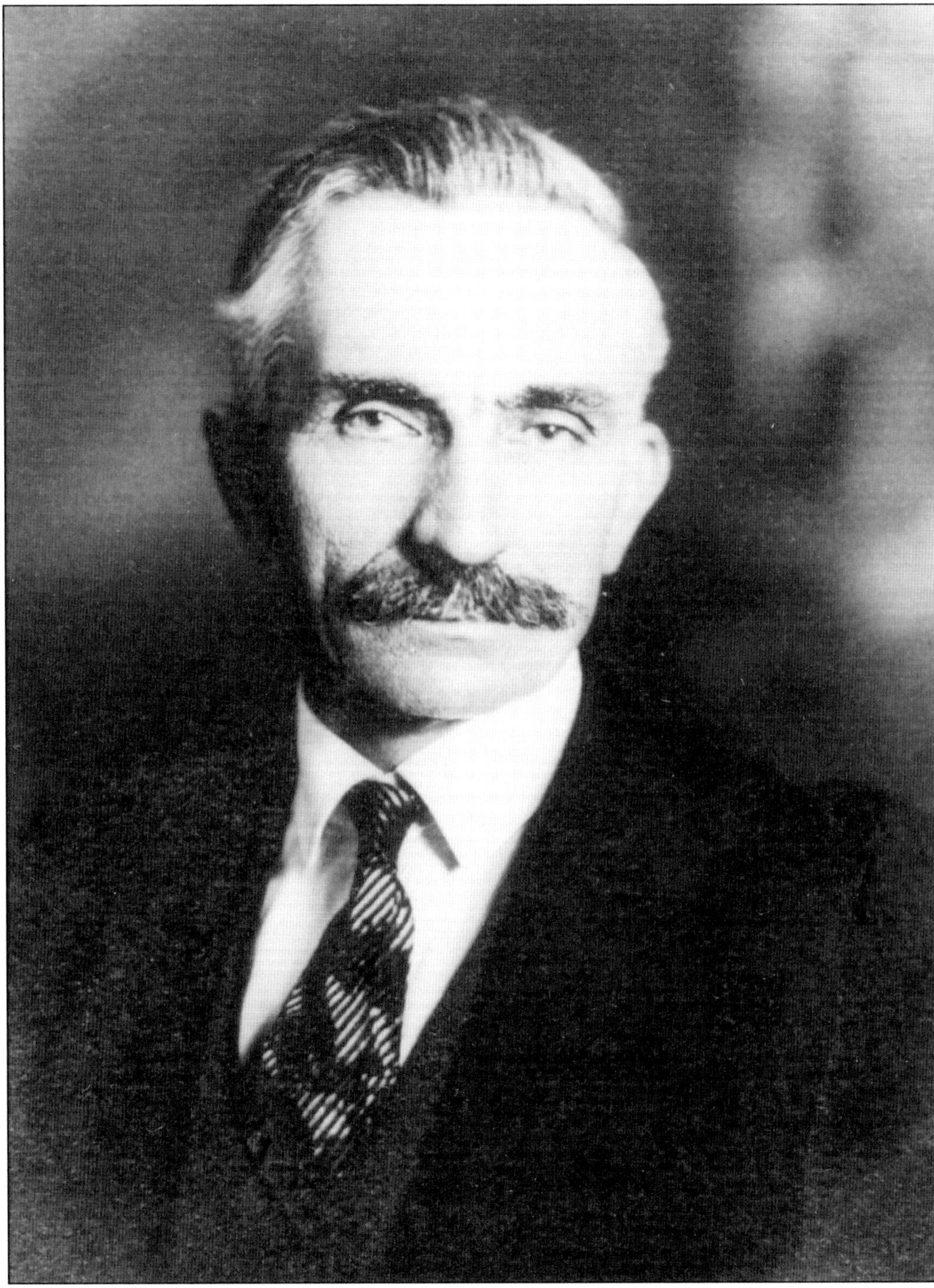

The late Leonidas Henry Oakes served as South Charleston mayor for 18 years. He served through its greatest expansion, taking advantage of the WPA, PWA, and other federal programs that brought South Charleston a new city hall, a recreation center, and a new football stadium, which bears his name. He was also instrumental in acquiring the much-needed Herbert J. Thomas Memorial Hospital, which was financed through federal funds. (Courtesy John and Betty Oakes.)

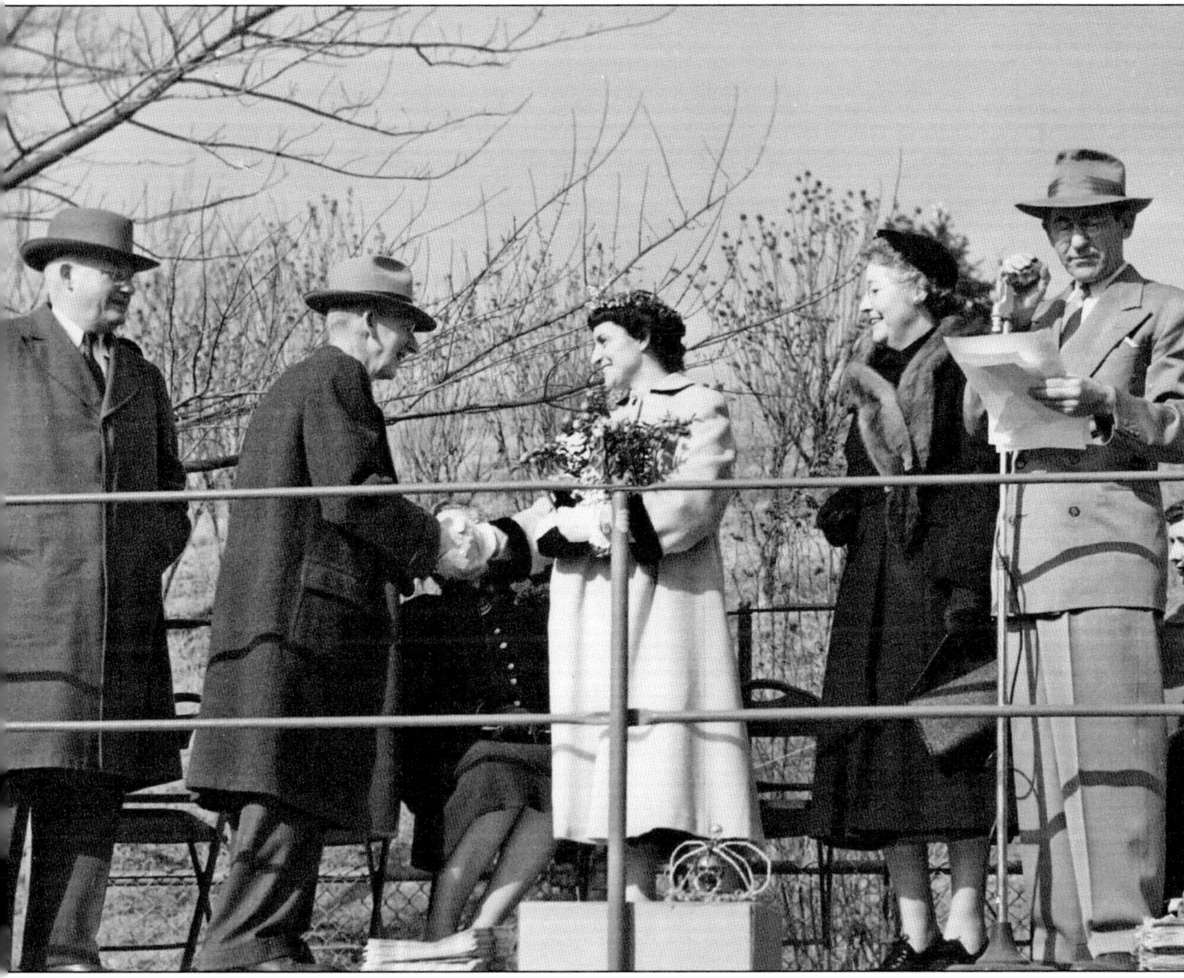

In the 1949 Christmas contest, A. V. Fitzwater, the mayor of South Charleston, and C. W. McClung, the winner of "Mr. Merry Christmas," are shaking the hand of Mary Helen Edge, the winner of "Ms. Merry Christmas." On the far right is Cliff Beckett, the editor of the *Free Press*, master of ceremonies, and producer of the contest. This donated picture is from the Free Press Publishing Company. (Courtesy South Charleston Museum.)

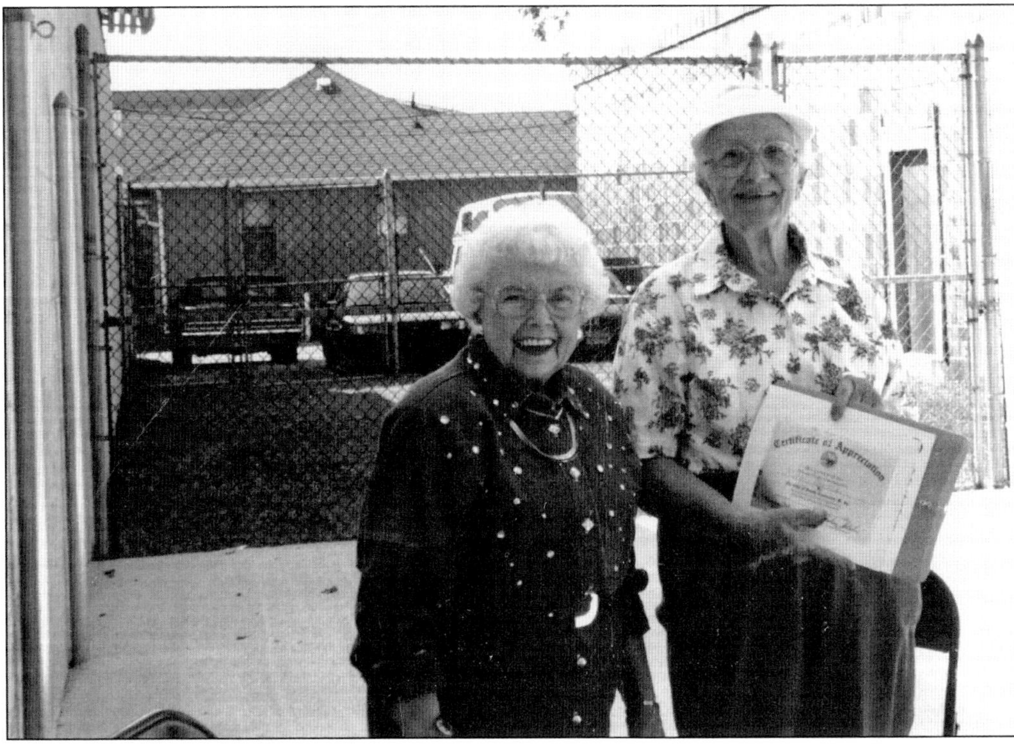

Ruth Sheltz was 75 years old in 1994, and the city of South Charleston shared her birthday. Mayor Robb signed a proclamation, and Frances Bowers Price presented it to Ruth. Cake and punch were served on D Street. (Courtesy South Charleston Museum.)

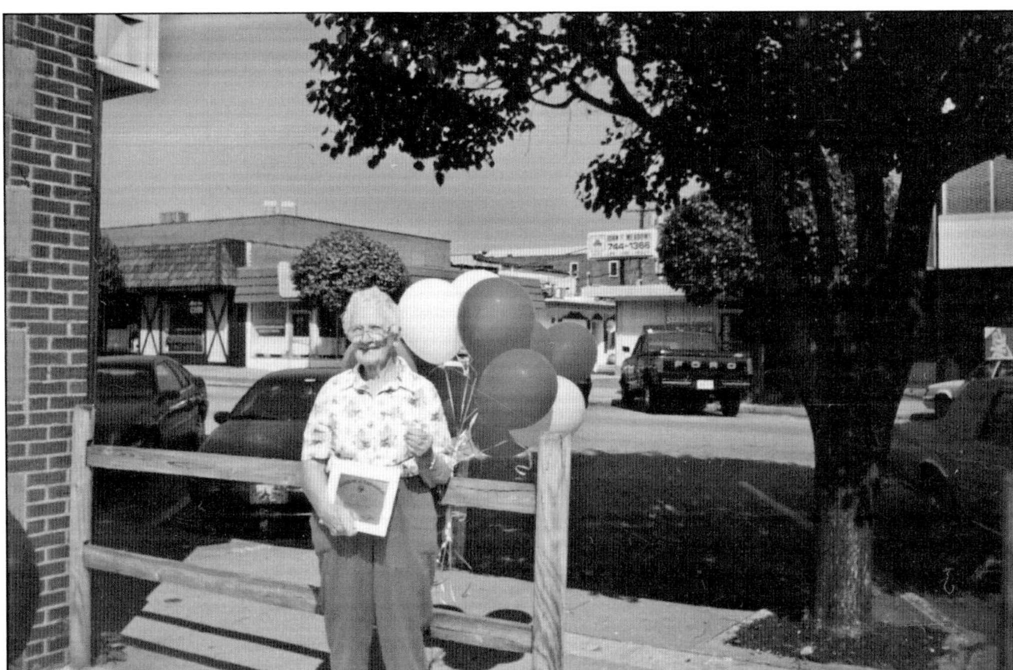

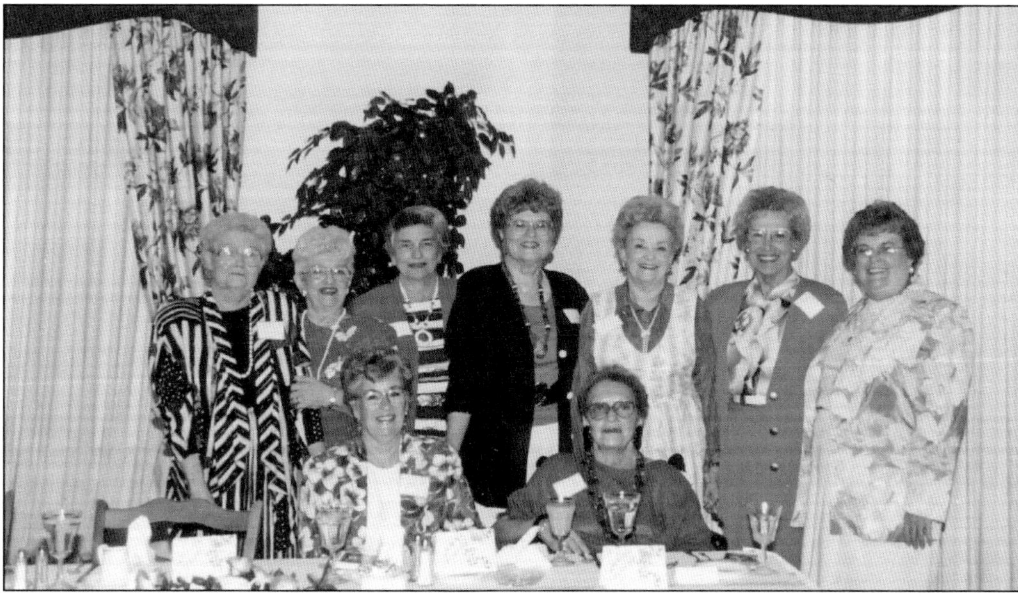

This is the Woman's Club of South Charleston. Past presidents are, from left to right, (first row) Mary Bright, 1963–1965; and Libby Rude, 1992–1993; (second row) "Boots" King, 1976–1978; Nancy Ruddle, 1963; Lura Watkins, 1968–1970 and 1990–1992; Phillis Shawver, 1980–1982; Lois Phillips, 1970–1972; Barbara Grose, 1966–1968; and Alma Brough, 1986–1988. Founded in 1919, the Woman's Club helped the city with many projects and improvements over the years. (Courtesy Phillis Shawver.)

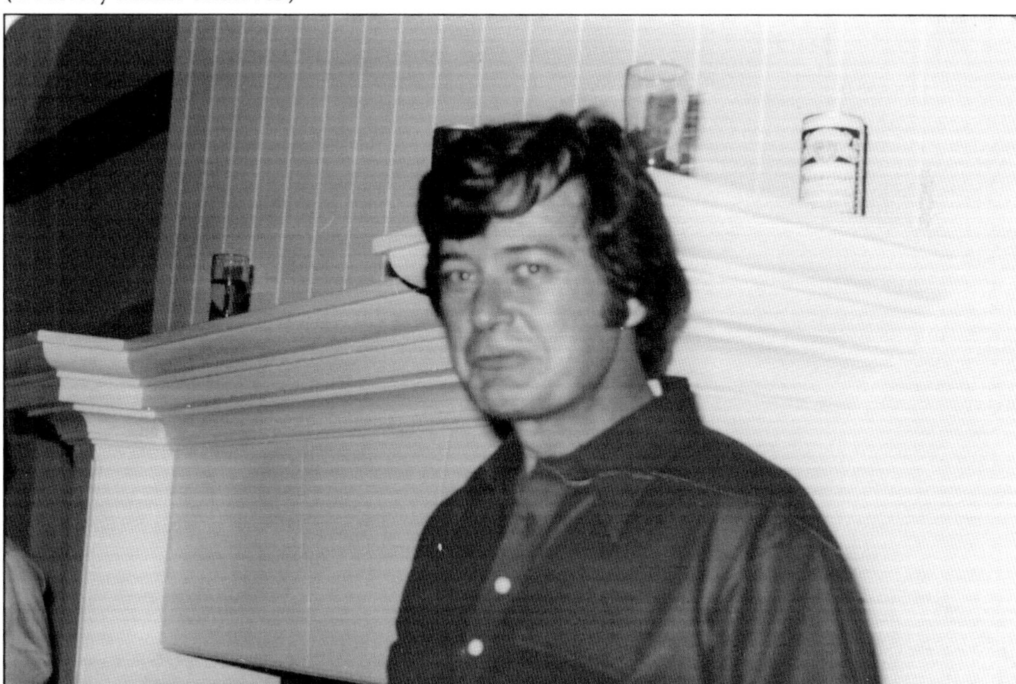

Delbert Kidd is at his class reunion at the Kanawha Country Club. He played basketball for South Charleston High School and loves golf. (Courtesy Judy Romano.)

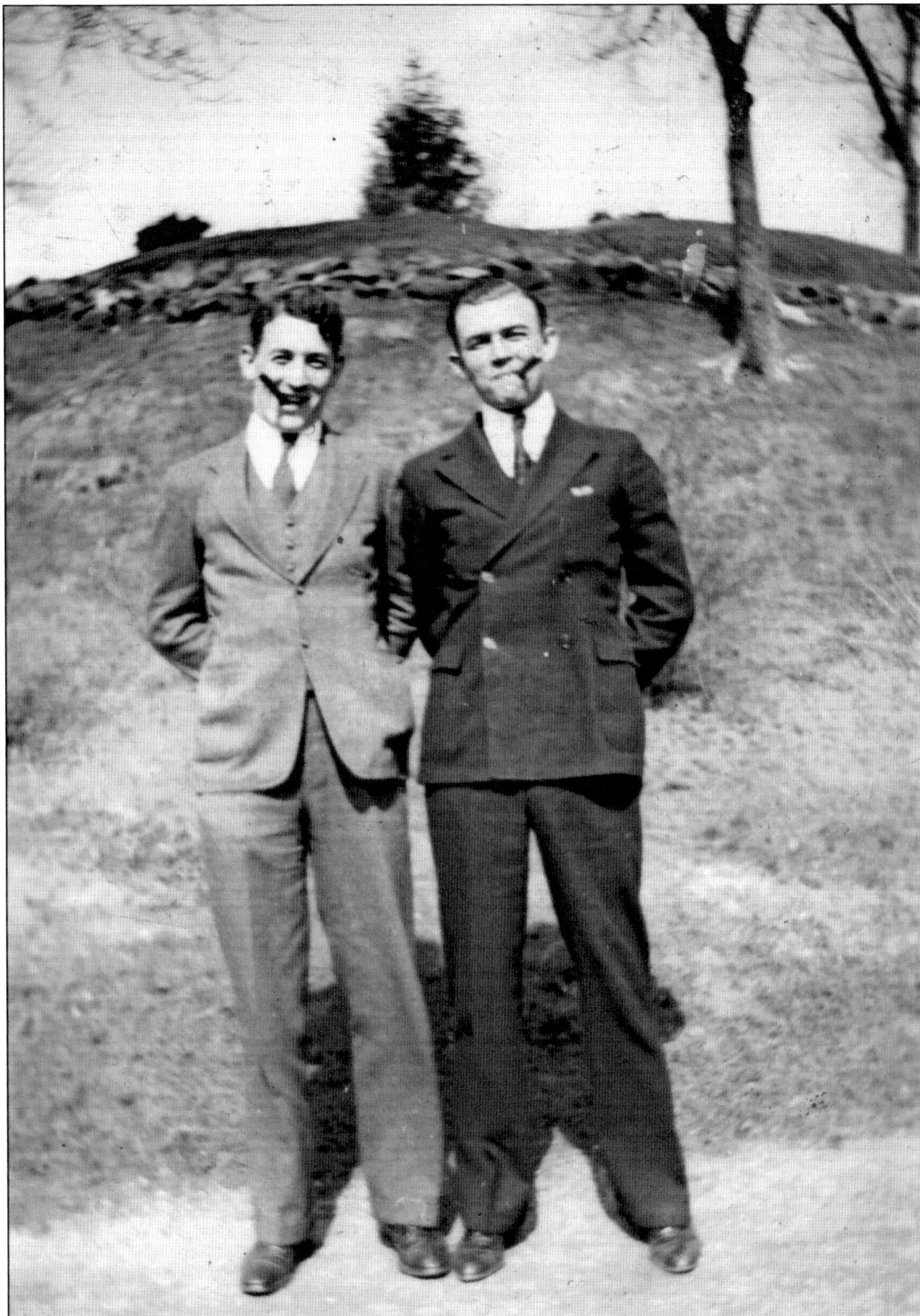

In the 1940s, two unidentified men enjoy their cigars in front of the Criel Mound at the end of D Street. (Courtesy South Charleston Museum.)

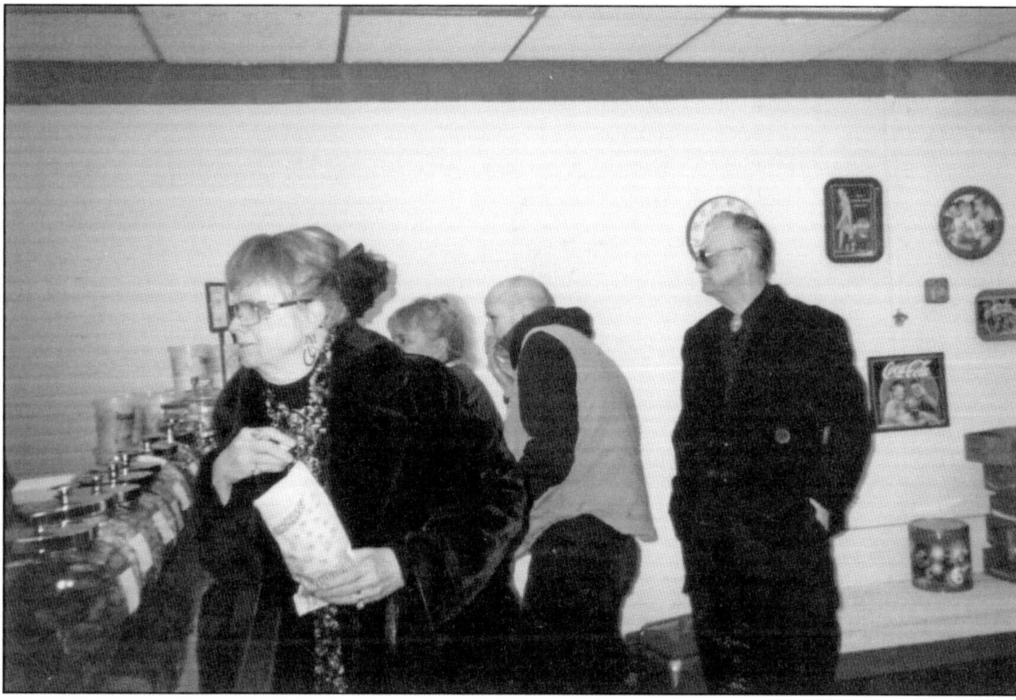

Lucie Mellert, a photographer for the Charleston newspapers and the South Charleston Convention and Vistors Bureau (SCCVB), is attending a grand opening of Happy Days Café (above) and riding in a car with Bob Anderson, the SCCVB director, at the annual Christmas parade (below). (Both courtesy Bob Anderson.)

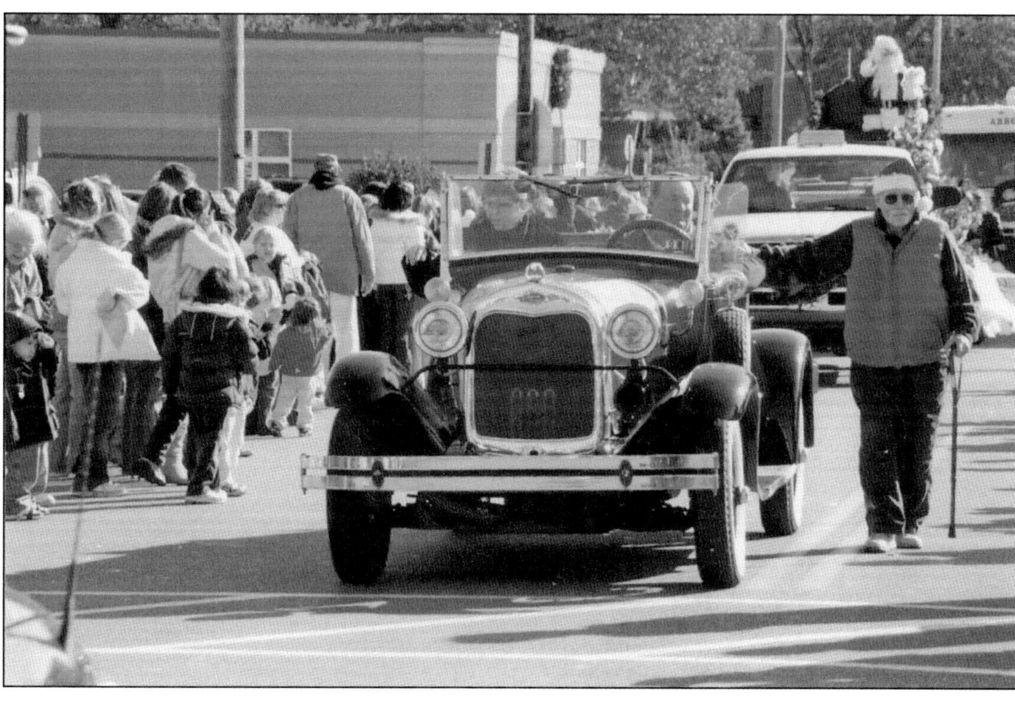

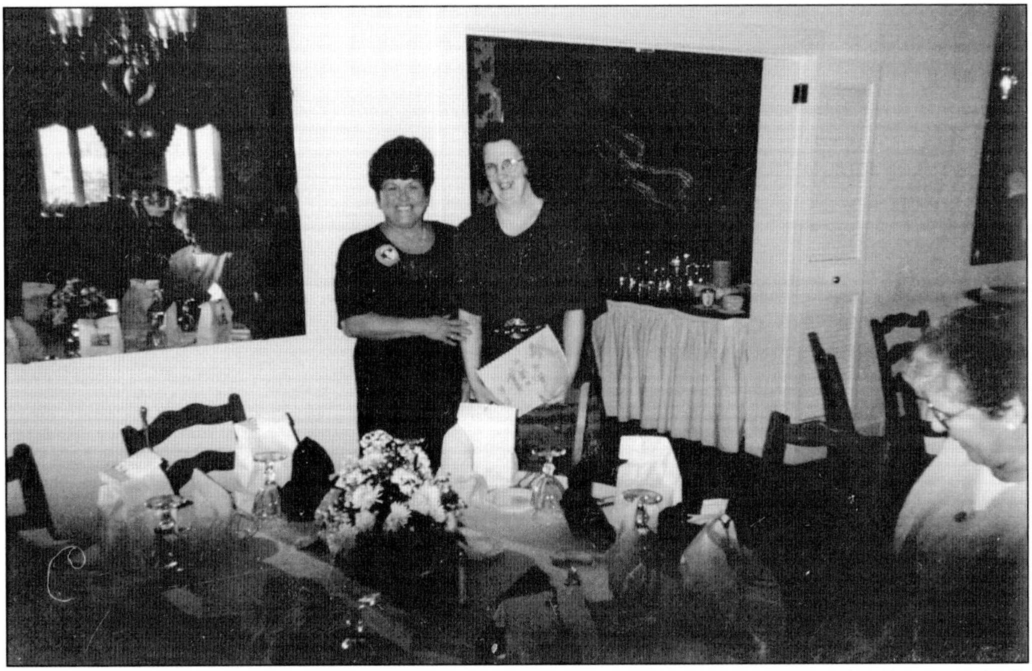

Bonnie Brenneman and Judy Romano are at their 25th class reunion at Kanawha Country Club in 1983. (Courtesy Judy Romano.)

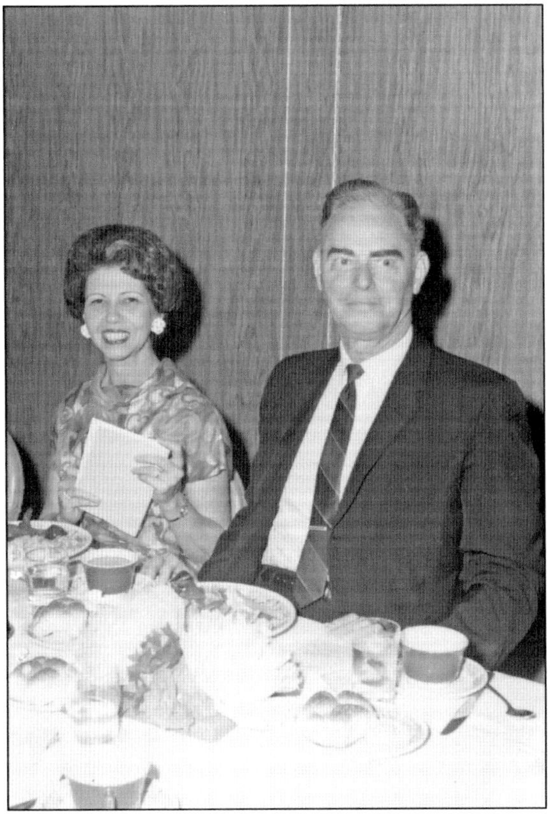

Former mayor J. Alfred Poe and his wife, Maxine, are at his retirement party from South Charleston Junior High School. He served as principal for 30 years and as a teacher for 10 years. Poe was mayor of South Charleston from 1971 to 1975. He passed away March 14, 1994, at age 90. *The History of South Charleston* book was dedicated to Poe. (Courtesy South Charleston Museum.)

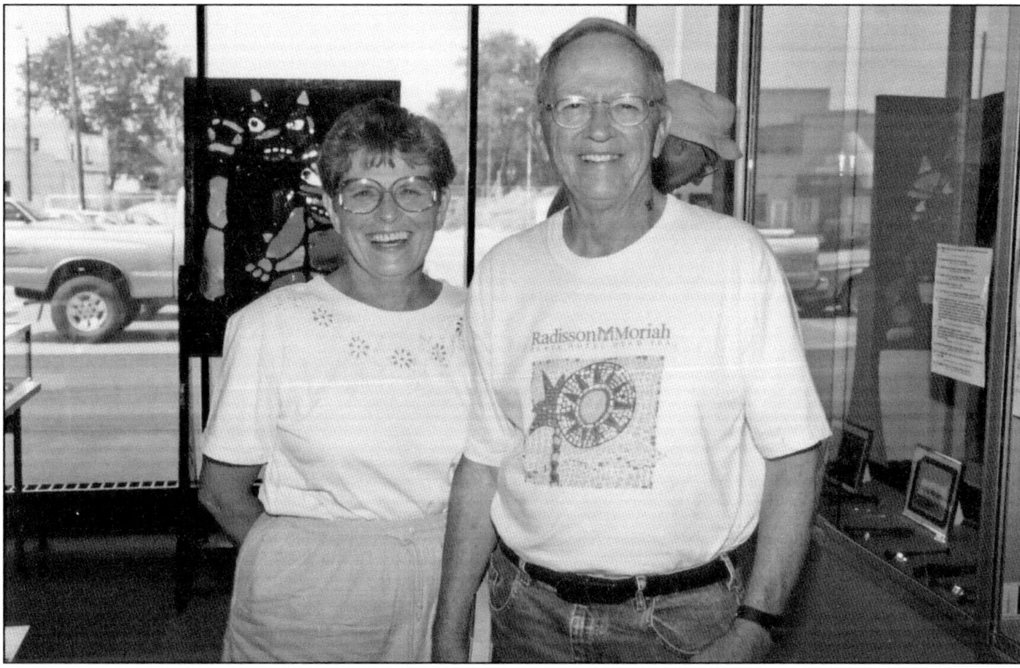

John and Betty Oakes are visiting the South Charleston Museum at the library on Fourth Avenue. Betty and John have always supported functions sponsored by the South Charleston Museum. (Courtesy South Charleston Museum.)

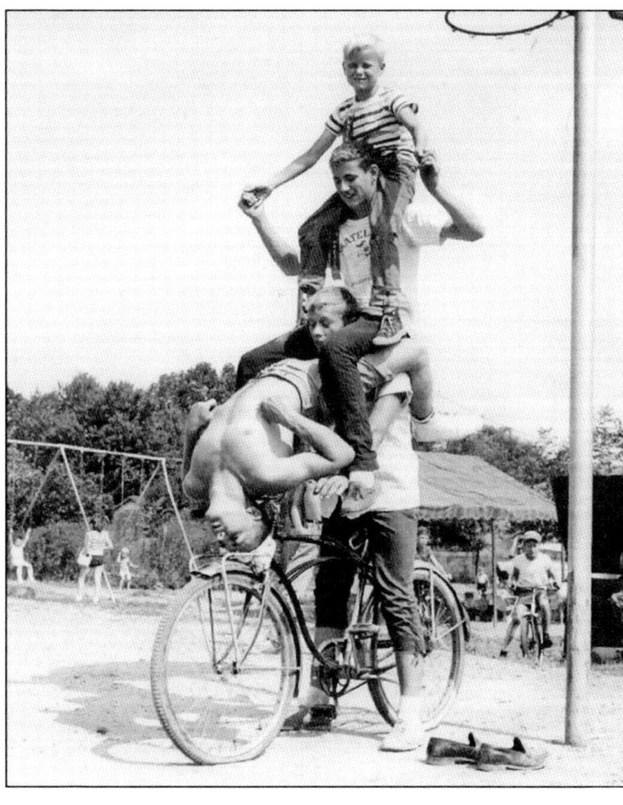

Skip Hawkins and his brother Alex pose on a bike with two other unidentified boys. Alex Hawkins played in the NFL, was a four-letter athlete from South Charleston High School, and authored three books. (Courtesy South Charleston Museum.)

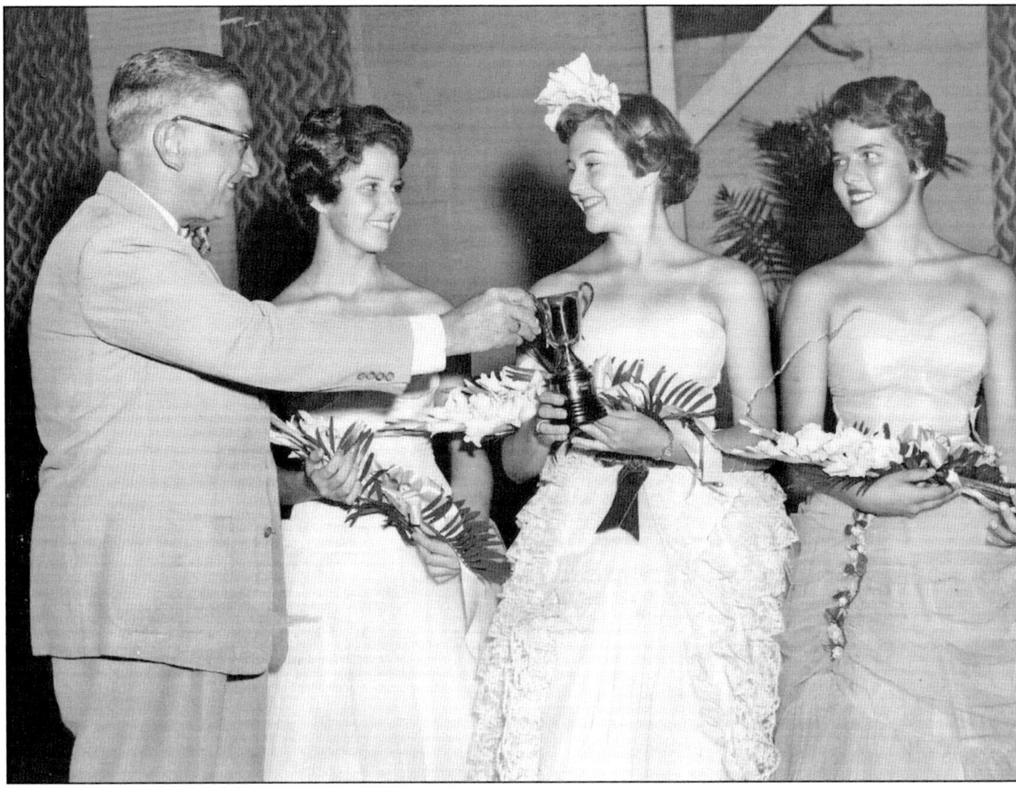

Mayor Londeree presented a trophy to Carolyn Sparks as she was crowned Miss South Charleston in 1953, with Patty Sutton (left) and Judy Bowen (right) as runners-up. (Courtesy South Charleston Museum.)

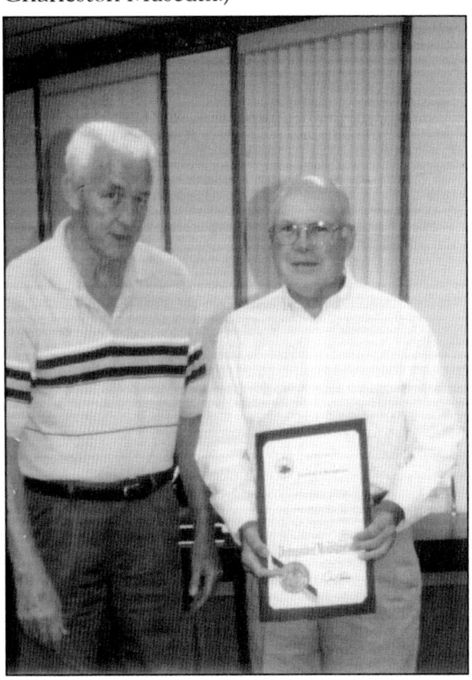

City councilman Sonny Holstine presents a "Distinguished Mountaineer Award" to Ken Samples. (Courtesy South Charleston Museum.)

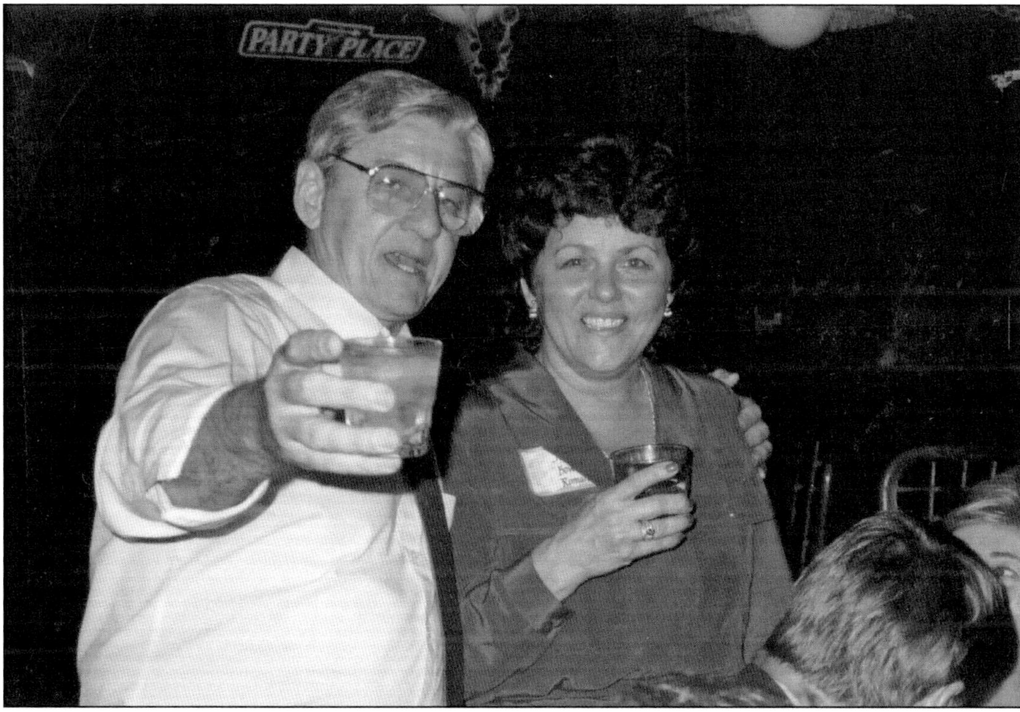

Deiter Garrett and Judy Romano are at the 25th reunion of the class of 1958. Deiter married Carolyn Sparks from South Charleston. (Courtesy Judy Romano.)

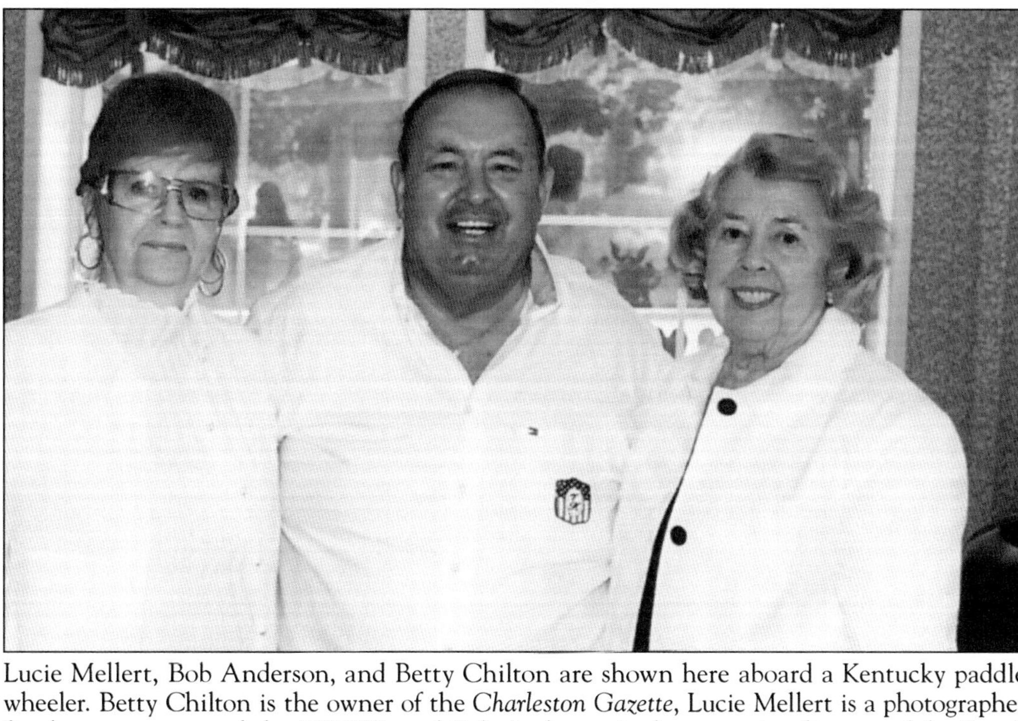

Lucie Mellert, Bob Anderson, and Betty Chilton are shown here aboard a Kentucky paddle wheeler. Betty Chilton is the owner of the *Charleston Gazette*, Lucie Mellert is a photographer for the newspaper and the SCCVB, and Bob Anderson is the executive director of the South Charleston Convention and Visitors Bureau.

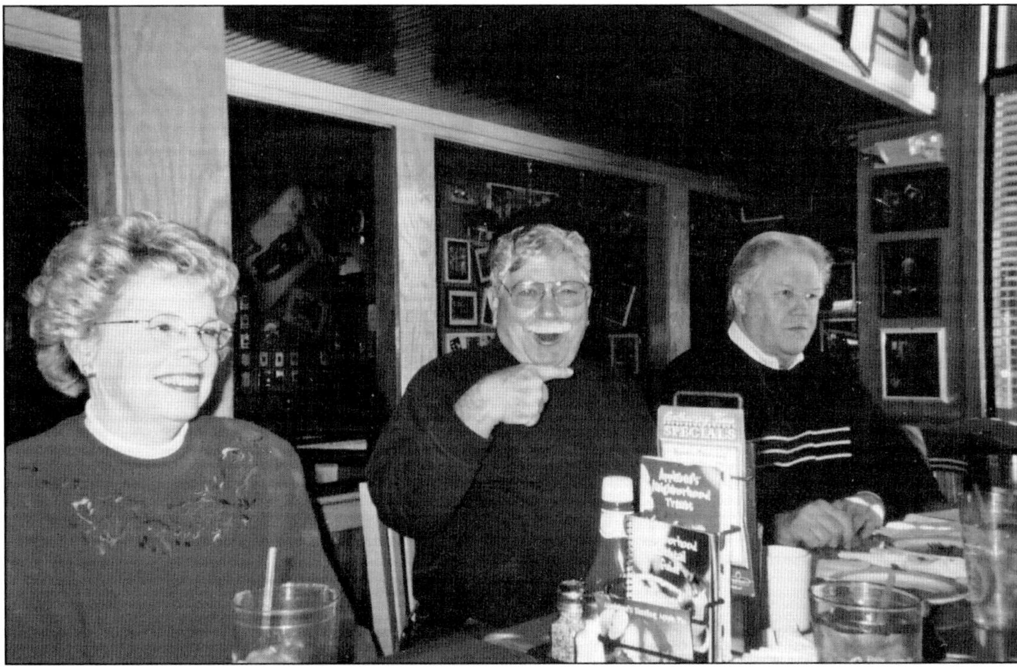

From left, Jo Ann Spitler, Donald Miller, and Butch Buckley are at Applebee's for their monthly luncheon for the South Charleston High School class of 1958. (Courtesy Judy Romano.)

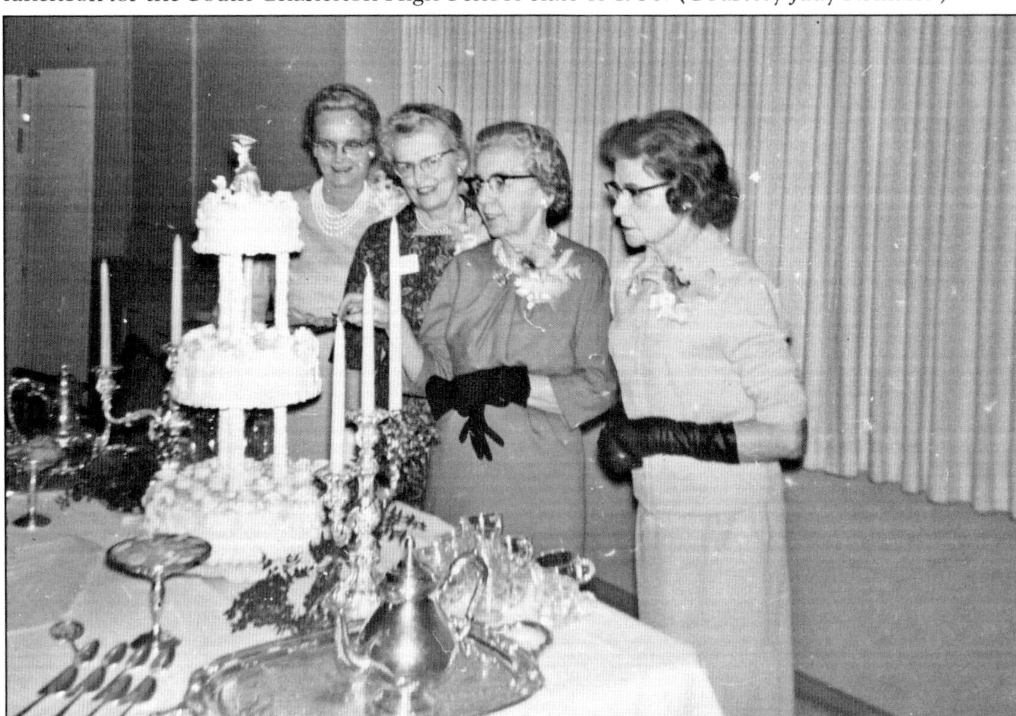

The wives of four previous mayors of South Charleston are, from left to right, Mrs. R. C. Jarrell, Mrs. Walter W. Kramer, Mrs. L. C. McIlwain, and Mrs. Joseph W. Londeree. They are attending a reception at the Woman's Club of South Charleston. (Courtesy South Charleston Museum.)

In this 1955 or 1956 picture, Joan Bennett Belcher is in her high school cheerleading uniform; she graduated in 1958. (Courtesy Judy Romano.)

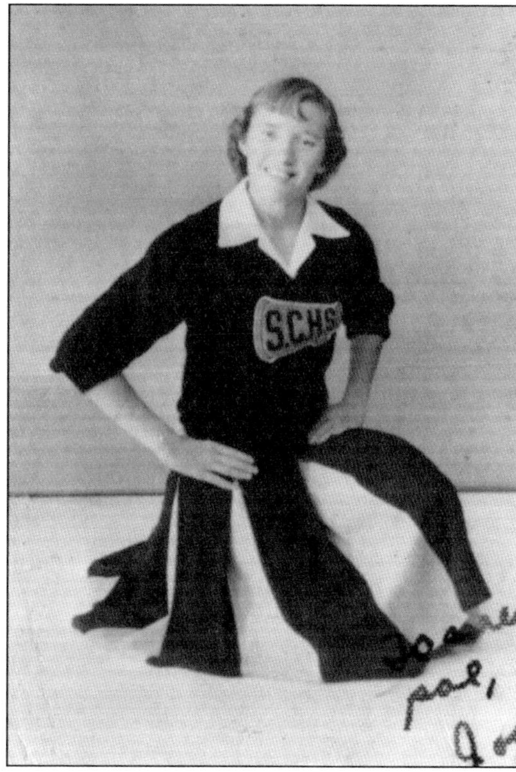

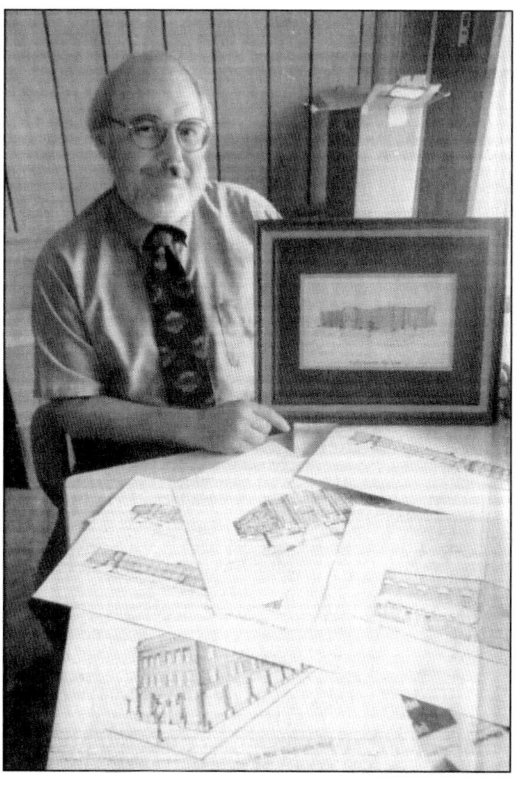

Don Evans of South Charleston discovered a talent for art in 1988, when he created a pen-and-ink drawing of the old South Charleston High School for his 30th class reunion. Since then, he has drawn several other historic buildings in the area. Along with being a talented artist, Don also builds homes and makes grandfather clocks. (Courtesy Charleston Newspapers, photograph by Ben Calwell.)

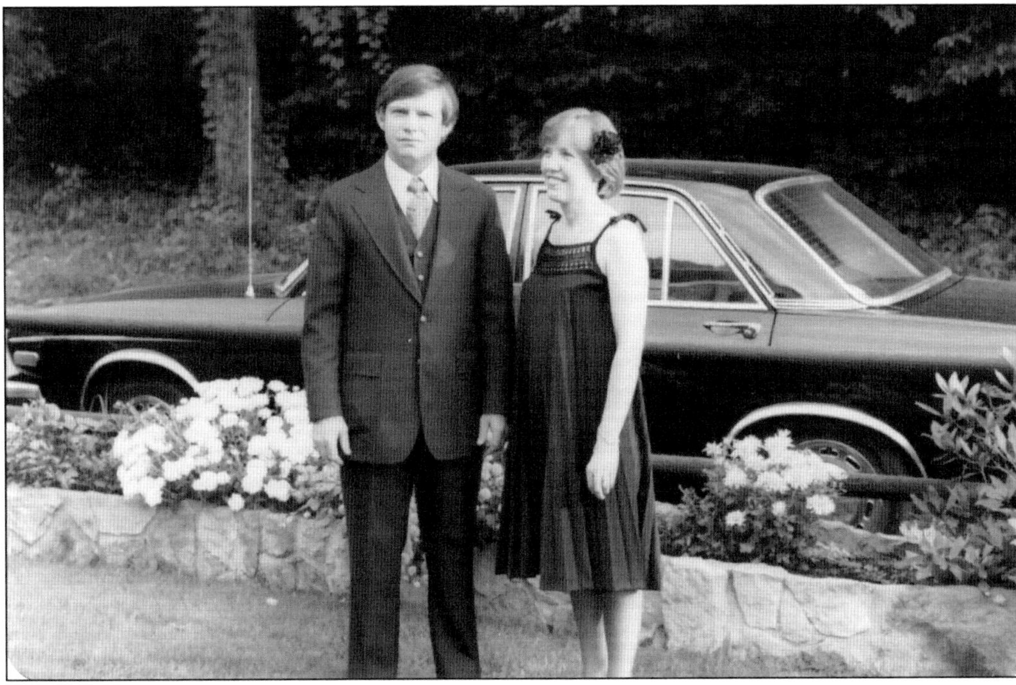

Gus and Joan Belcher are on their way to a reunion at Kanawha Country Club; this picture was taken in front of Jane and Fred Ferrell's home on Country Club Boulevard in 1983. (Courtesy Judy Romano.)

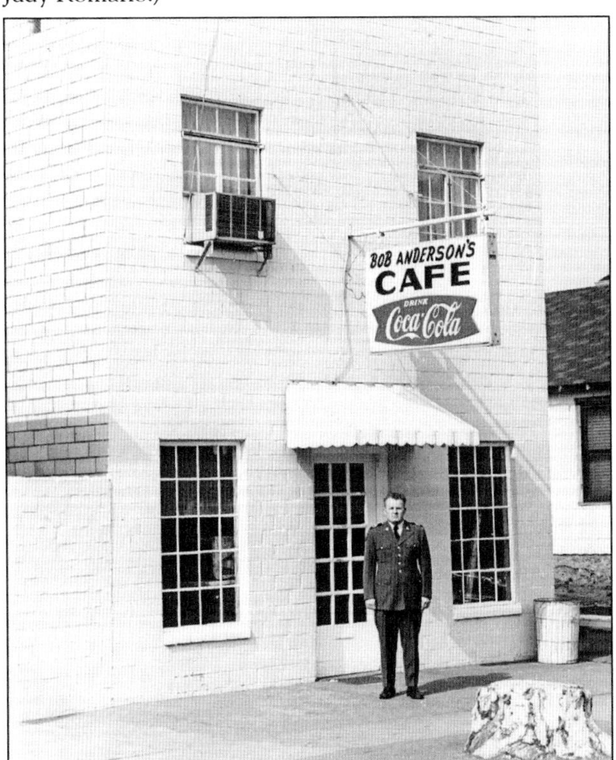

Bob Anderson is standing in front of the Bob Anderson Café on Third Avenue in his ROTC uniform from West Virginia State University. (Courtesy Bob Anderson.)

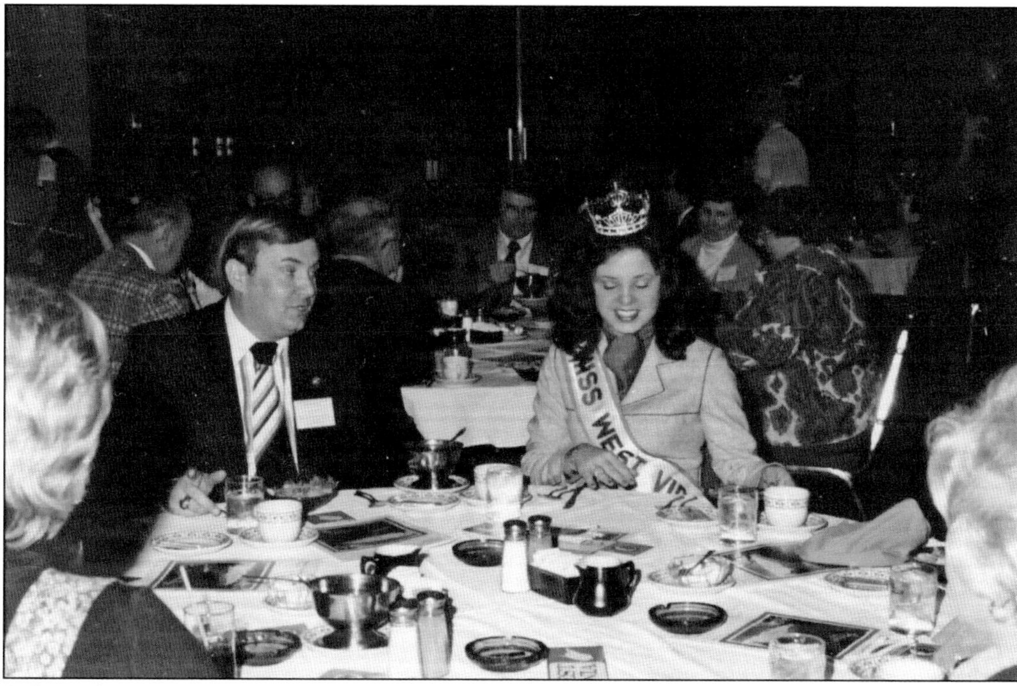

Bob Anderson is pictured here with Miss West Virginia, Patsy Ramsey, in 1978. Bob ran beauty contests in West Virginia for the Hawaiian Tropic tanning lotion company out of Daytona Beach, Florida. (Courtesy Bob Anderson.)

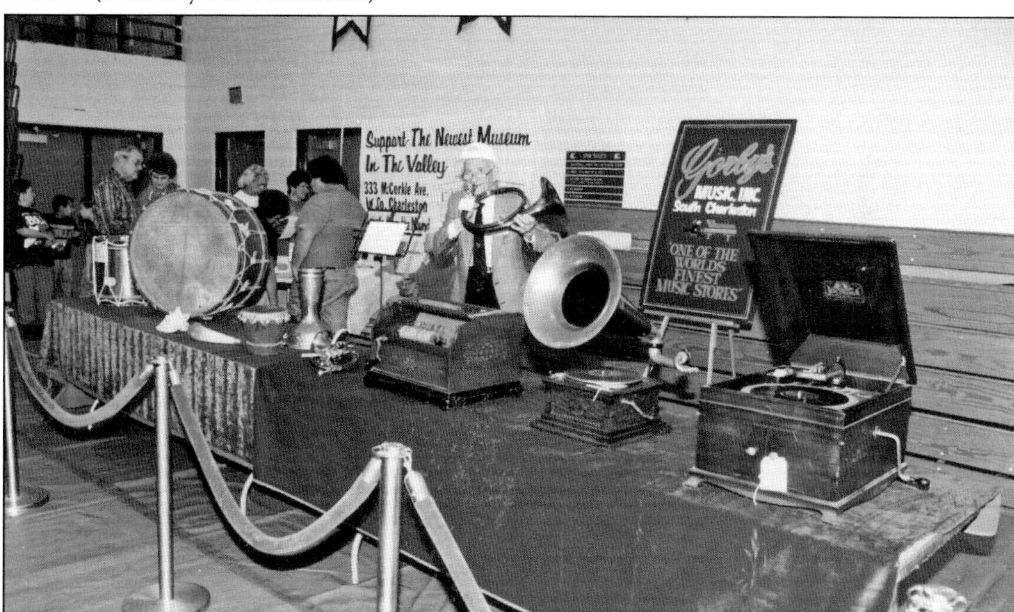

Charles Gorby passed away at age 94 on July 9, 2004. He served as the first band director at South Charleston High School and was the assistant football coach in the 1930s. Gorby owned and operated Gorby's Music Store on Seventh Avenue, was a member of the South Charleston Museum and the history book committee, and a collector of antique musical instruments. (Courtesy South Charleston Museum.)

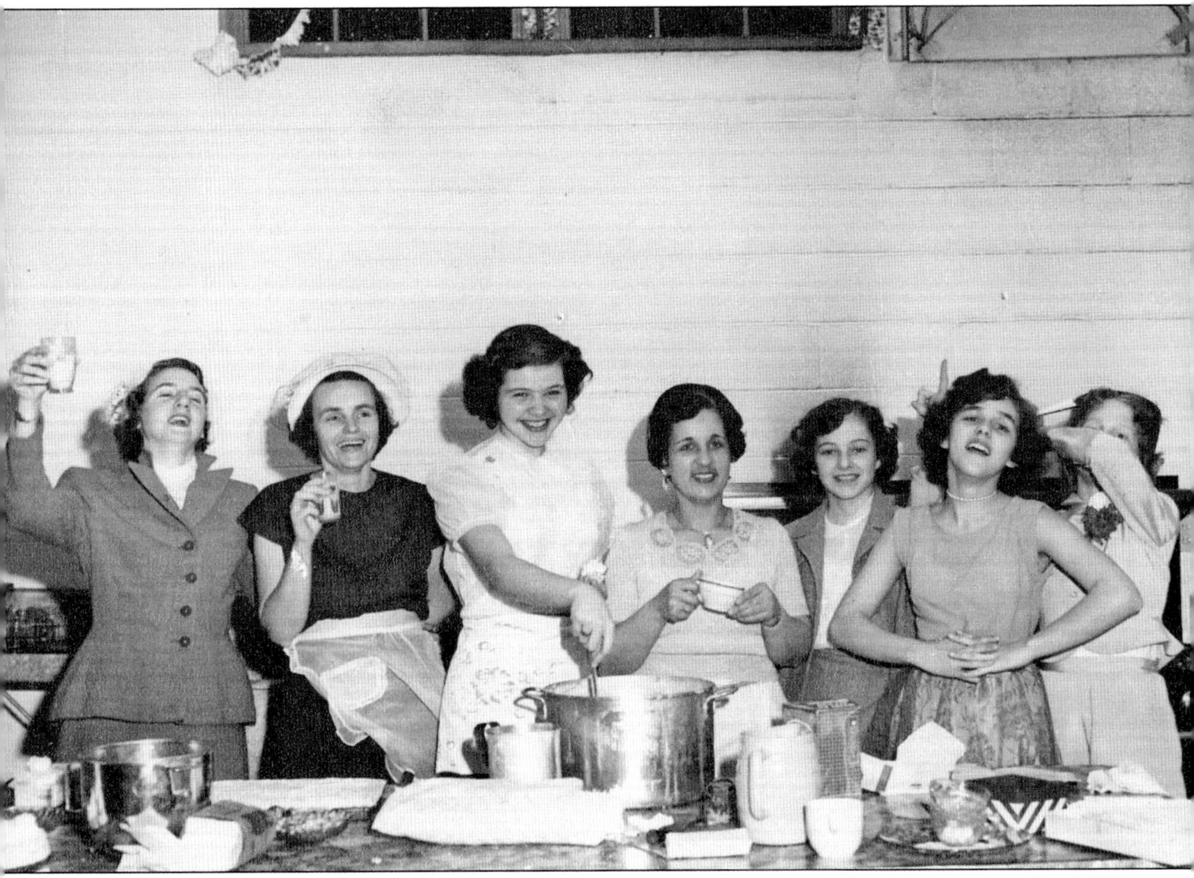

These women are in the kitchen at the First Baptist Church in South Charleston in the 1950s preparing for Clarence Dillon and Shirley Hill's wedding reception. Dillon retired as a minister. The ladies are, from left to right, unidentified, Edith Miller, Rosalie Newman, Audrey Bowen, Carolyn Sparks, Judy Bowen, and Jo Anne Hill (sister of the bride). (Courtesy of Judy Bowen Romano.)

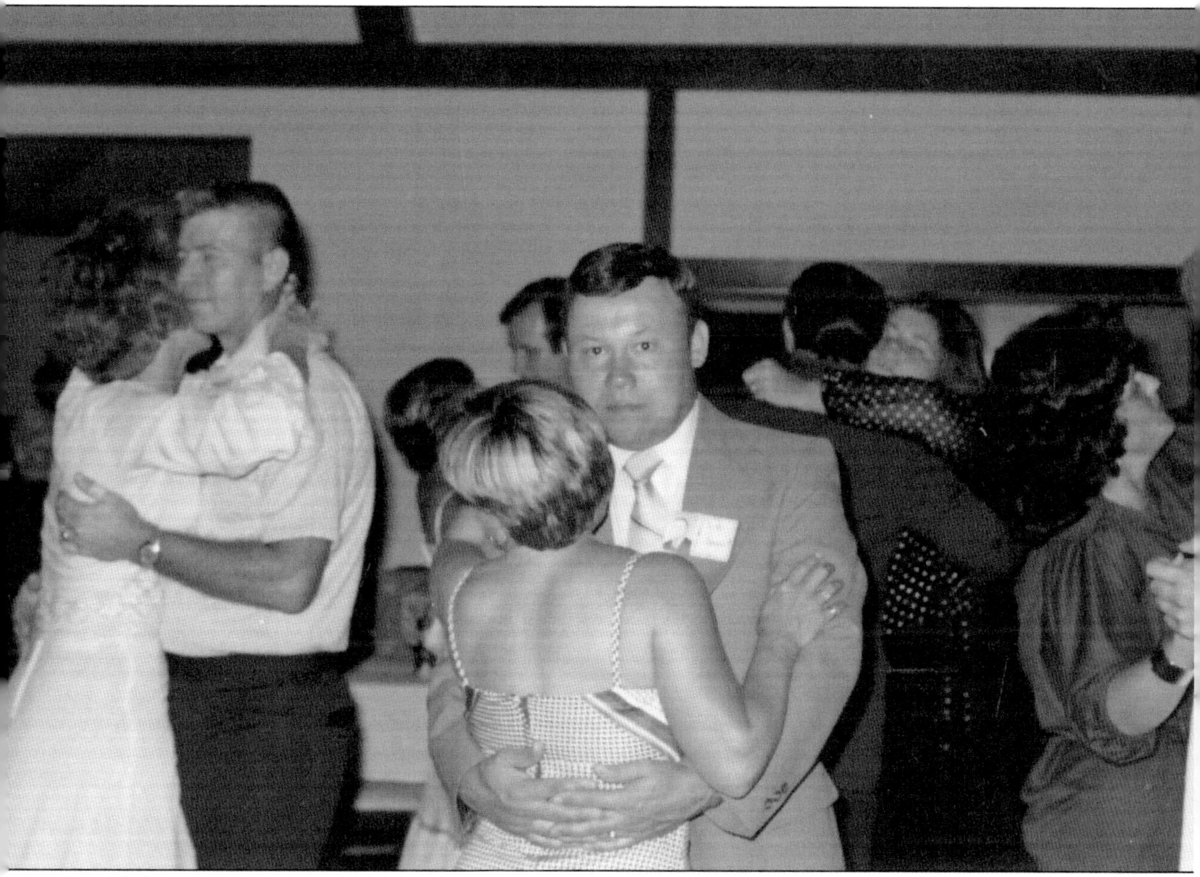

From left to right, Joann and Jim Dement and R. M. and Susie Brewer are dancing at their 25th class reunion at Kanawha Country Club. (Courtesy Judy Romano.)

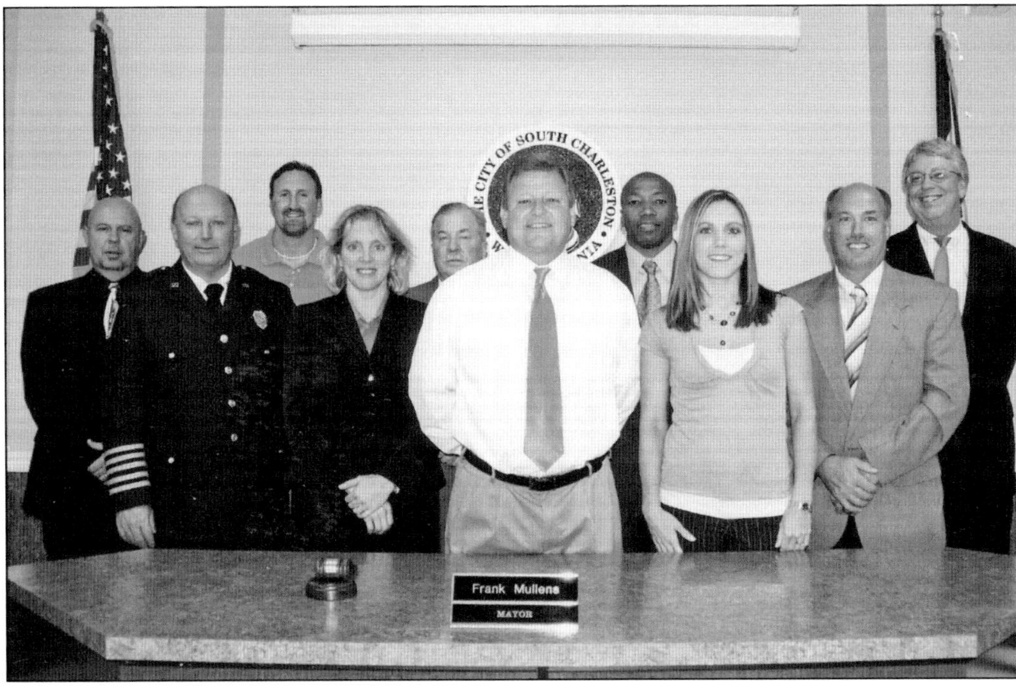

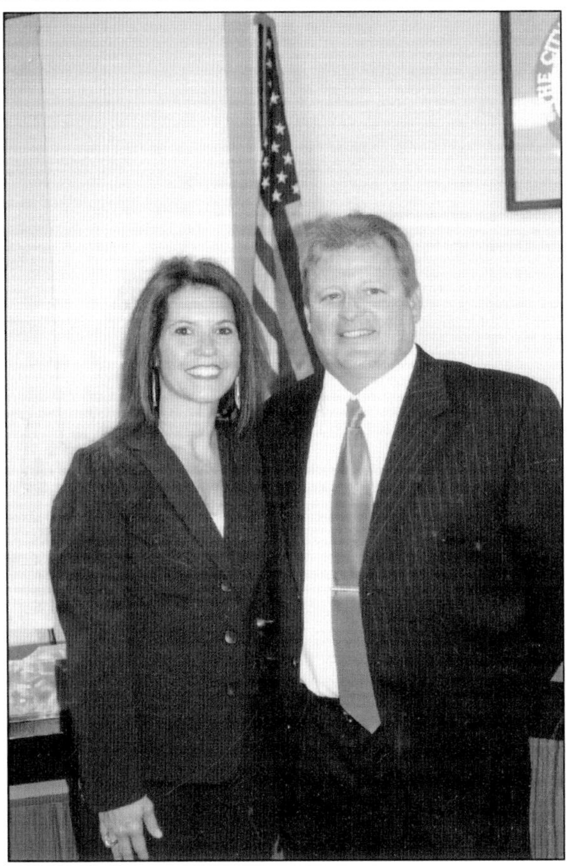

Mayor Frank Mullens is with his department heads. From left to right are (first row) James Wood, fire chief; Susan J. Riggs, attorney; Mayor Frank Mullens; Hannah Pettit, city treasurer; and Gerald Burgy, Public Works director; (second row) Steve DeBarr, engineer and sanitary board director; Danny Smith, recreation director; Brad Rhinehart, chief of police; Carlton Lee, city manager; and Mark D. Clark, city attorney. Mullens began as mayor of South Charleston in 2007. He is pictured at left with his lovely wife, Sherri, who sings the national anthem at many South Charleston functions. (Courtesy Bob Anderson.)

Five

MILITARY

South Charleston residents have served in many conflicts throughout American history. The *Charleston Gazette* Sunday newspaper honors servicemen from Kanawha County each year by publishing photographs of the men and women who have served their country. Ken Samples of Spring Hill collects photographs from area servicemen and sends them to the newspaper so they can be recognized. Ken is a very proud person and his nephew visits area schools and talks to the students about military service. In South Charleston, there are many commemorative statues and plaques to honor the men and women who have served their country in conflicts.

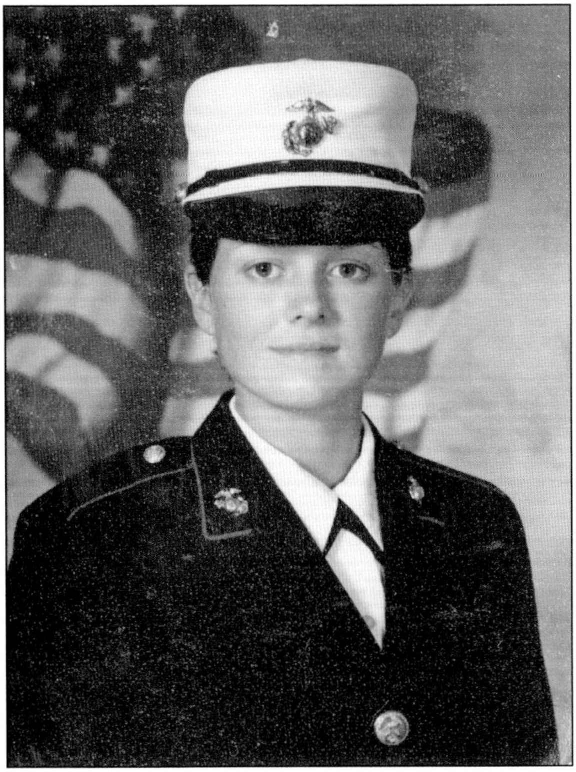

Sgt. Sally Chandler, U.S. Marines (left), and Frank Burgess, U.S. Air Force (below), served in Vietnam in the 1960s. (Both courtesy Ken Samples.)

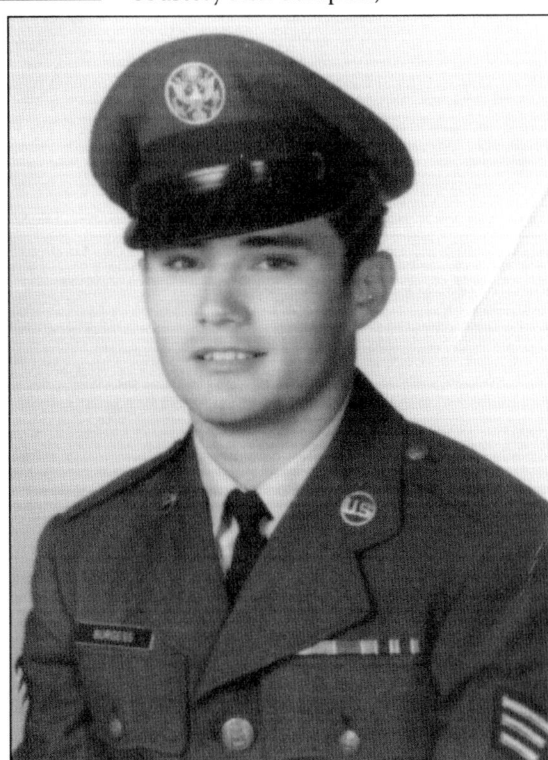

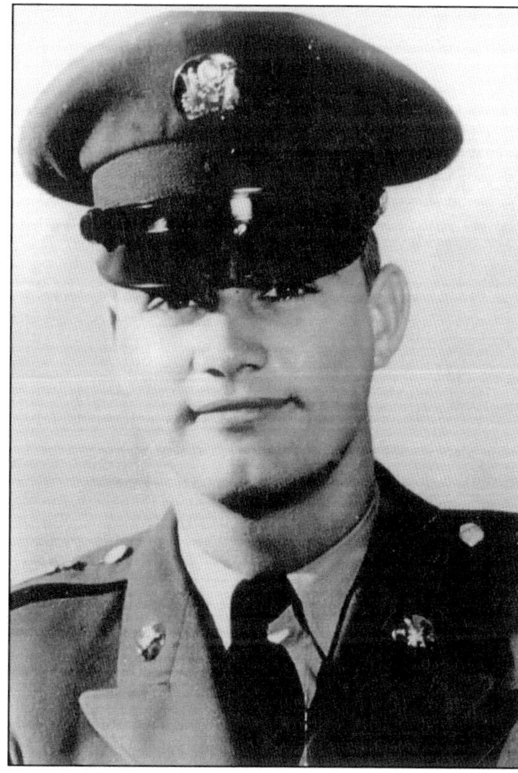

David C. Lucas, U.S. Army (right), and his wife, Barbara, now reside in Roanoke, West Virginia. Sid Mallory (below) served in the U.S. Army. (Both courtesy Ken Samples.)

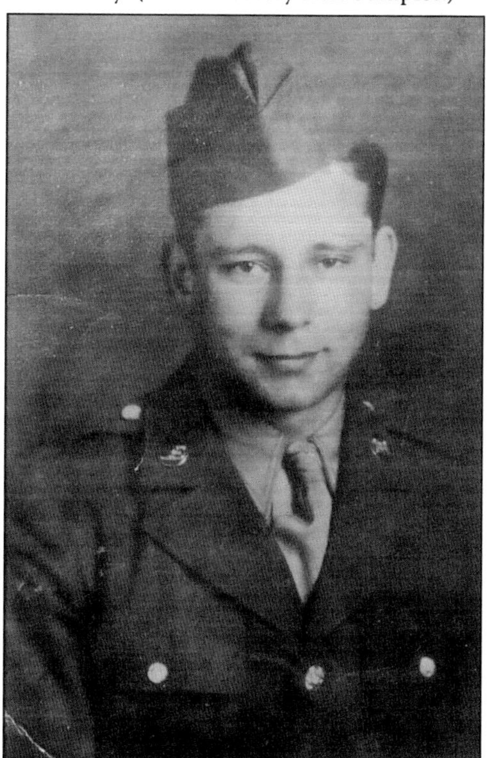

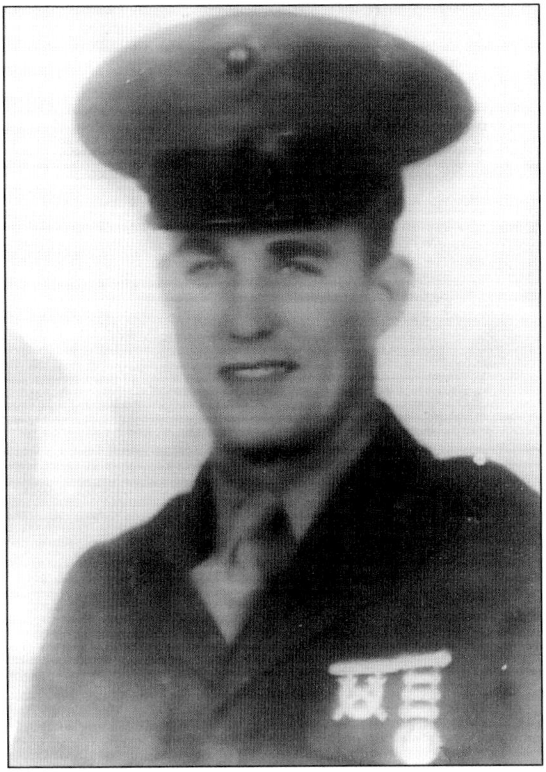

William Mason Lucas, U.S. Marines (left), served in World War II. Glen Williams, U.S. Air Force (below), served in Vietnam, and his brother Jack was in the U.S. Marine Corps. (Courtesy Ken Samples.)

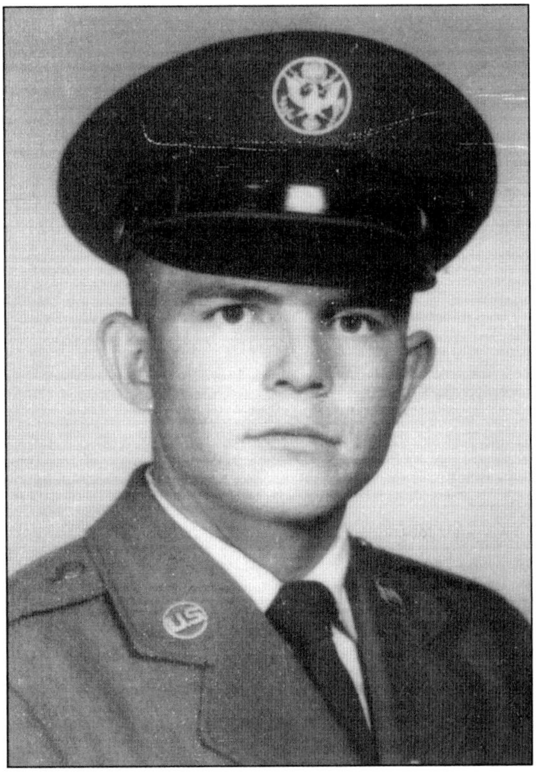

Steven Williams served with the U.S. Army in Germany. (Courtesy Ken Samples.)

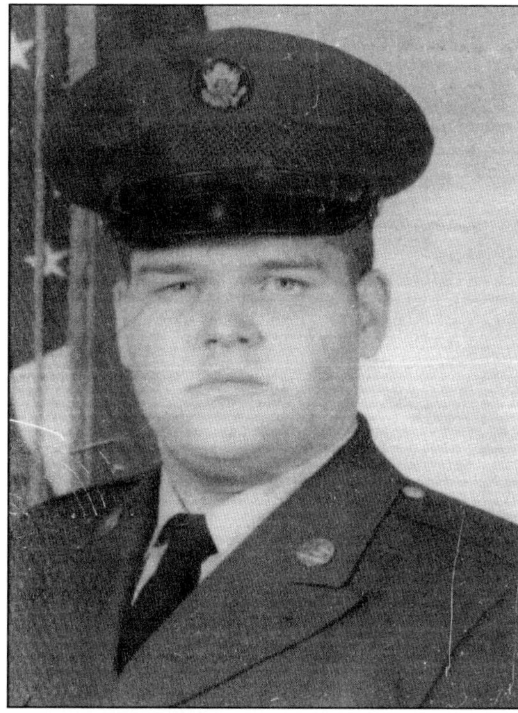

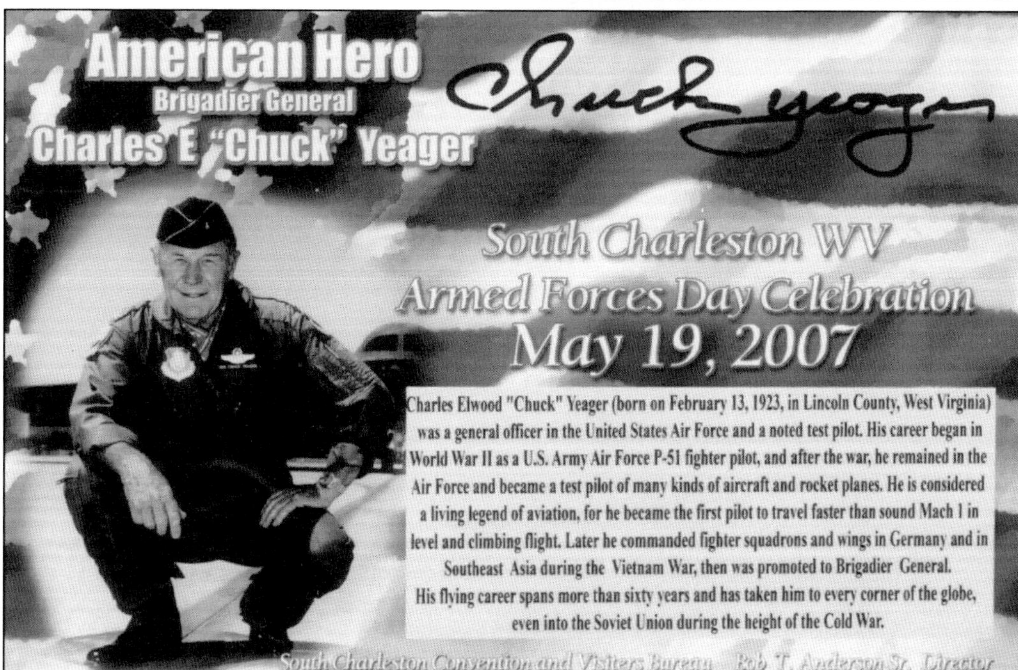

South Charleston has honored the military for more than 50 years. Brig. Gen. Charles E. "Chuck" Yeager was the parade grand marshal in 2007. He was the first pilot to travel faster than sound. In 2009, South Charleston was honored by a resolution introduced by the late senator Robert C. Byrd in Washington, D.C., for the 50th Armed Forces Day Celebration honoring the military. (Courtesy Bob Anderson.)

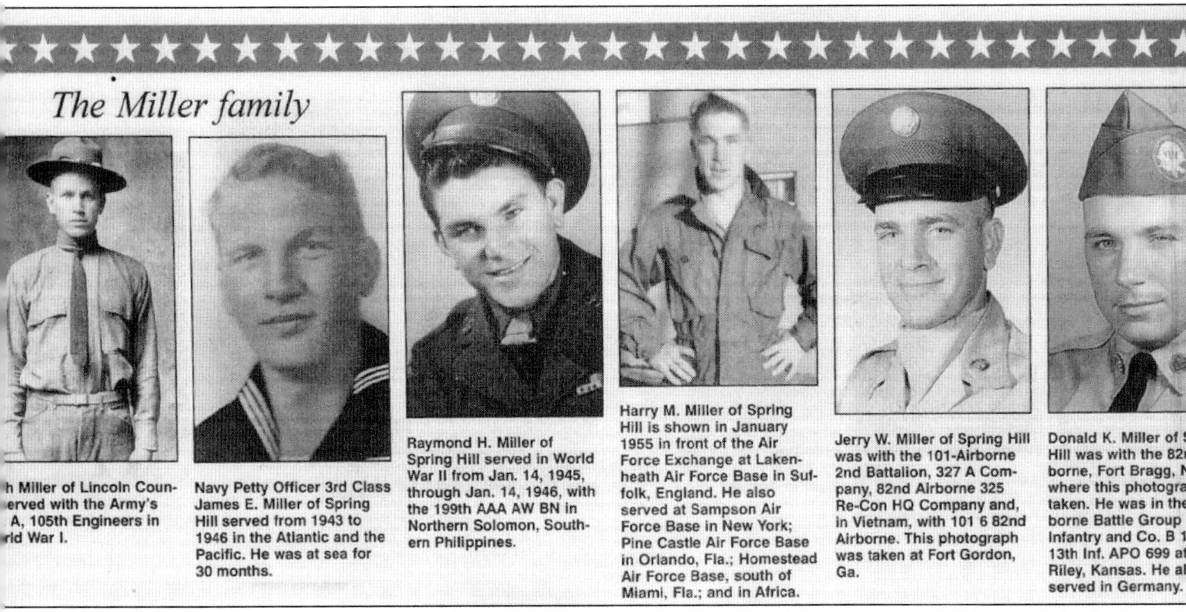

The Miller family

h Miller of Lincoln Coun- erved with the Army's A, 105th Engineers in rld War I.

Navy Petty Officer 3rd Class James E. Miller of Spring Hill served from 1943 to 1946 in the Atlantic and the Pacific. He was at sea for 30 months.

Raymond H. Miller of Spring Hill served in World War II from Jan. 14, 1945, through Jan. 14, 1946, with the 199th AAA AW BN in Northern Solomon, Southern Philippines.

Harry M. Miller of Spring Hill is shown in January 1955 in front of the Air Force Exchange at Lakenheath Air Force Base in Suffolk, England. He also served at Sampson Air Force Base in New York; Pine Castle Air Force Base in Orlando, Fla.; Homestead Air Force Base, south of Miami, Fla.; and in Africa.

Jerry W. Miller of Spring Hill was with the 101-Airborne 2nd Battalion, 327 A Company, 82nd Airborne 325 Re-Con HQ Company and, in Vietnam, with 101 6 82nd Airborne. This photograph was taken at Fort Gordon, Ga.

Donald K. Miller of S Hill was with the 82n borne, Fort Bragg, N where this photogra taken. He was in the borne Battle Group 1 Infantry and Co. B 1s 13th Inf. APO 699 at Riley, Kansas. He als served in Germany.

The Miller family of Spring Hill sent five sons to serve the country. Navy Petty Officer 3rd Class James Miller served from 1943 to 1946 in the Atlantic and Pacific. He was at sea for 30 months. Raymond served from 1945 through 1946 during World War II, with the 199th AAA AW BN in Northern Solomon, Southern Philippines. Harry is shown in front of the Air Force Exchange in England. He also served at Sampson Air Force Base in New York, and in Florida and Africa. Jerry was with the 101st Airborne 2nd Battalion, 327 A company, and in Vietnam was with the 101 6 82nd Airborne. Donald was with the 82nd Airborne, Fort Bragg, North Carolina; he was in the 1st Airborne battle group 187th infantry and Co. B 1st BG 13th Inf. APO 699 at Fort Riley, Kansas, and also served in Germany. Their father, Arch Miller, of Lincoln County, who later moved to Spring Hill, also served in the Army's Company A, 105th Engineers in World War I. (Courtesy Donald Miller.)

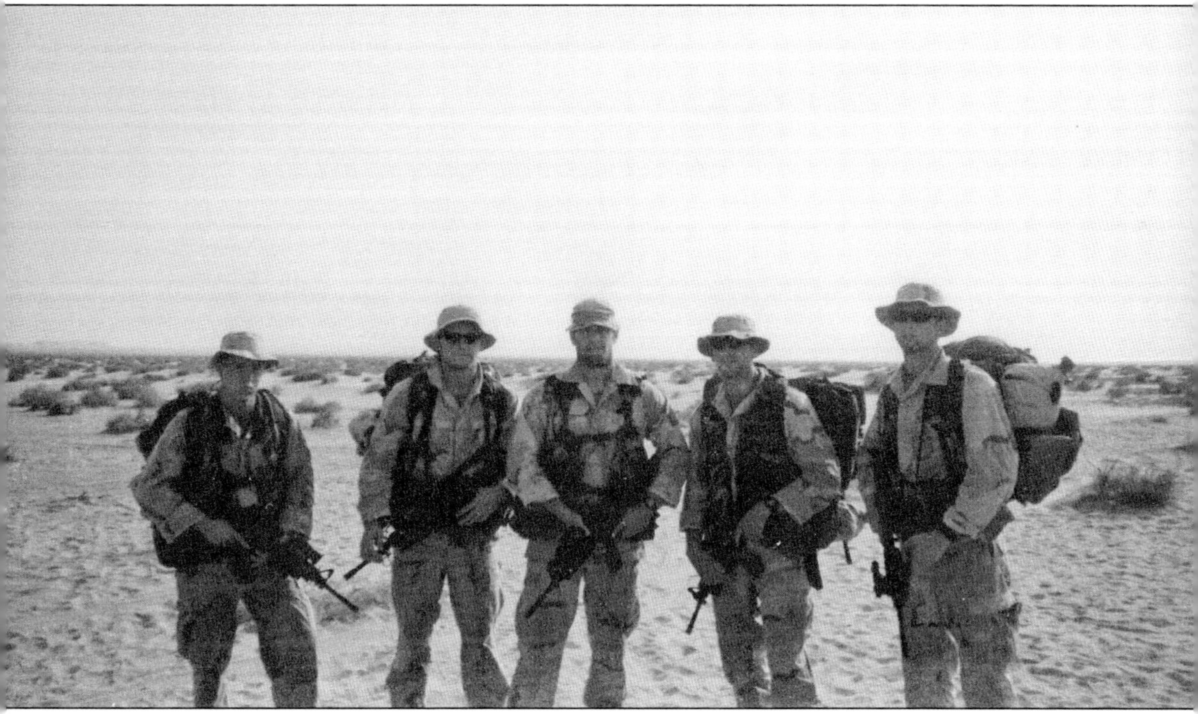

Matt Leavitt, U.S. Army sergeant 2001–2004 Iraq, IE Company, LRRP 51st Ranger, is the center soldier. (Courtesy Ken Samples.)

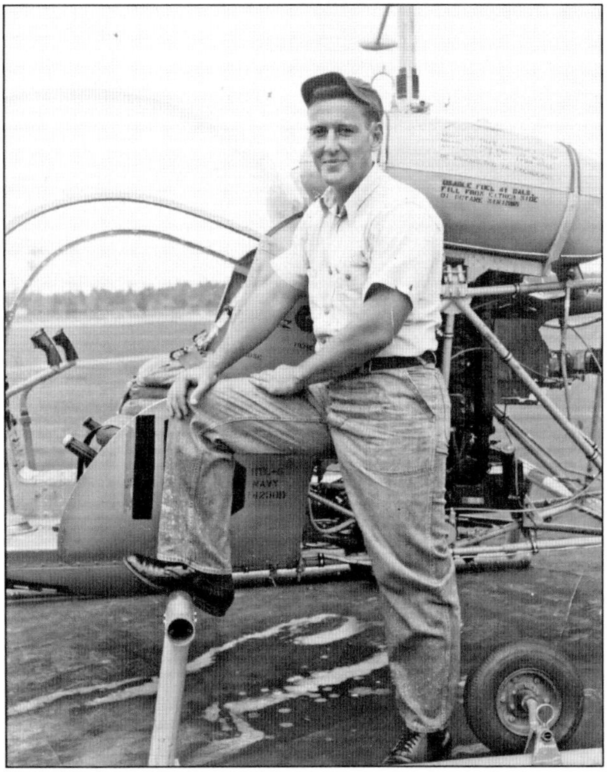

Paul Fox of South Charleston (left) served in the U.S. Navy during the Korean War and his daughter Julia (below) served in the U.S. Army during the Gulf War. (Courtesy Ken Samples and Nancy Fox.)

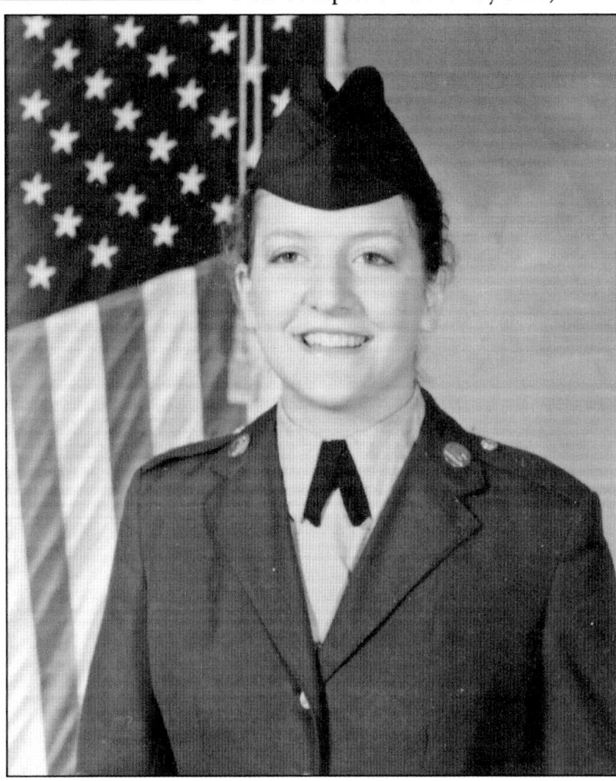

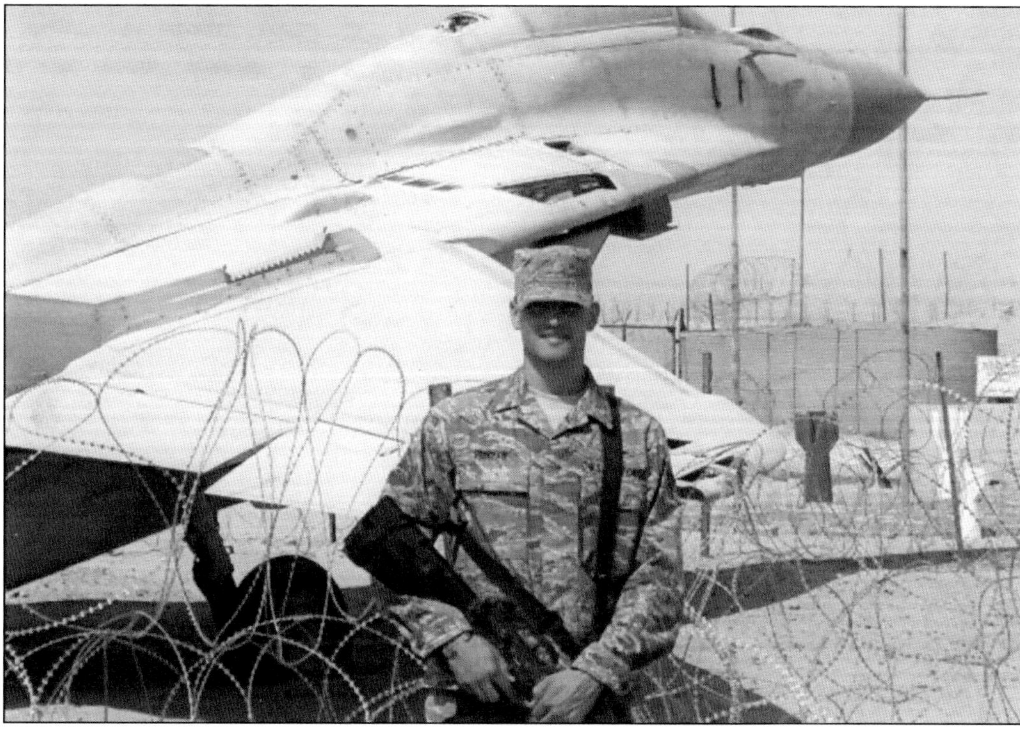

Adam Runyan (above), U.S. Air Force, served in Iraq. Charlie Miller (right), 87 Infantry, Rhineland, Germany, received the Purple Heart and the Bronze Star. (Both courtesy Ken Samples.)

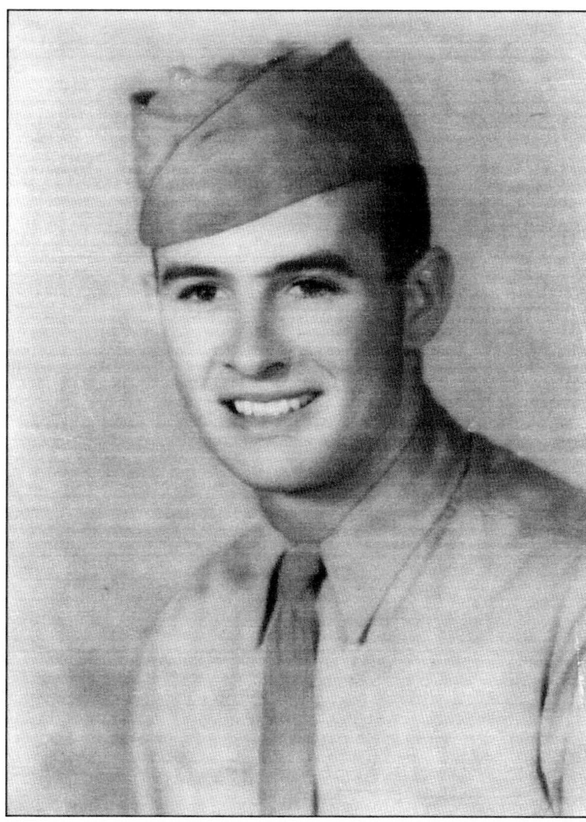

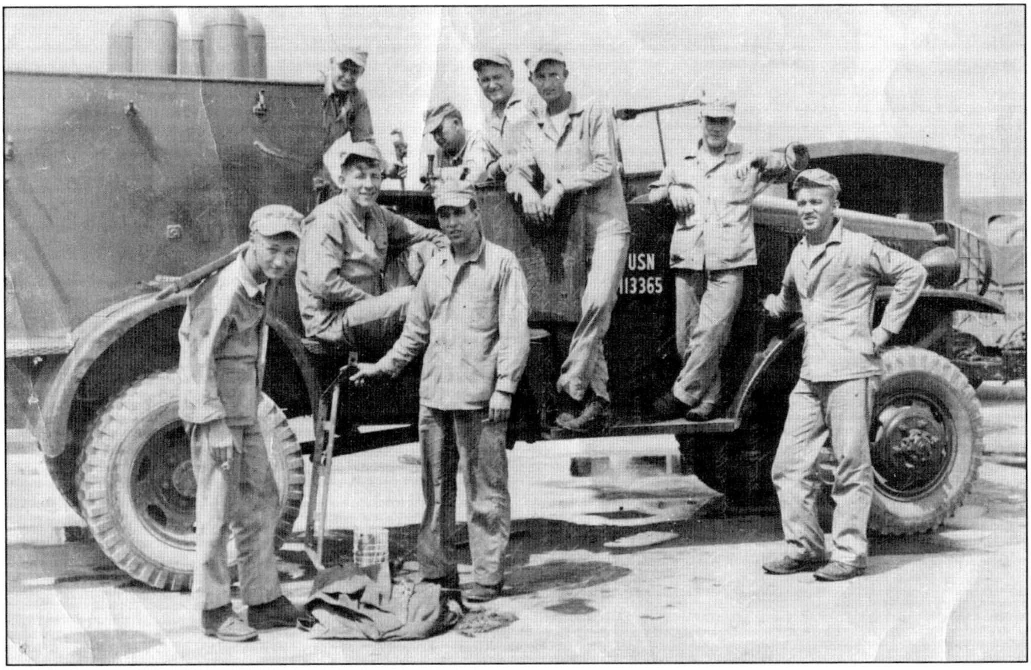

Benny Mallory is the second serviceman from the left sitting on the vehicle. He served with the U.S. Marines from 1952 to 1954. His training in the Marines helped him to build his flying dream. Benny fulfilled his dream of opening an airport in Spring Hill, West Virginia, and called it Mallory Airport. He now serves as West Virginia's aeronautical chairman. (Courtesy Ken Samples.)

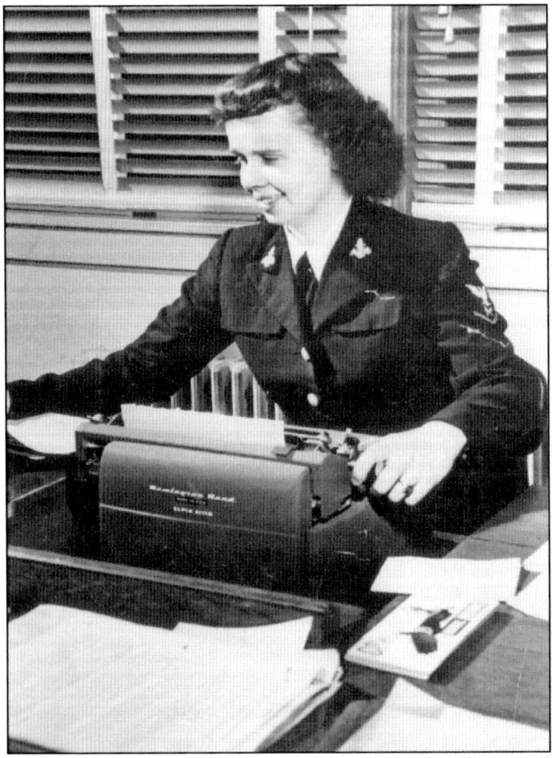

Lucie Frame Mellert, YNT3, of Quarrier Street spent Tuesday evenings doing office work and taking training at the Naval Reserve Training Center in South Charleston. She now takes pictures for the local newspaper and for the SCCVB. (Courtesy Lucie Mellert.)

William E. "Butch" Buckley served in the U.S. Army and is now the manager of the South Charleston Memorial Ice Arena on Corridor G in South Charleston. (Courtesy South Charleston Museum.)

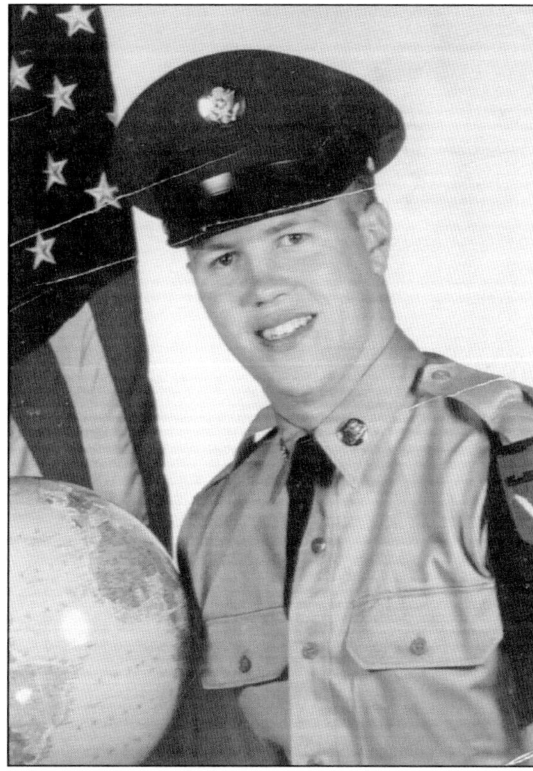

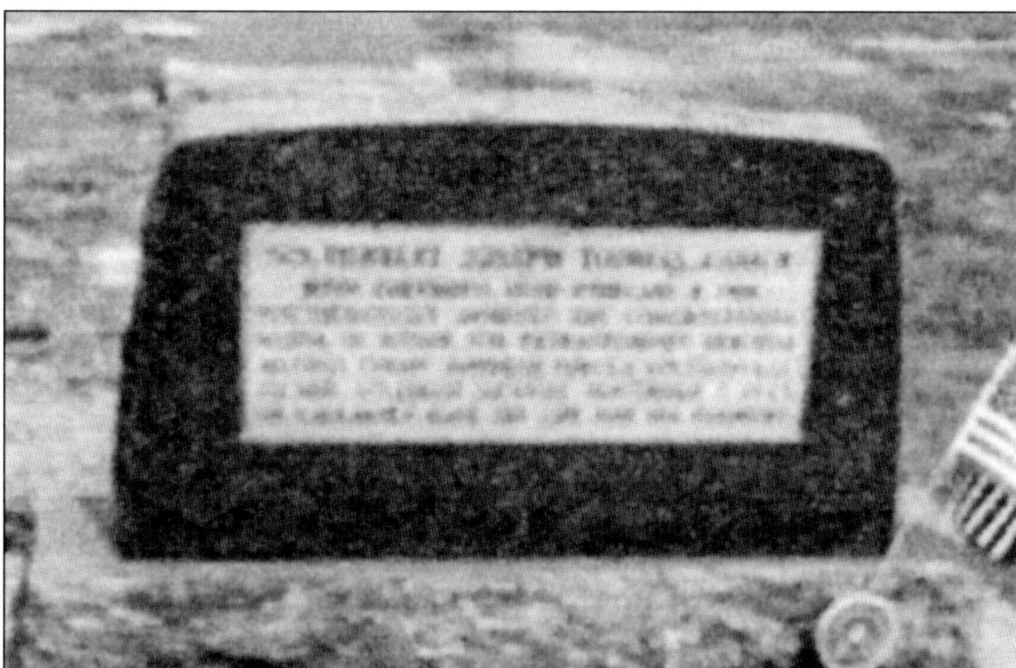

Herbert Joseph Thomas Jr. was honored by South Charleston when the hospital was named in his honor. On March 26, 1945, the government named a destroyer, the *U.S.S. Herbert J. Thomas*, in his memory, and his sister Audrey christened it. (Courtesy South Charleston Museum.)

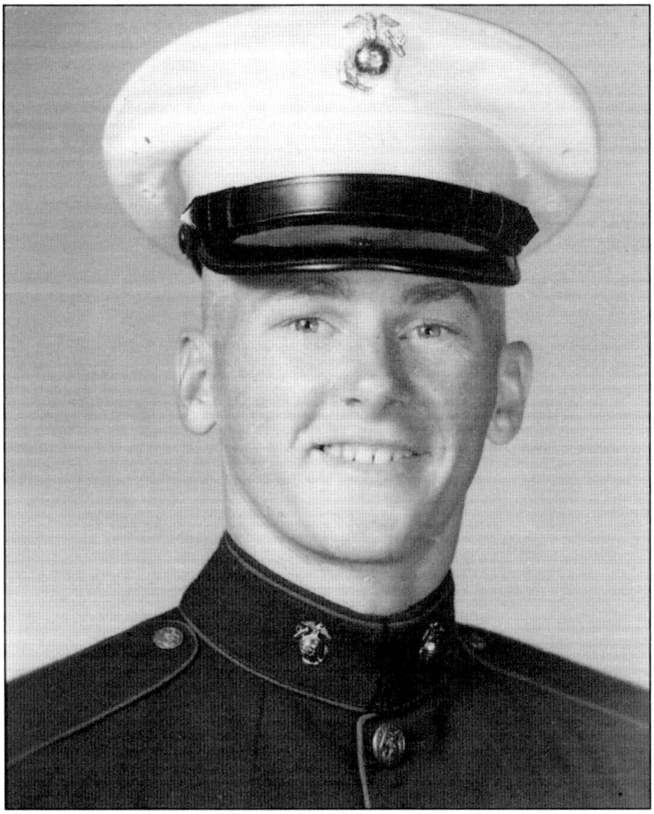

Jerry Lee Billups served in the U.S. Marines, and two of his daughters live in South Charleston, Vicki Lee Vaughan and Gina Louann Billups. His son, Jerry Lee Billups Jr., lives in Florida. (Courtesy Gina Billups.)

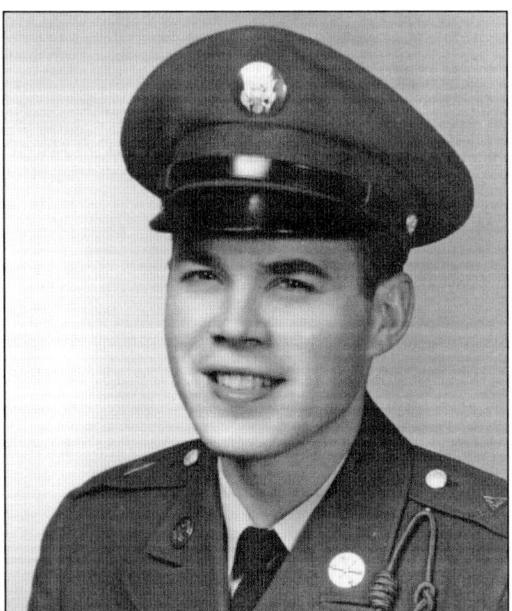

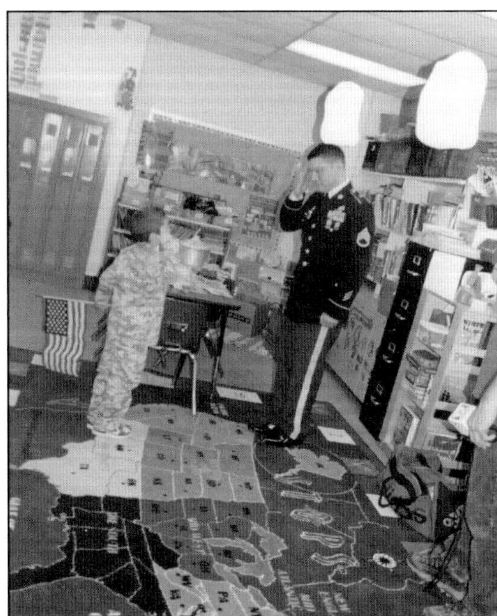

Ken Samples (left) served in the U.S. Army and his nephew, Joseph Allan Samples (right), also served in the U.S. Army, spending two terms in Iraq. He communicated with students from area elementary schools while serving his country. (Courtesy Ken Samples.)

Six

Businesses

Several South Charleston businesses have been in the city for more than 50 years. The ordnance facility was built during World War I, and today serves as a complex for several businesses and is owned by the Park Corporation. Several chemical companies came to South Charleston in the 1920s, and two glass companies opened in the early 1900s. Broyles Jewelry Store in the Spring Hill area and Evans Lumber Company on D Street have operated for more than 50 years. Joe Holland Chevrolet bought Rhodes Walker Chevrolet in the 1960s.

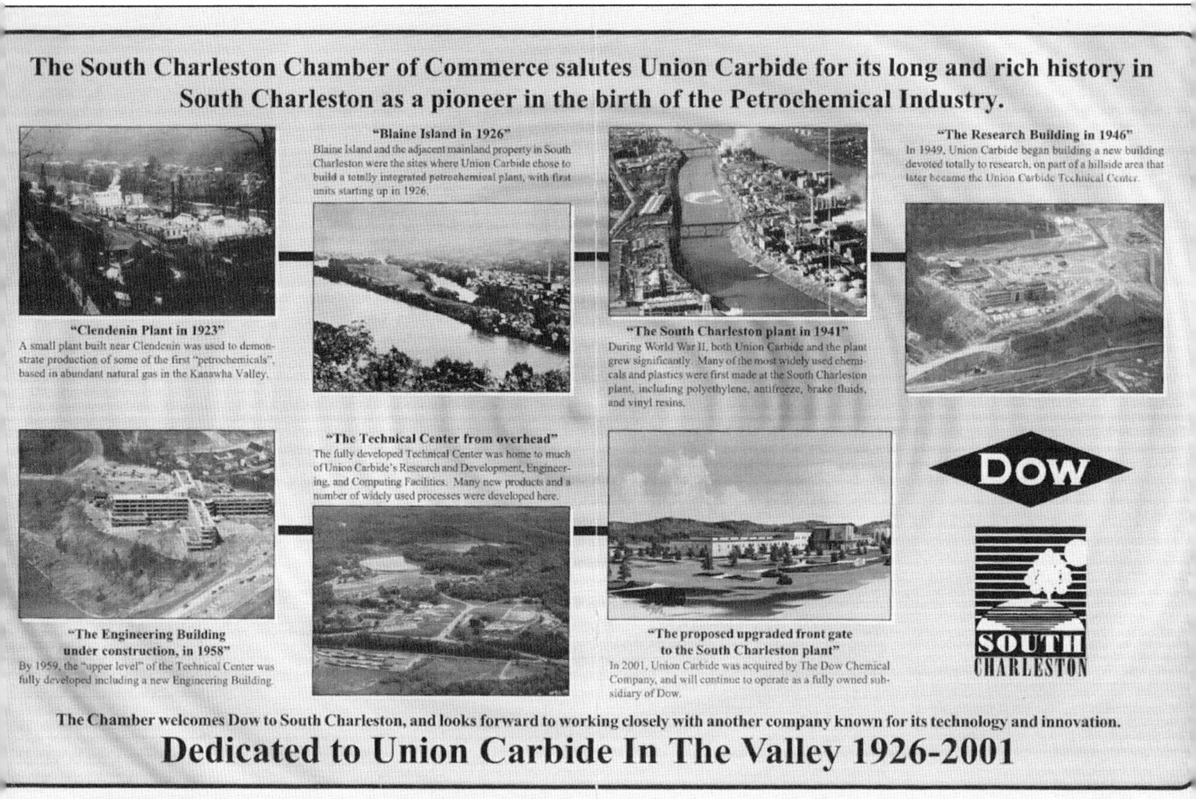

An early Union Carbide publication stated: "The initial contract at South Charleston called for taking possession as of November 30, 1923, and covered a five year period with option to renew and option to purchase." In early 1924, a construction crew was at work, cleaning out the old buildings and making the site ready for occupation. Today Union Carbide is a wholly owned subsidiary of the Dow Chemical Corporation and was purchased in 2001. (Courtesy South Charleston Museum.)

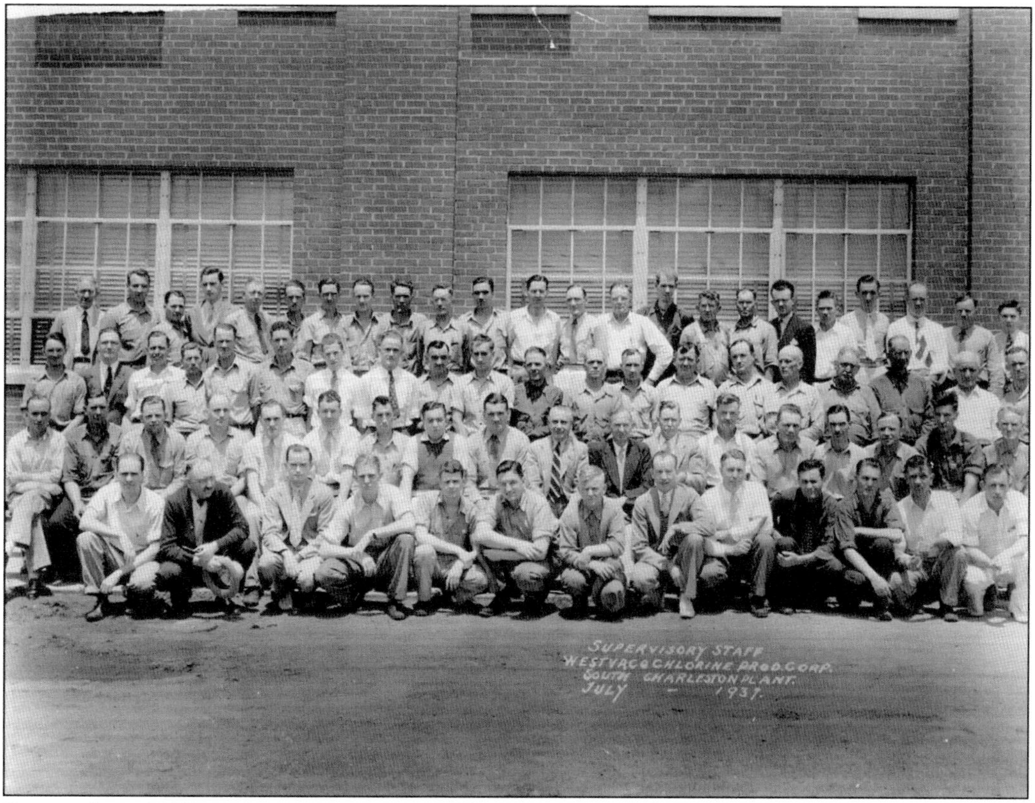

Pictured in 1937 is the supervisory staff of Westvaco Chlorine Products Corporation at the South Charleston Plant. Westvaco employed many local residents. (Courtesy South Charleston Museum.)

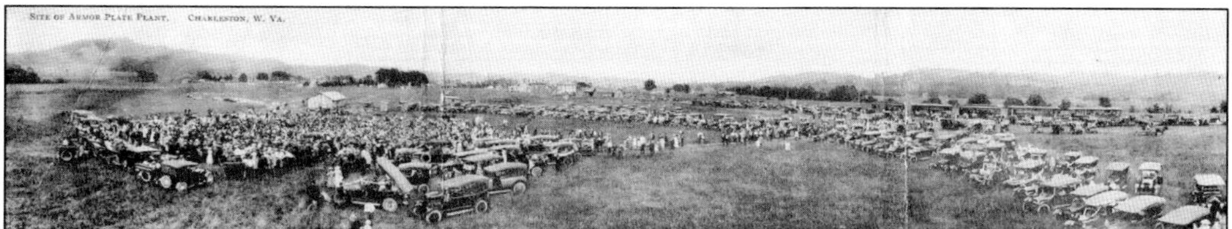

This postcard from the early 1900s shows the Naval Ordnance site, referred to as the site of the Armor Plate Plant, in Charleston, West Virginia. (Courtesy South Charleston Museum.)

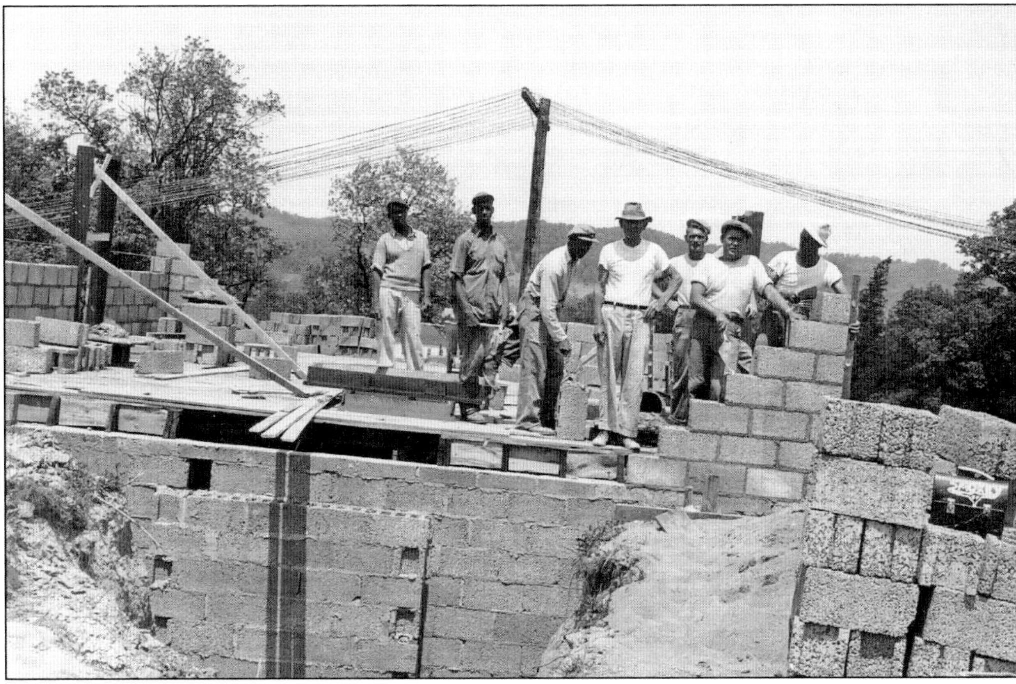

A new building is going up in South Charleston in the 1940s. Workers, from left to right, are Bill Duckwyler, Smokey Duckwyler (lunchbox on the blocks to the right), George Richardson, Clarence Dillon, Junior Reynolds, "Tucker" Bowen, and Kermit Bowen. (Courtesy Judy Romano.)

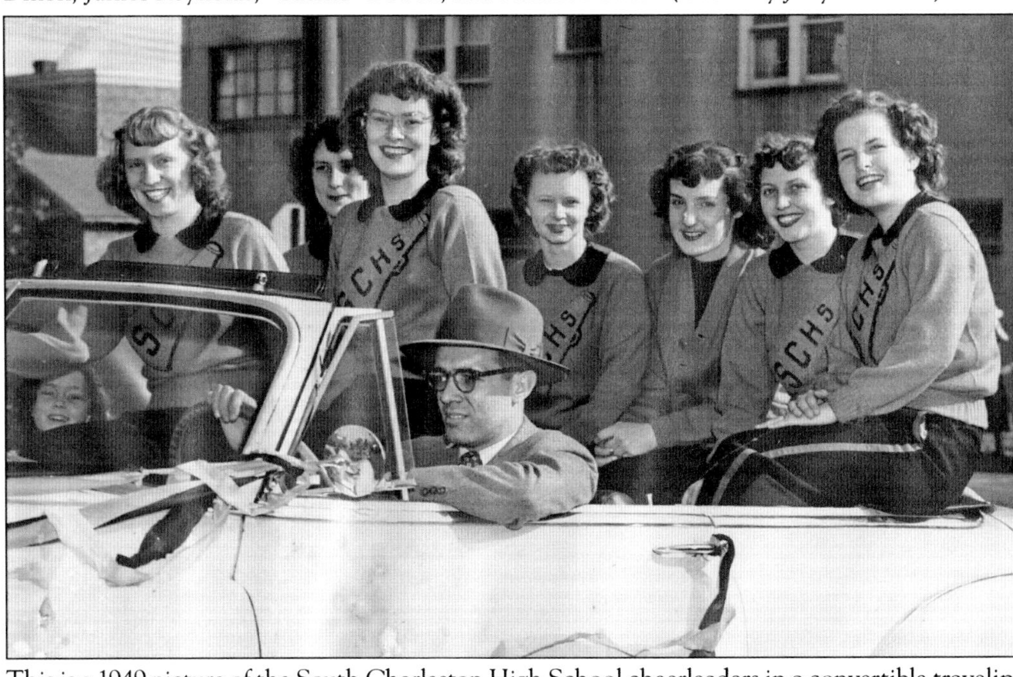

This is a 1949 picture of the South Charleston High School cheerleaders in a convertible traveling down D Street at the annual homecoming parade. Pictured in the car are Patty Coffman, Marjorie Coen, Joy Loftis, Sara Barker, Pat Durrett, and Maxine Dent (Crawford). (Courtesy South Charleston Museum.)

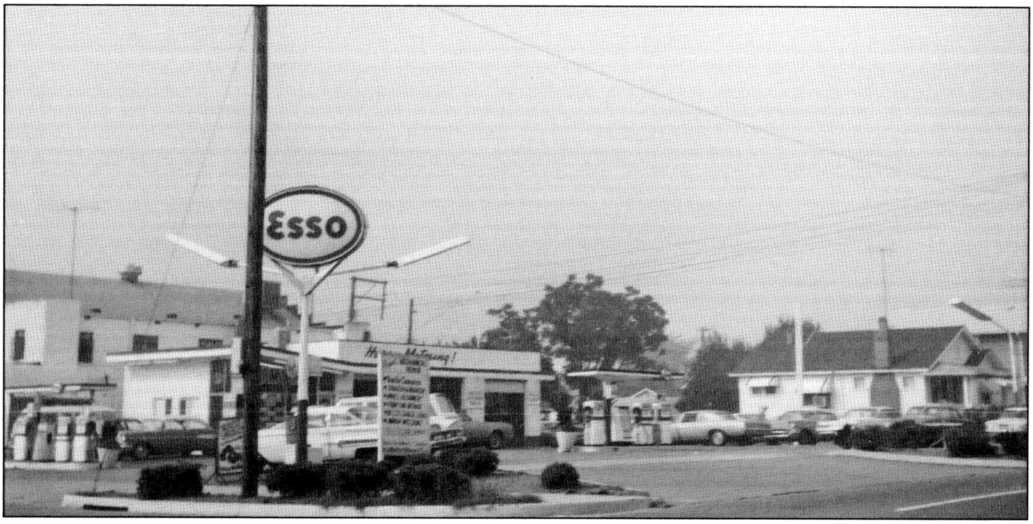

The city of South Charleston bought this property in 1997, which was once home to Ben Paul's Esso service station. Ben Paul operated this business from 1963 until 1989. The property now houses the Regional Intergovernmental Council, which faces D Street. Ben's station was on the corner of D Street and Fourth Avenue. (Courtesy Ben Paul.)

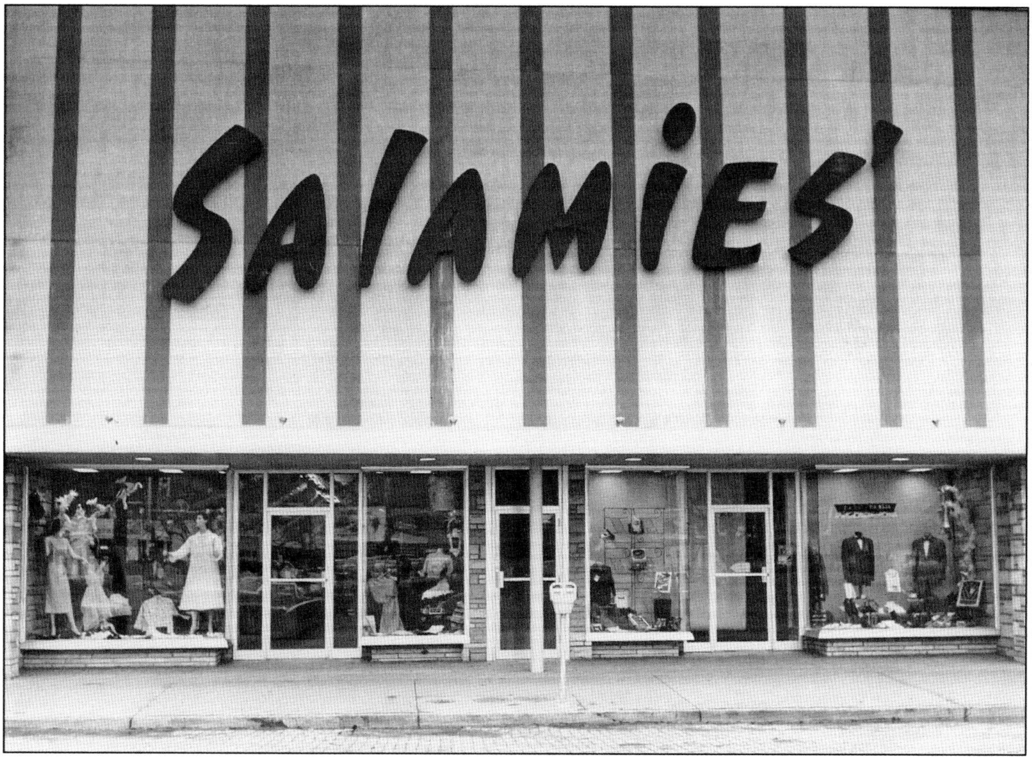

In the late 1950s, the Salamie family changed the appearance of Seventh Avenue when they remodeled and changed their store from working men and women, church, and housedresses to a fashion store for men and women. The twins, Don and Dale, along with their siblings Juanita and Dick ran the store for many years. Their parents, George and Sadie, came to South Charleston as newly weds in the 1920s and opened this store. (Courtesy Diana Salamie.)

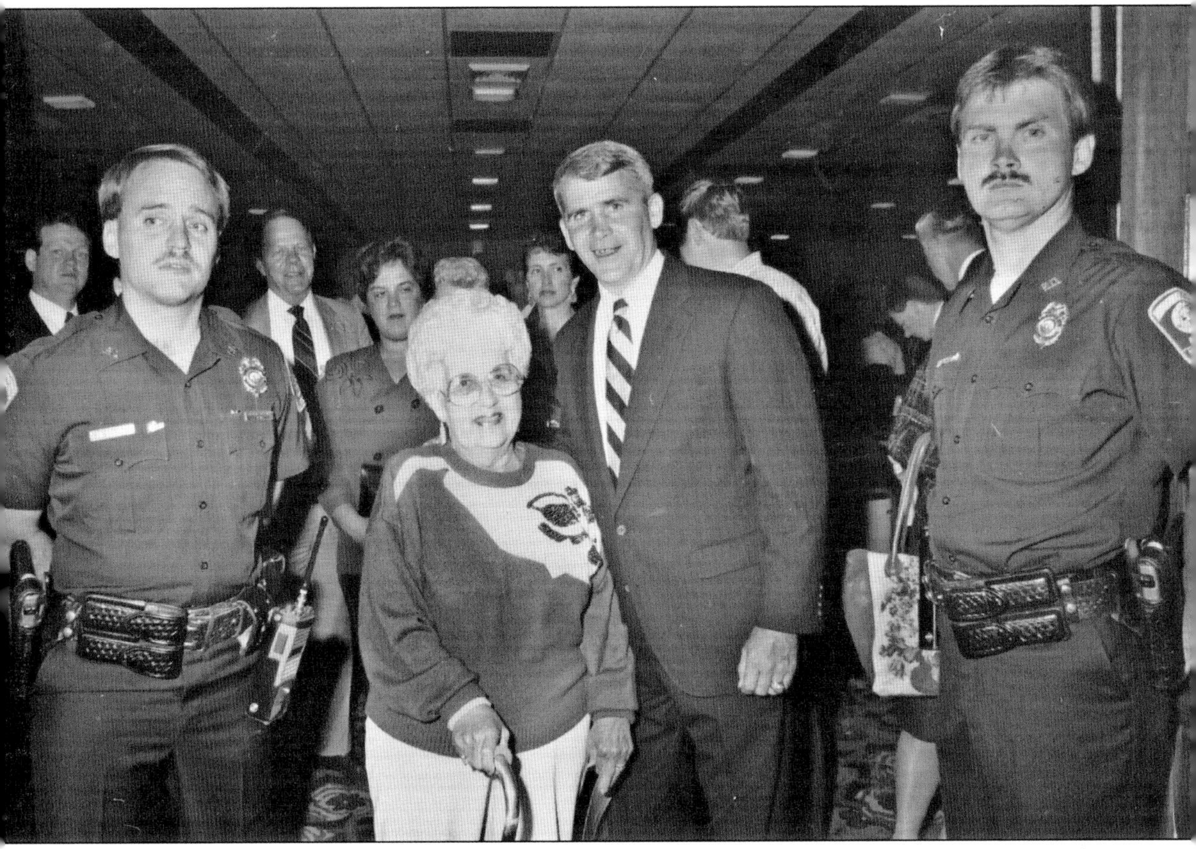

Audrey Bowen, a registrar for the South Charleston Convention Bureau in the 1990s, is shown here with Col. Oliver North. The South Charleston Police Department invited North to speak at their convention held at the South Charleston Ramada Inn. (Courtesy South Charleston Museum.)

Seven

SCHOOLS AND SPORTS

South Charleston High School opened in 1926 in a distinctive five-sided building on Third Avenue and played its first basketball and football games that year. The first yearbook was the *Loudspeaker*, renamed the *Pentagon* in 1929. The first class ring was worn until 1971. In 1933–1934, the school was named South Charleston High School, orange and black were chosen for the school colors, and the black eagle as the school's mascot. The first Miss Black Eagle was Carolyn Hoover, and the first Miss Kanawha Majorette was Dolores (Blackwell) Thompson.

South Charleston High School State Championships:

1940 boy's golf
1941 boy's golf
1942 boy's golf
1945–1946 football
1958–1959 boy's basketball
1976–1977 baseball
1977–1978 baseball
1994–1995 AAA football
2003 AAA girl's basketball
2008 AAA football
2008 girl's tennis

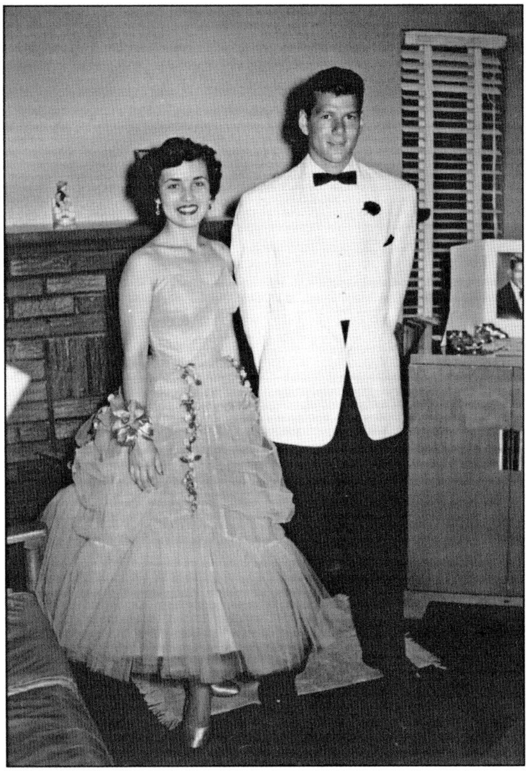

Luana Bowen and Jerry Chandler are on their way to the prom at South Charleston High School. Chandler graduated from South Charleston High School in 1954 and went on to play basketball at Morris Harvey College, now the University of Charleston. Jerry and Luana married and moved to Daytona Beach, Florida, in 1960 with Coach Jack Surette. Jerry has been with Seabreeze High School for over 50 years. (Courtesy Luana Bowen Chandler.)

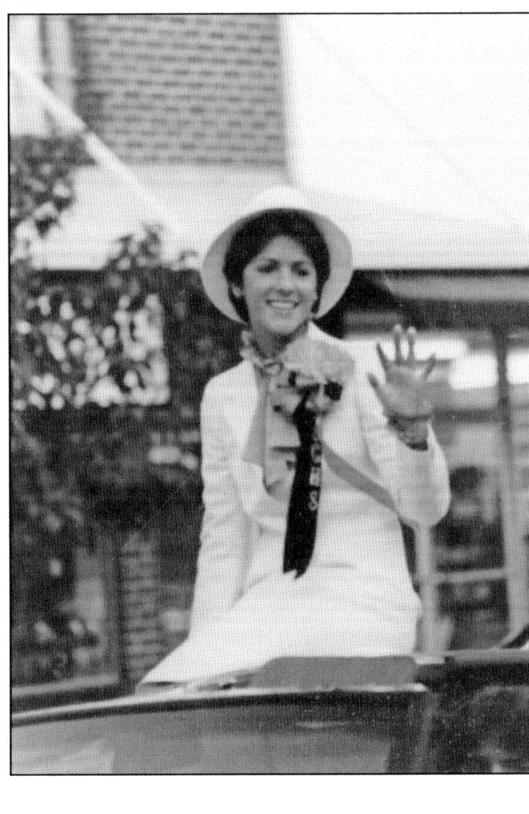

Paula Romano waves at the crowd at the homecoming parade in South Charleston. She was chosen by her class to be the South Charleston High School Homecoming Queen attendant in 1982. (Courtesy South Charleston Museum.)

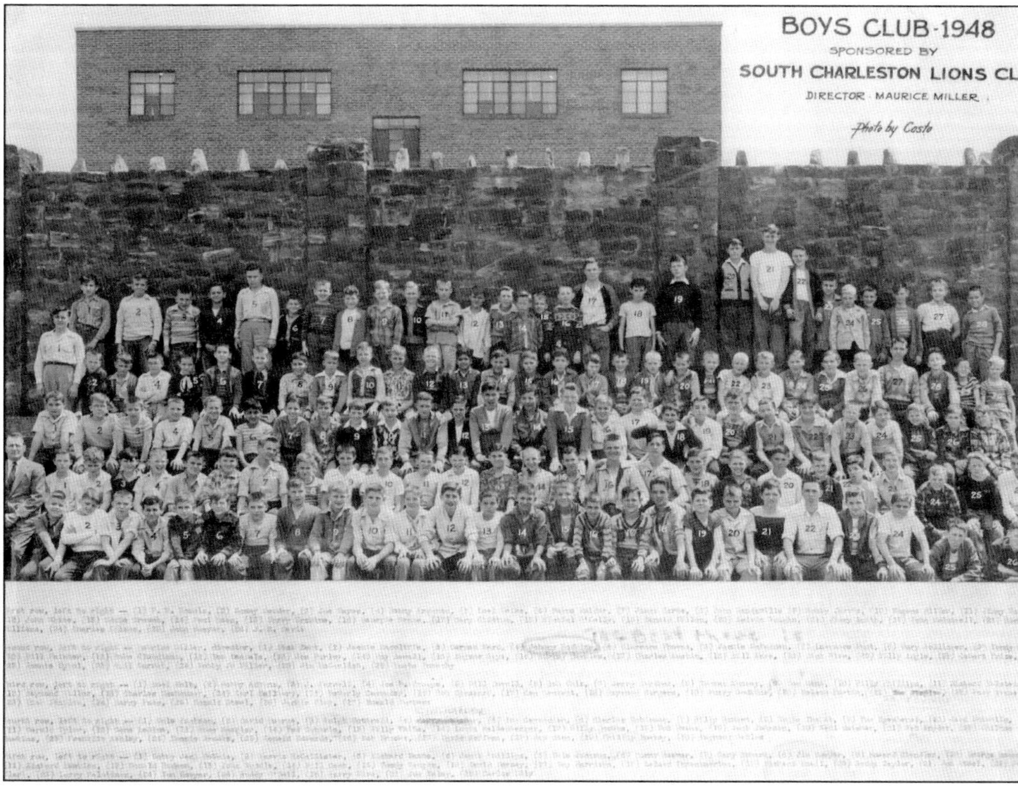

The 1948 Boys Club was sponsored by the South Charleston Lions Club director Maurice Miller. (Courtesy South Charleston Museum.)

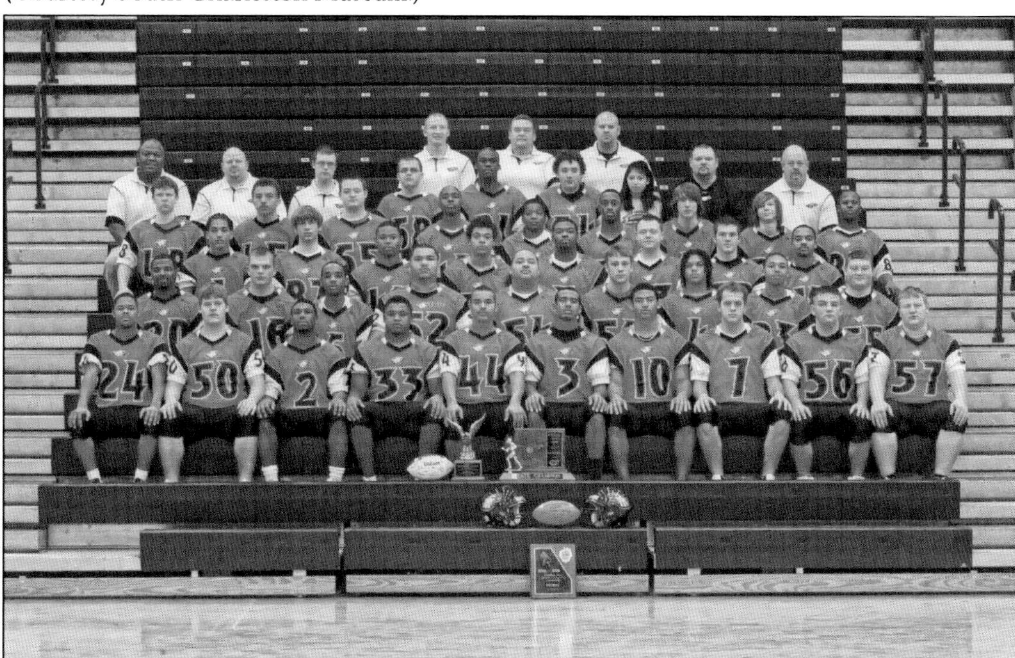

The 2008 AAA state football champions, with a 14–0 record. (Courtesy Ken Samples.)

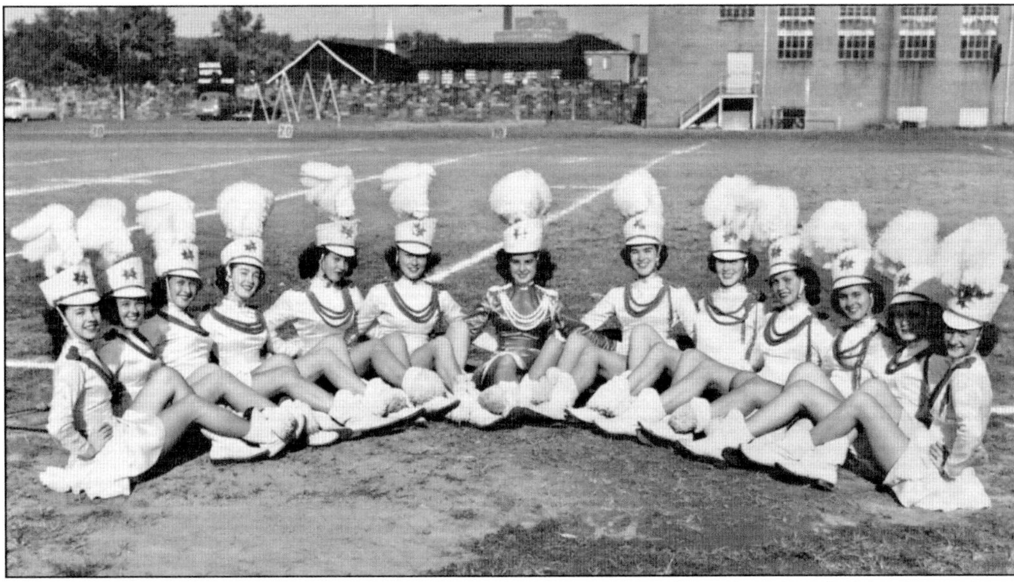

Pictured are the South Charleston High School majorettes in the 1950s. South Charleston High School's Delores Thompson was the very first Miss Kanawha Majorette. The *Charleston Daily Mail* has sponsored the Kanawha County Majorette festival for many years, and the school is proud to say their majorette was the first to be honored. (Courtesy South Charleston Museum.)

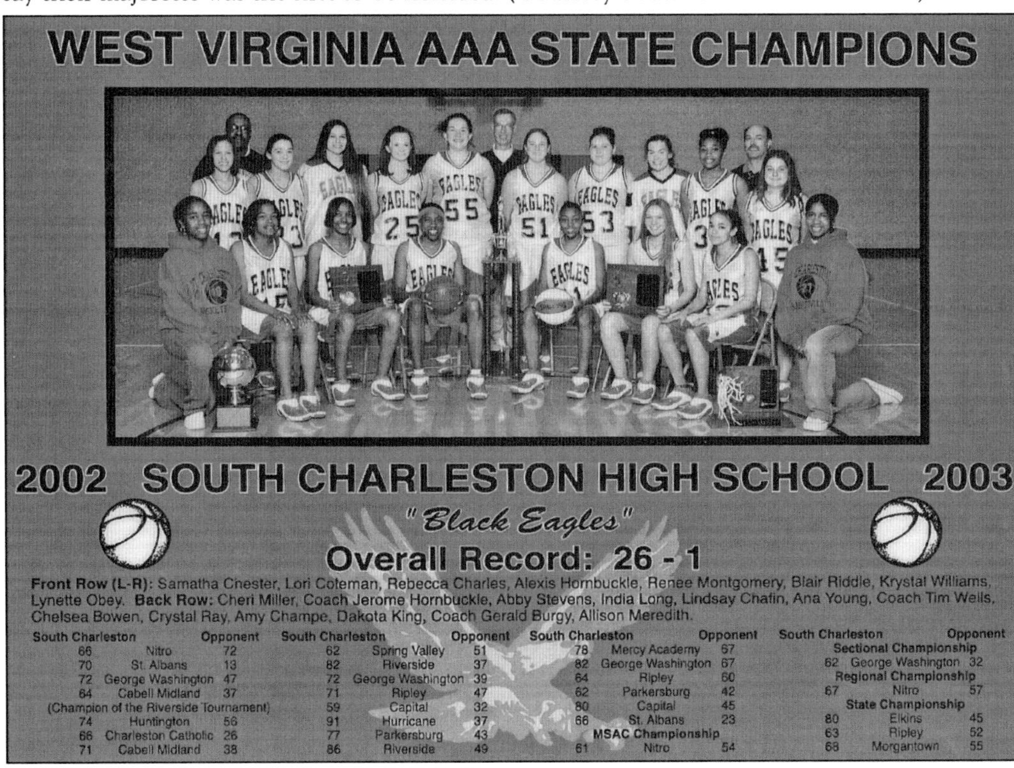

The South Charleston High School 2002–2003 girl's basketball team were the West Virginia AAA state champions with a 26–1 record. Two players went on to play college basketball. (Courtesy Ken Samples.)

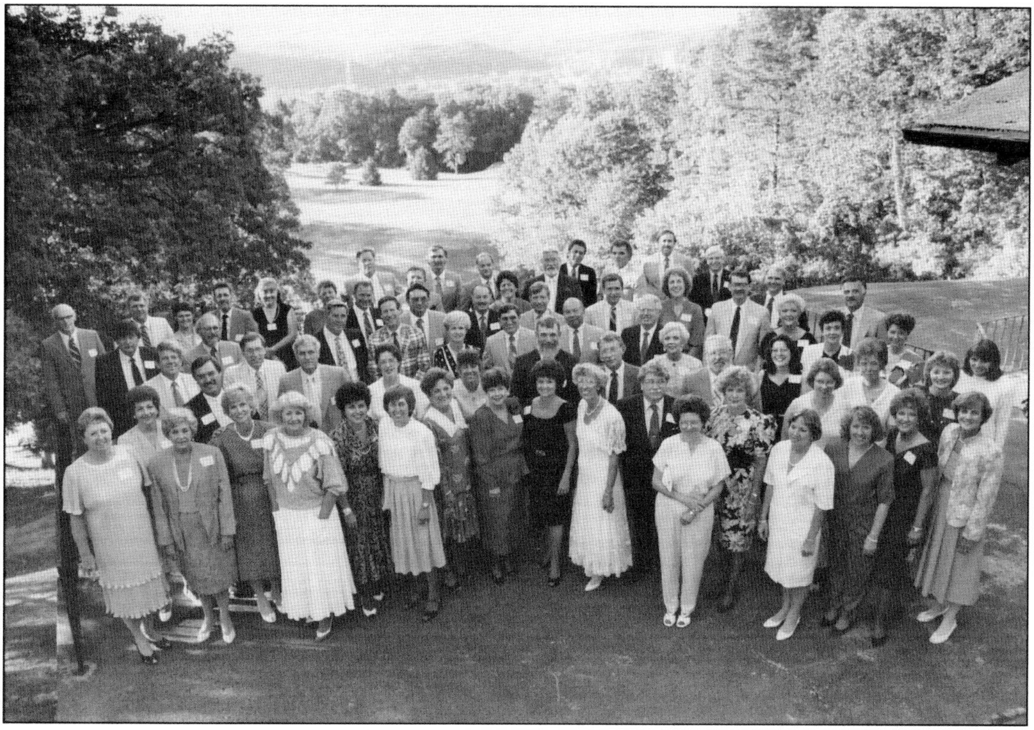

The South Charleston High School class of 1958 is pictured at their 30-year (above) and 25-year (below) reunions. (Courtesy South Charleston Museum.)

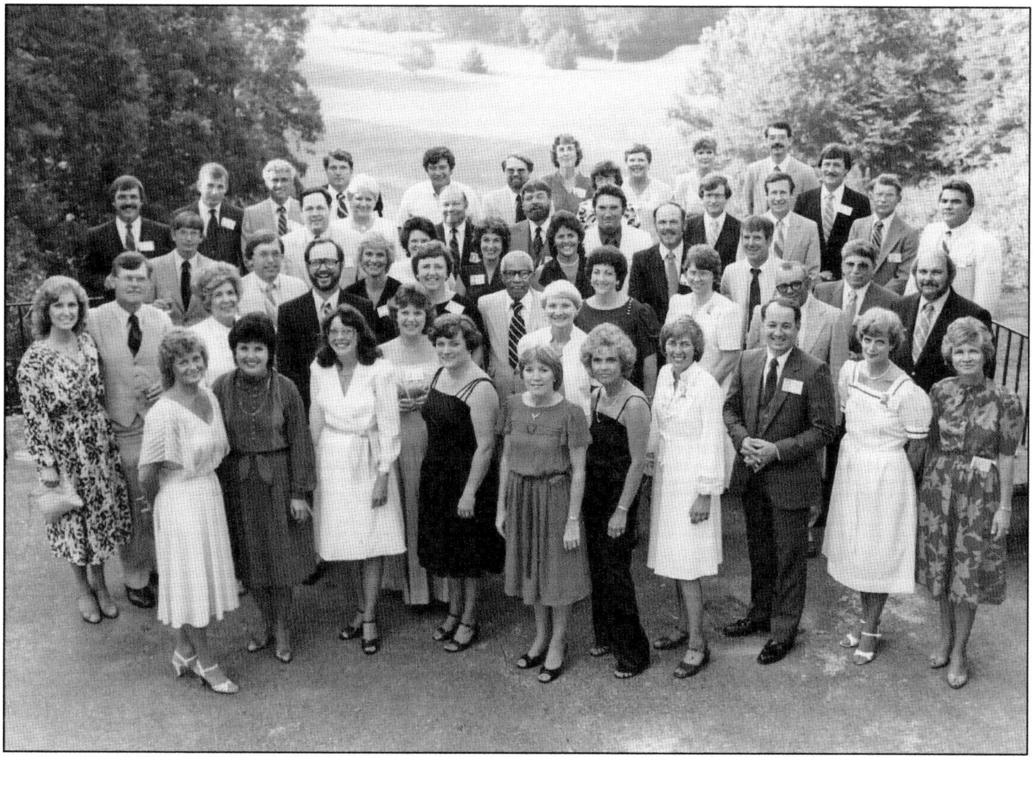

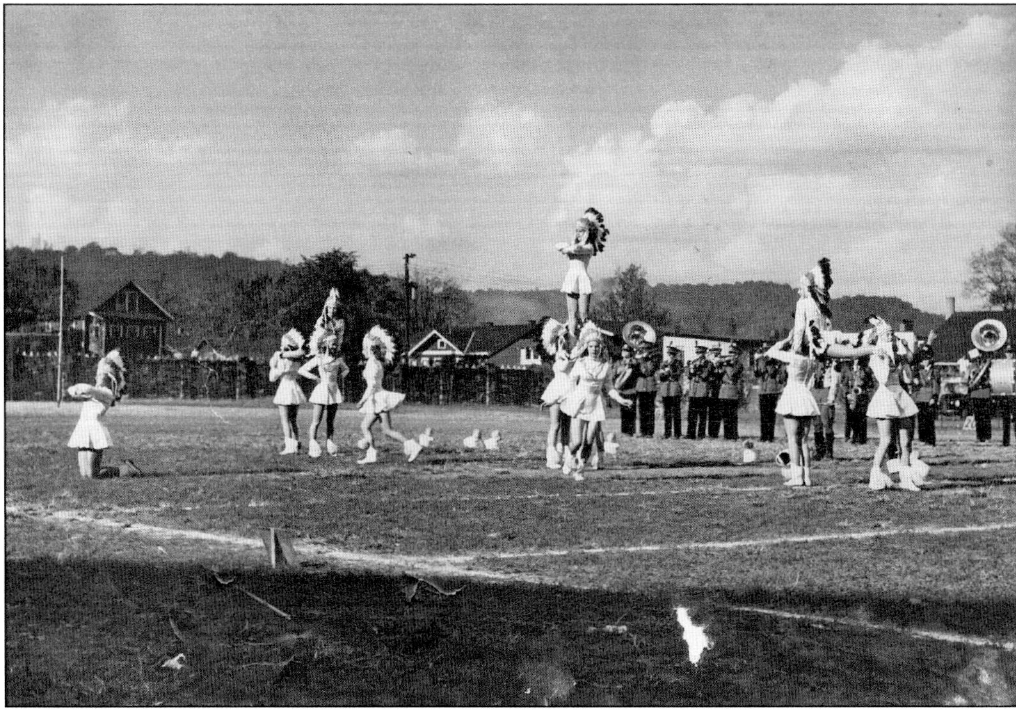

The South Charleston High School majorettes perform a routine with the band. (Courtesy South Charleston Museum.)

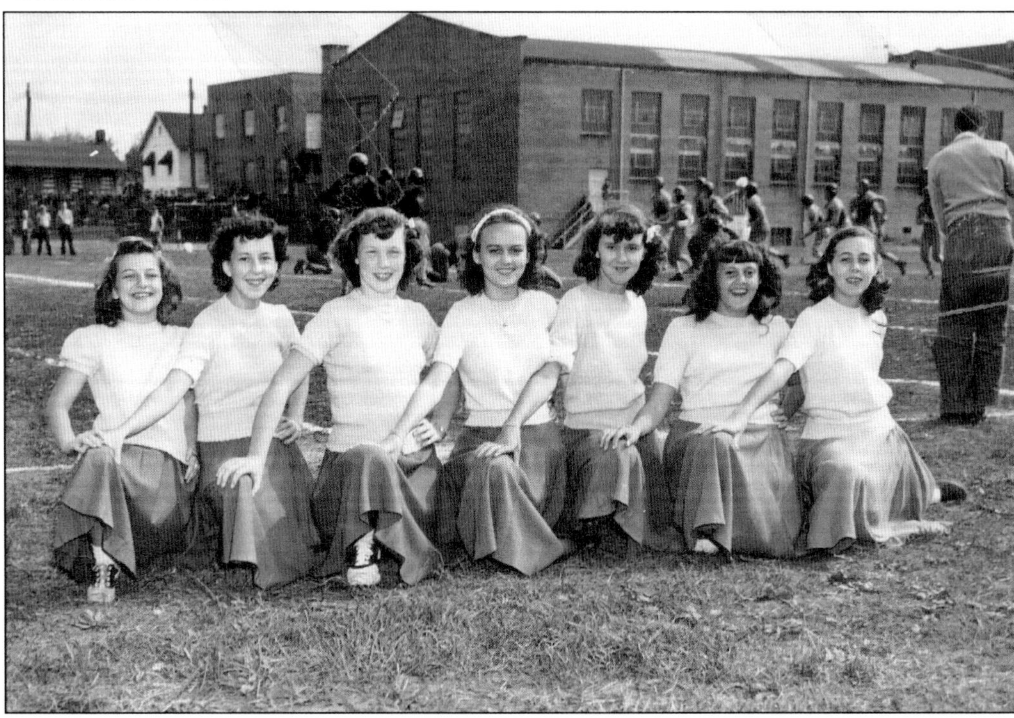

In the 1940s, the South Charleston Junior High cheerleaders are posing on the football field. Edith Jean Scott is on the left. The others are unidentified. (Courtesy South Charleston Museum.)

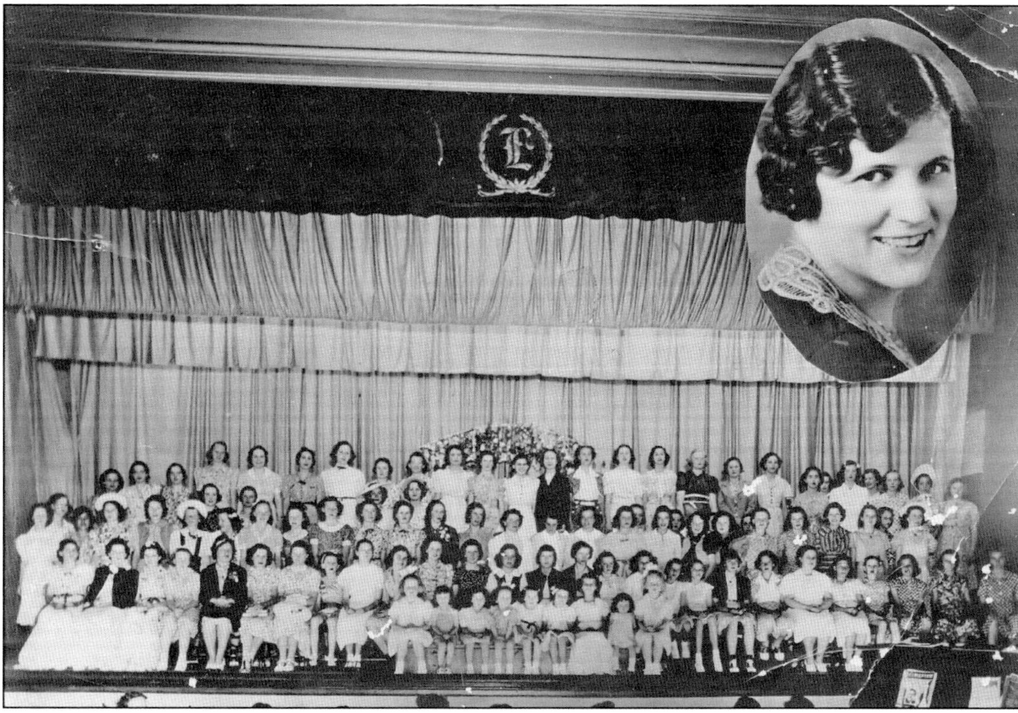

The 1936–1937 South Charleston High School sewing class won awards for their garments, and their parents attended this presentation. The home economics teacher is in the inset. (Courtesy South Charleston Museum.)

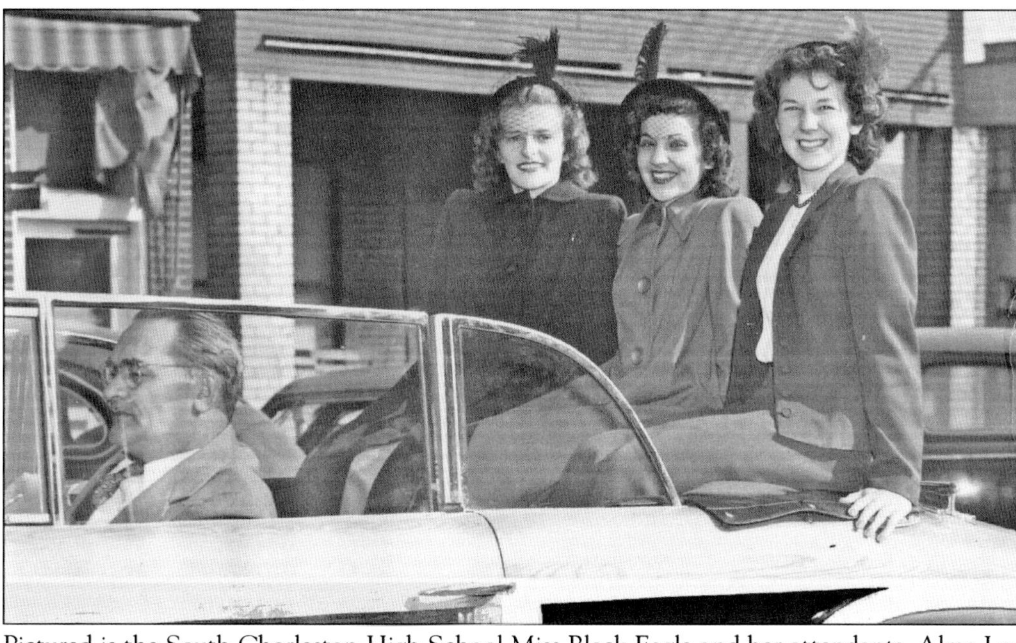

Pictured is the South Charleston High School Miss Black Eagle and her attendants, Alma Lou Combs, Ruth Kinder, and Judy Gay. The driver of the convertible is unidentified. South Charleston loves parades, and each year they have a homecoming parade before the annual homecoming football game. (Courtesy South Charleston Museum.)

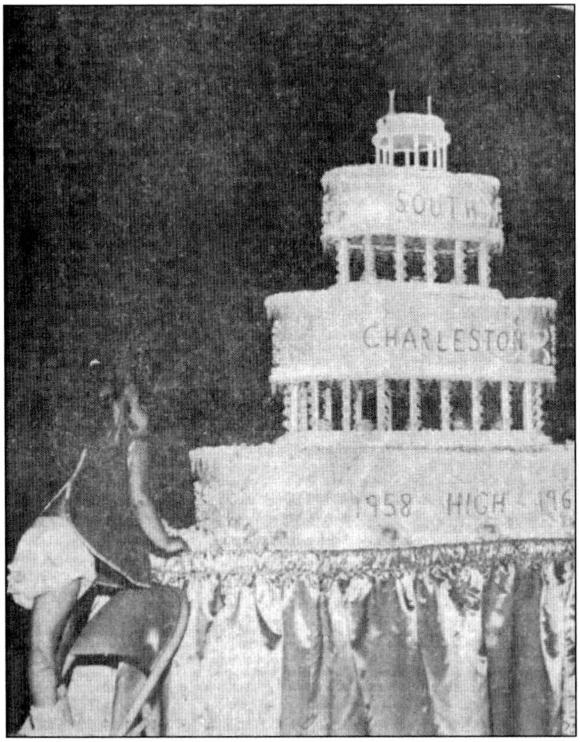

Chef Eric Crane of the Greenbrier Hotel prepared this cake for the South Charleston High School class of 1958 ten-year reunion. (Courtesy Charleston Newspapers.)

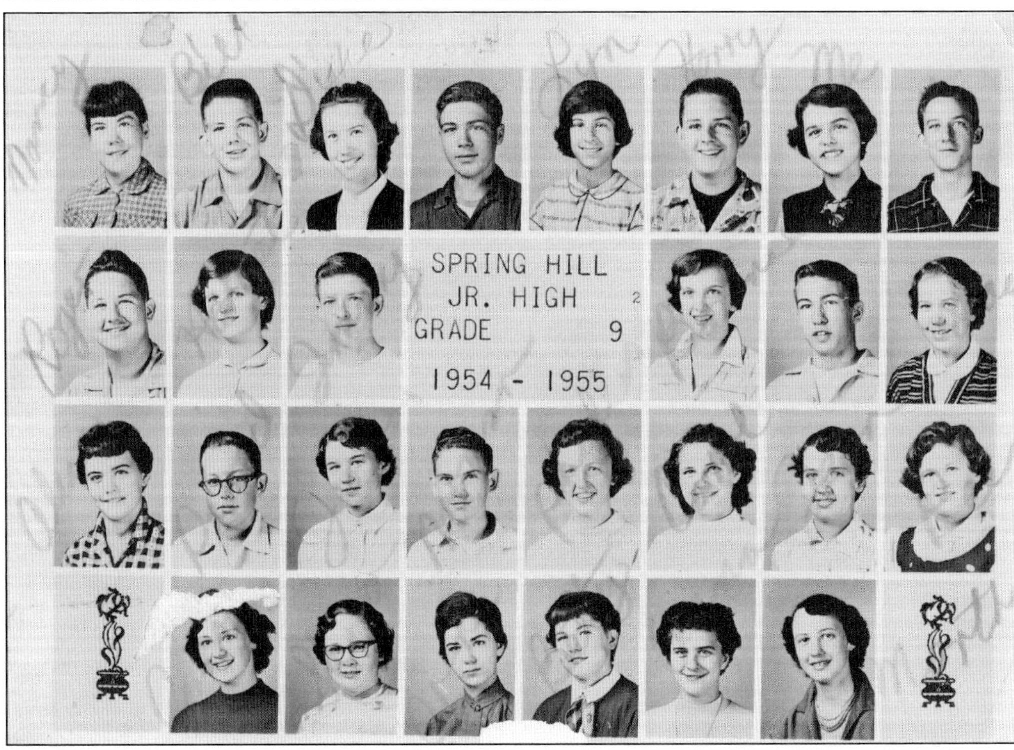

The 1954–1955 Spring Hill Junior High ninth grade class were the first graduates from the new school. In 1953, they attended South Charleston Junior High School. (Courtesy Judy Romano.)

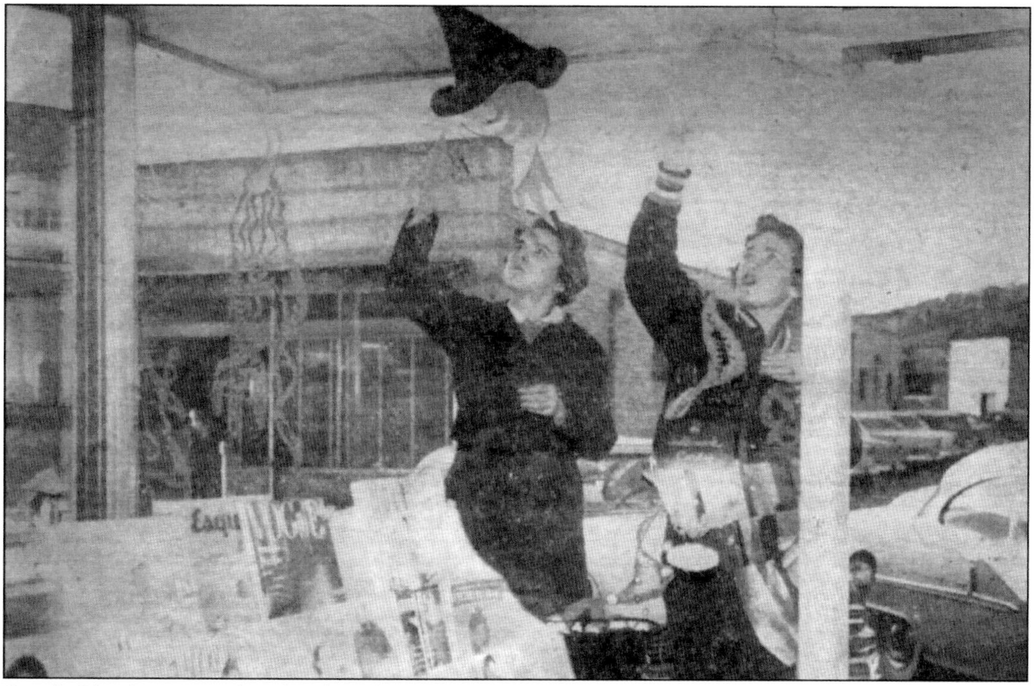

South Charleston High School students Judy Scholl and Luana Bowen are decorating the Copper Drugstore window on Seventh Avenue in South Charleston in the 1950s. They competed for a prize of $45. The contest was open to elementary, junior, and senior high students. (Courtesy Luana Bowen.)

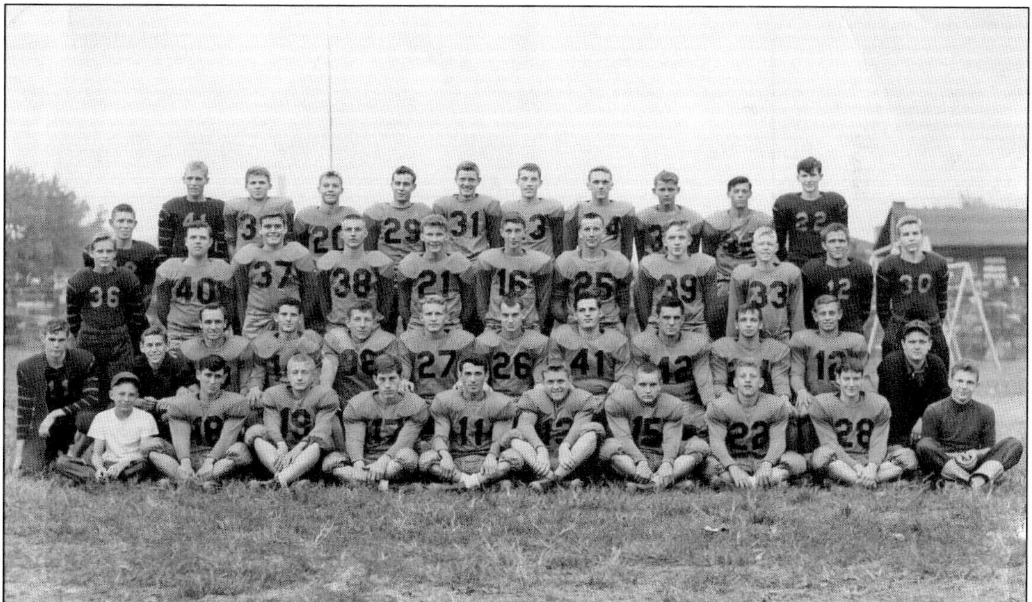

This is the 1951–1952 South Charleston High School football team. Included are No. 19 "Skippy" Hawkins, No. 17 Shot Mallory, No. 15 Ricky Fisher, No. 13 Eddie Garrett, No. 22 Bob Molle, No. 36 Benny Mallory, and their coach, Bill Weber. Other players are not identified. (Courtesy South Charleston Museum.)

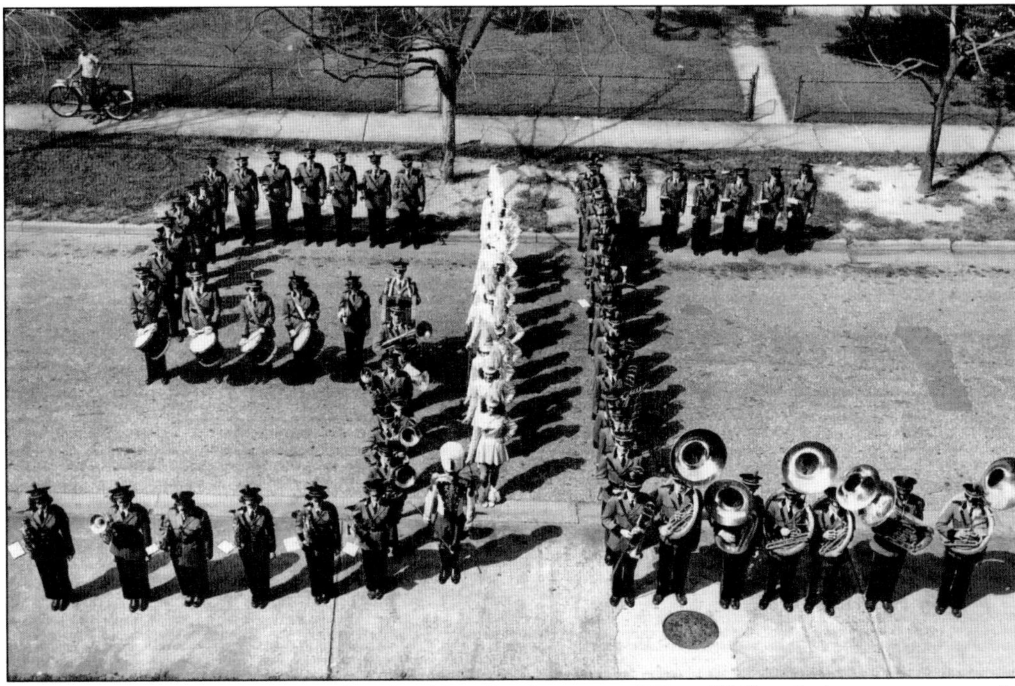

This is the South Charleston High School band in formation "S" and "C" with the majorettes in the center. The band won many awards for their formations. (Courtesy South Charleston Museum.)

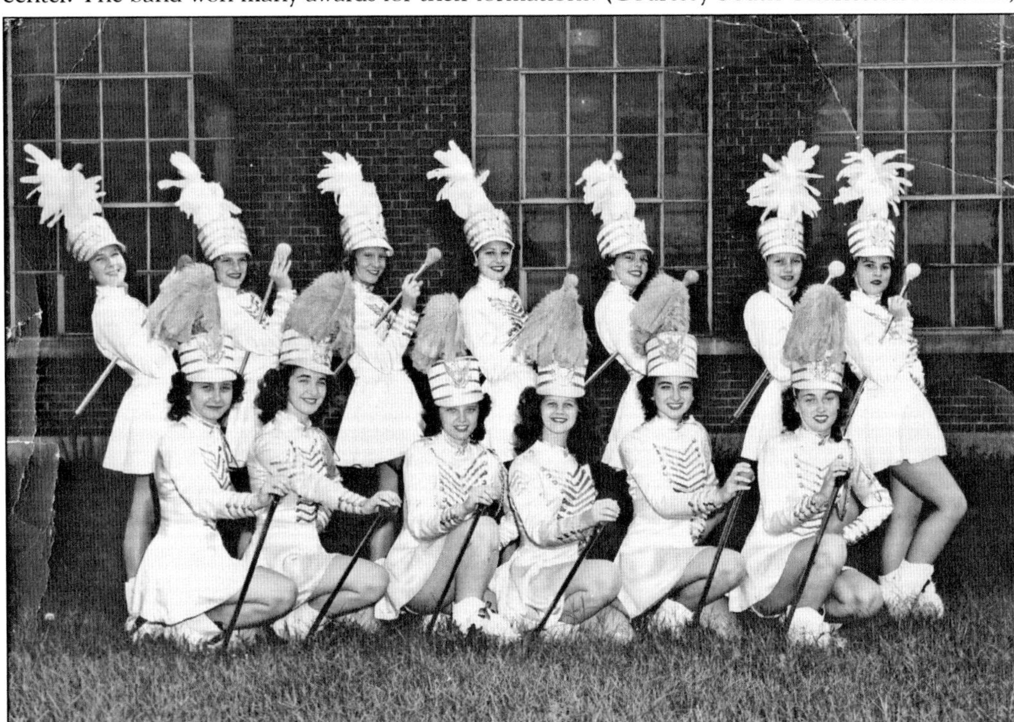

The South Charleston High School majorettes pose in front of the high school, bordered by Second and Third Avenues. (Courtesy South Charleston Museum.)

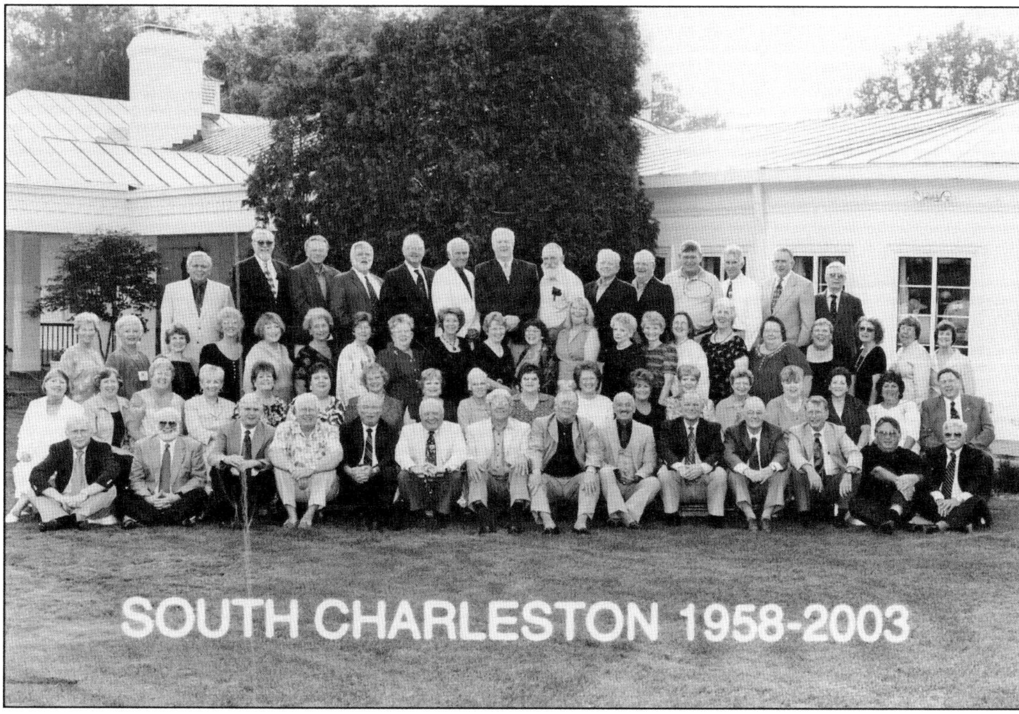

South Charleston High School students from the class of 1958 are shown here at their class reunions in 2003 (above) and 2008 (below). (Courtesy South Charleston Museum.)

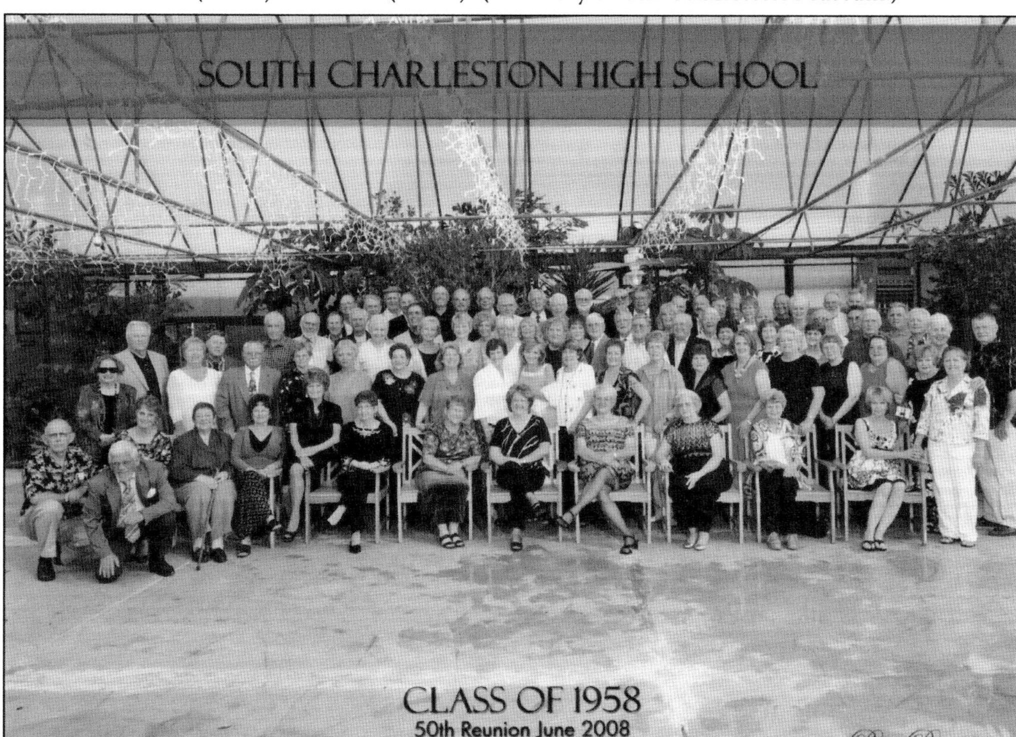

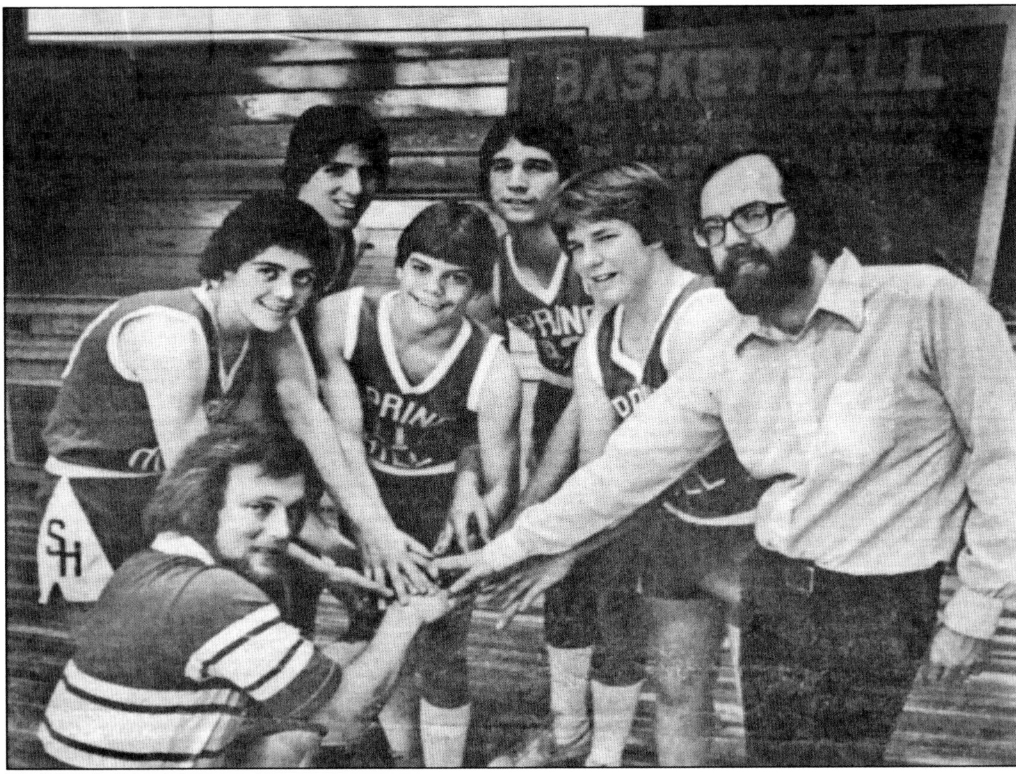

The 1981 Spring Hill Junior High basketball team members are, from left, Jim Gillespie, Gary Thompson, David Bradley, Mark Rucker, and Vic Green, with their coaches Bill Estep and Gary Green. (Courtesy the *Charleston Gazette*.)

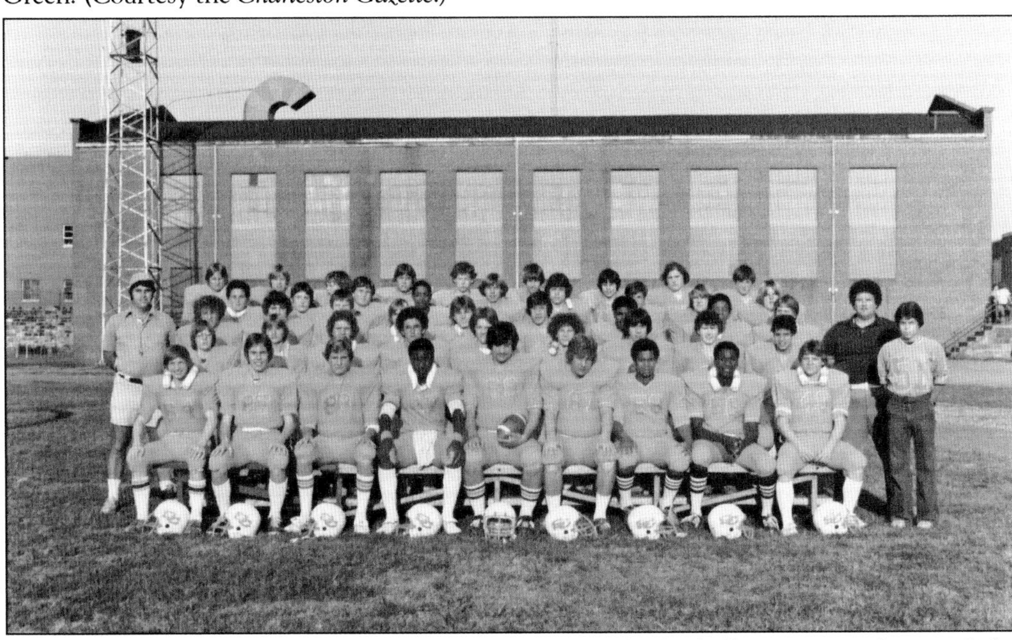

Pictured is the South Charleston Junior High Golden Cubs football team in uniform at Oakes Field. (Courtesy South Charleston Museum.)

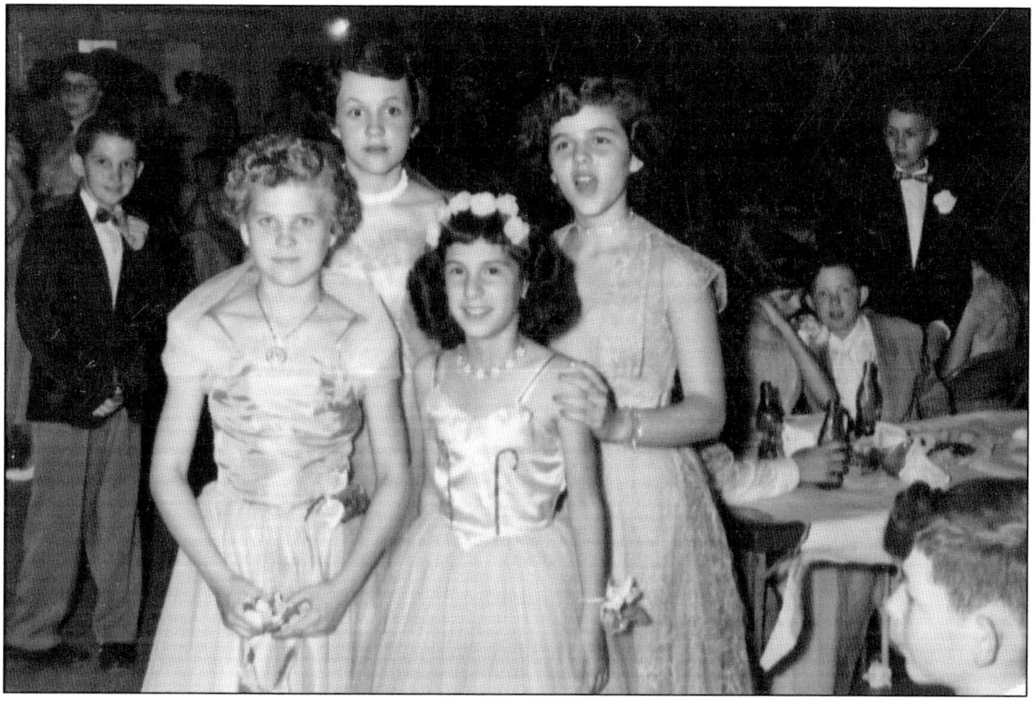

These South Charleston Junior High School students in 1953 are, from left to right, (first row) Linda Cole and Lyn Bailey; (second row) Sheila Hamrick and Judy Bowen. Merrill McIlwain donated the picture as he was the student's homeroom teacher. (Courtesy Merrill McIlwain.)

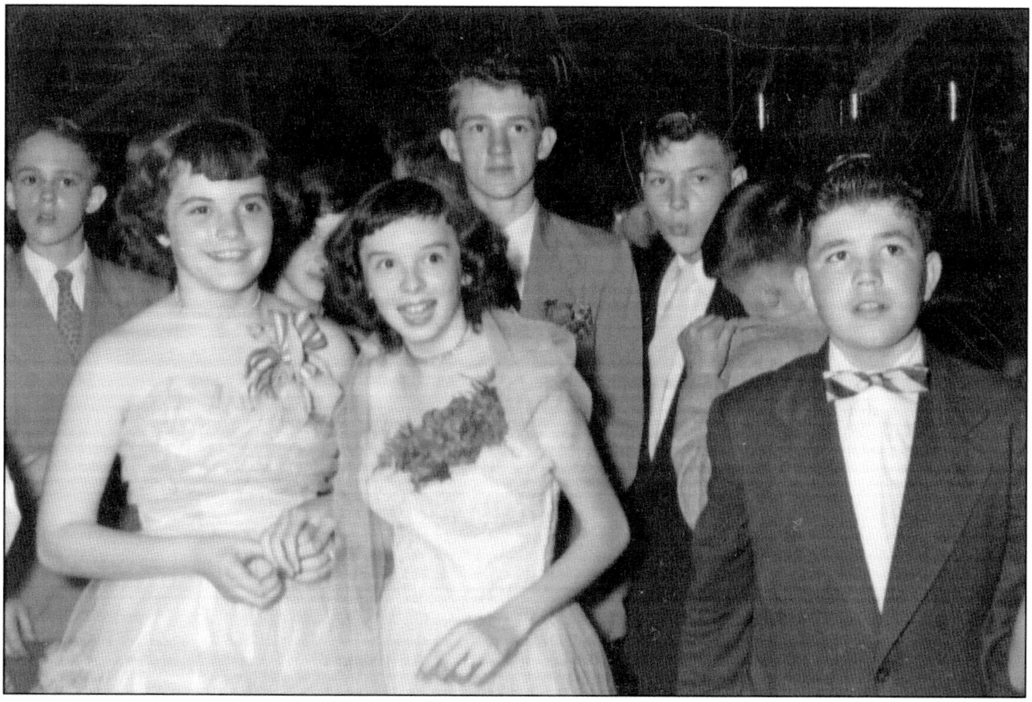

Alice Durrett (left) and Barbara Schoonover attend a dance at the gym on Third Avenue, beside South Charleston Junior High, in 1953. (Courtesy Merrill McIlwain.)

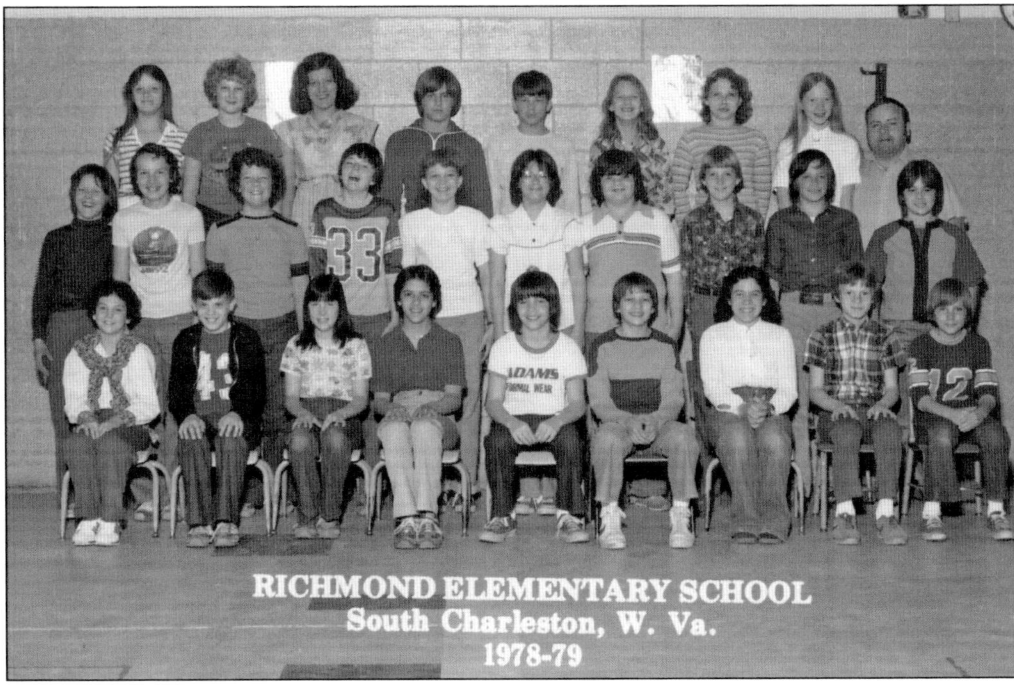

Pictured are the Richmond Elementary fifth-grade students from 1978–1979. Richmond Elementary is located in the Spring Hill section of South Charleston and is near Little Creek Park and Little Creek golf course. (Courtesy Judy Romano.)

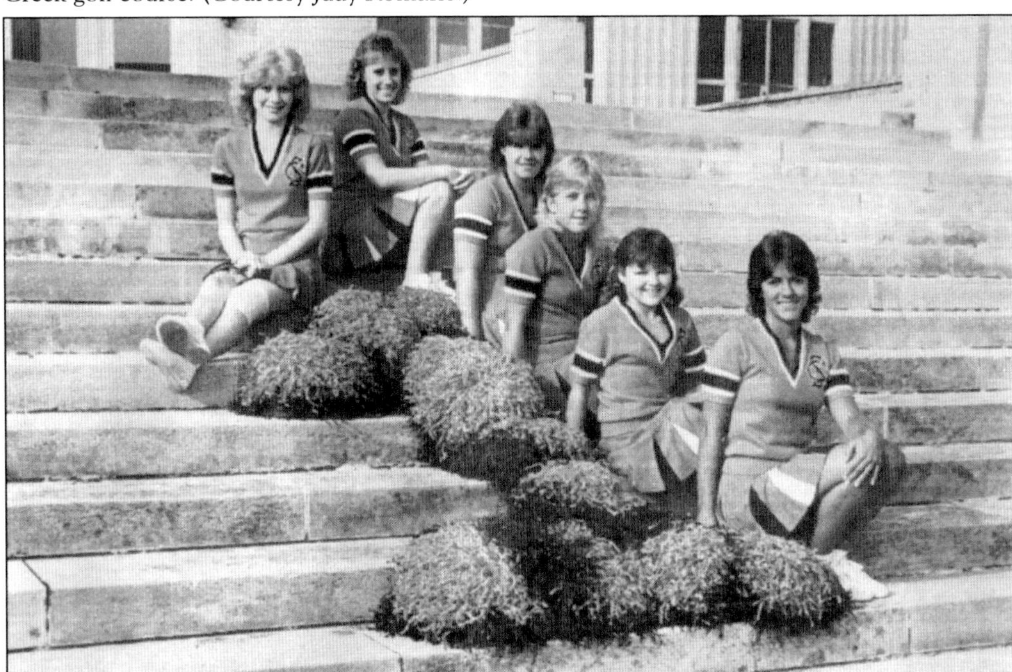

The 1984 South Charleston High School cheerleaders are, from the top, Kelly Payne, Sheryl Raymond, Elaine Bean, Cari Hundley, Julie Rowsey, and Paula Romano. (Courtesy South Charleston Museum.)

The South Charleston Junior High School achievement award winners pictured here are Chip Watkins in math and William Landolt in science. (Courtesy South Charleston Museum.)

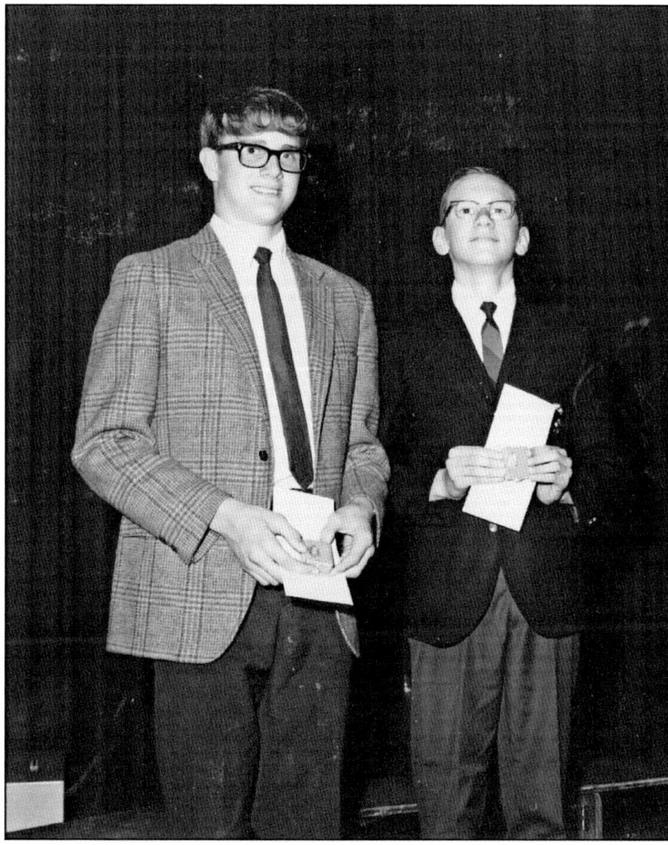

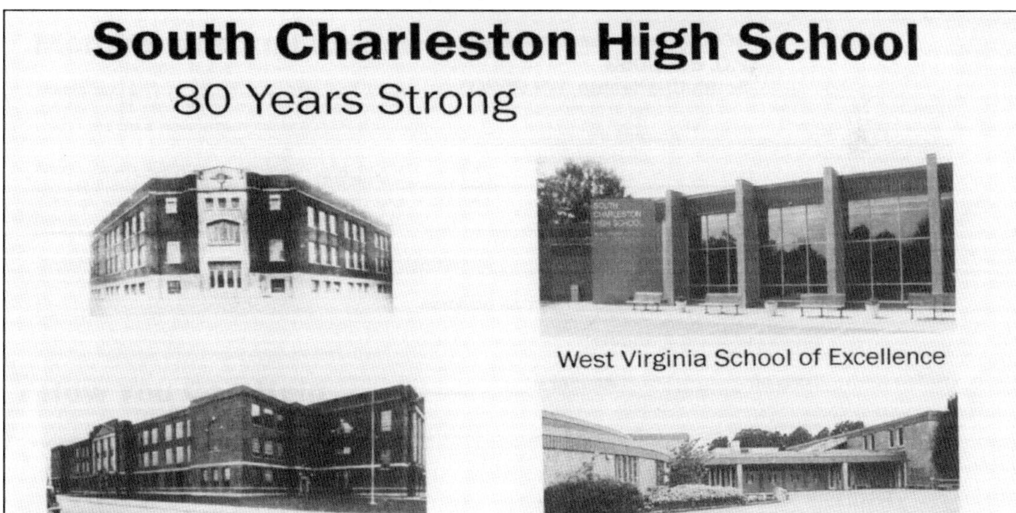

In 2006, the South Charleston High School Alumni Association had its Grand Reunion. Pictured here are the three buildings that have been home to South Charleston High School. The first location (upper left) was on Third Avenue. The second high school (lower left) was bordered by Second and Third Avenues. The West Virginia School of Excellence (right) is on One Eagle Way in the Spring Hill section. (Courtesy Judy Romano.)

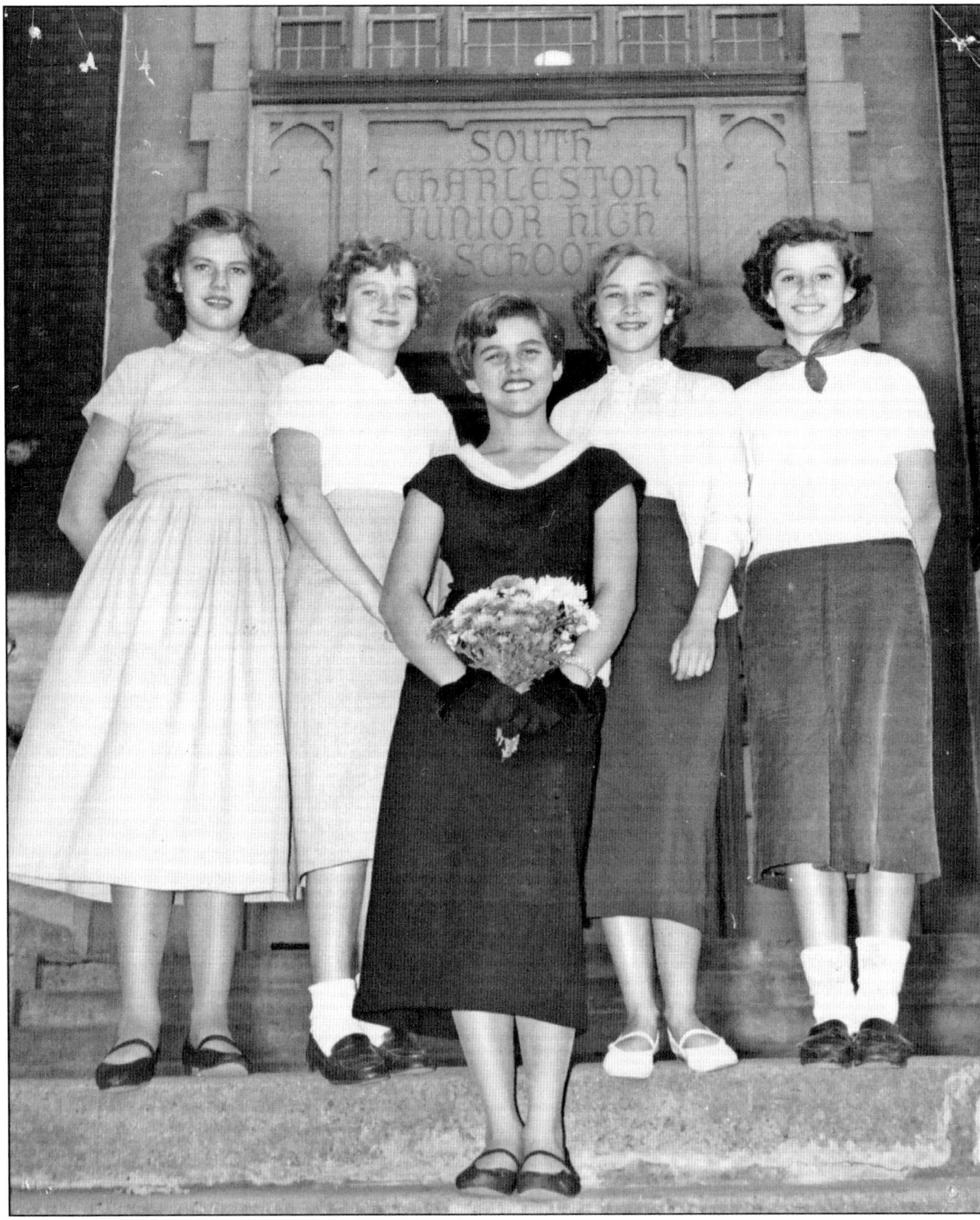

South Charleston Junior High School Miss Golden Cub 1954 was Judy Bowen, and her attendants were, from left to right, Janet Turley, Blanche Ewart, Carolyn Nelson, and Patty Sutton. (Courtesy South Charleston Museum.)

Sports greats from South Charleston High School include Alex Hawkins (1953; pictured), Robert Alexander (1977), Carl Lee (1979), Gay Elmore (1982), Alexis Hornbuckle (2004), Renee Montgomery (2005), Aaron Dobson (2009), Aaron Slusher (2009), Blake Brooks (2010) and Tyler Harris (2010). (Courtesy South Charleston Alumni Association.)

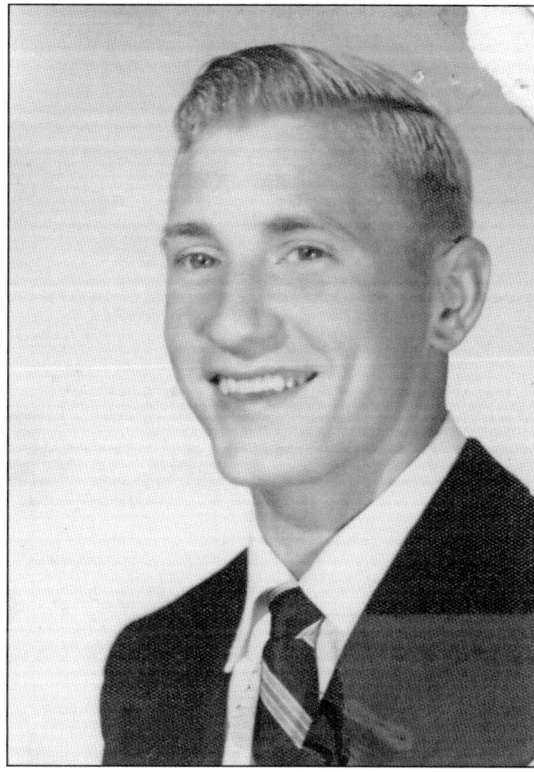

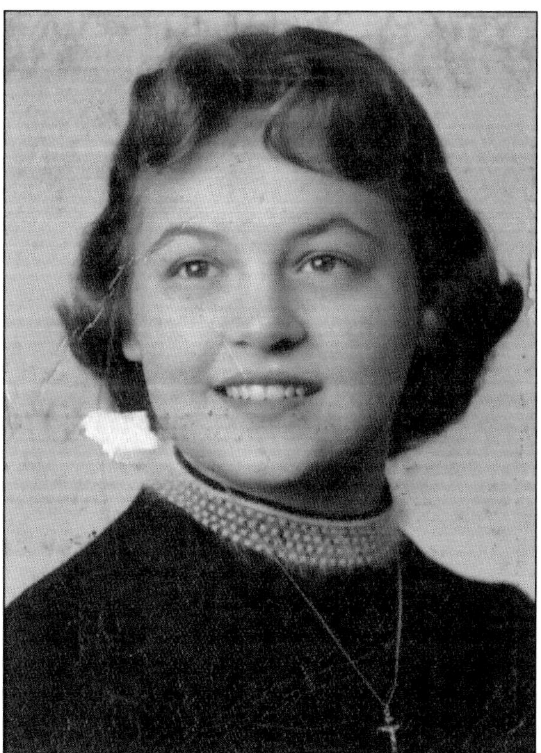

This is Judy Rousseaux's 1956 class picture. Judy's ancestors worked in the glass plants in South Charleston in the early 1900s. (Courtesy Judy Romano.)

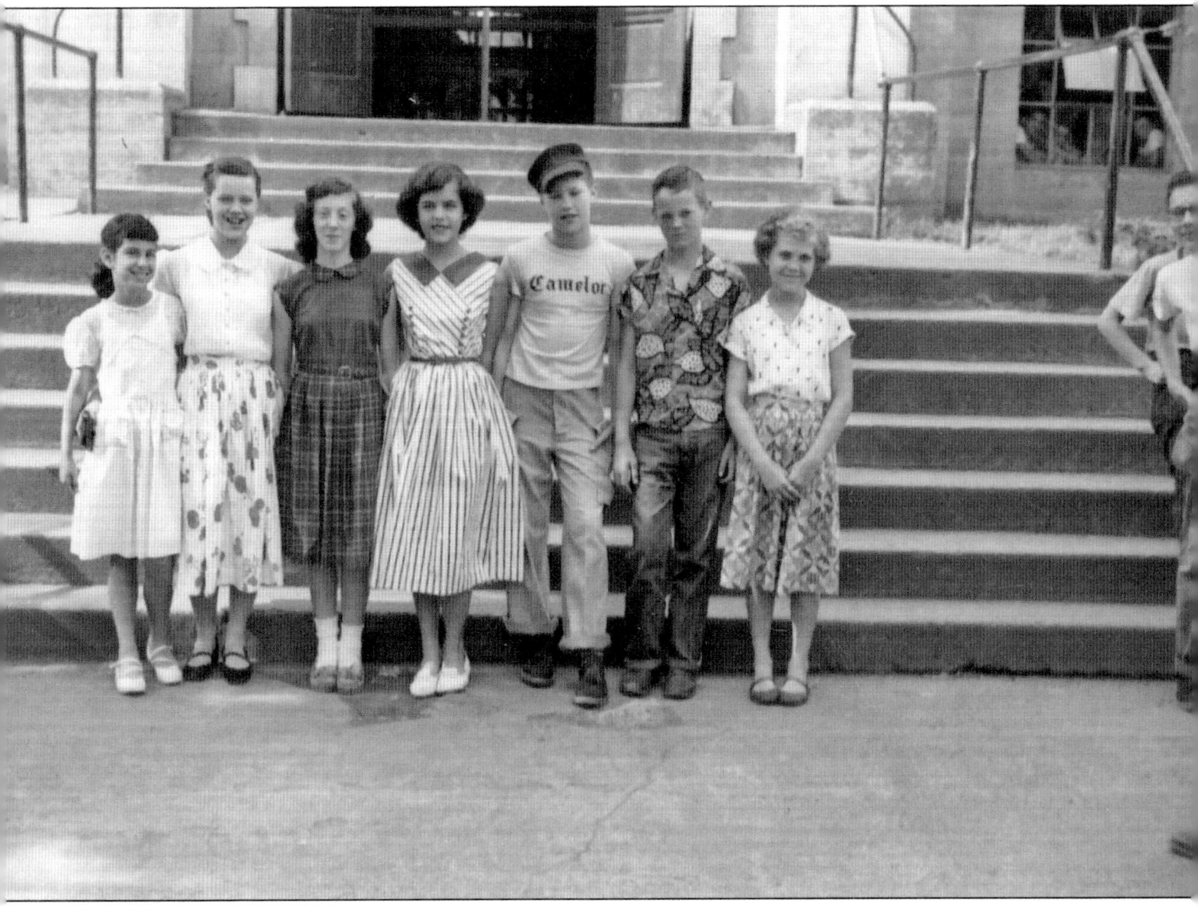

South Charleston Junior High School students are pictured in front of their school in 1953. From left to right are Lyn Bailey, Barbara Bates, Beverly Bickerstaff, Judy Bowen, William E. "Butch" Buckley, Monte Chittum, and Linda Cole. Tommy Field is peeking in on the side of the picture. (Courtesy Merrill McIwain.)

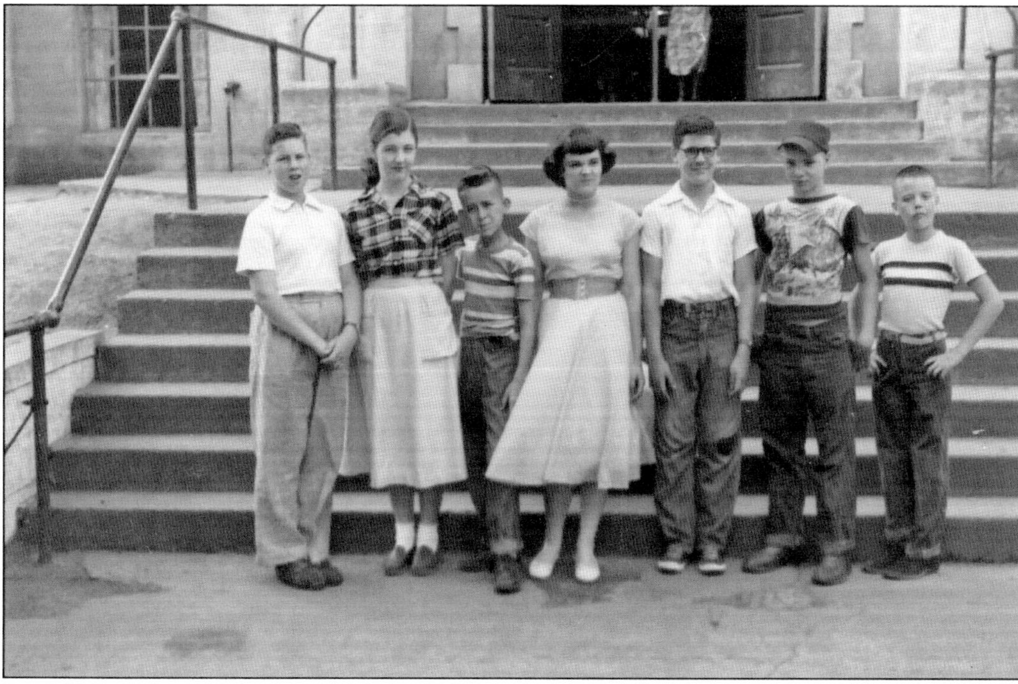

In 1953, Eric Crane, Connie Daugherty, Charlie Dement, Alice Durrett, Tom Fields, Jim Garber, and Harold Hackney are pictured in front of the junior high. (Courtesy Merrill S. McIlwain.)

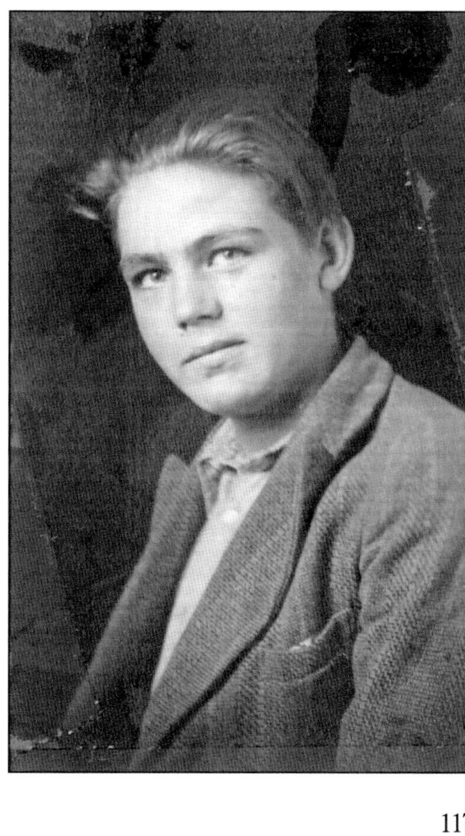

Francis L. "Tucker" Bowen's class picture at South Charleston High School dates to 1930; he played on the baseball team and the football team. (Courtesy Judy Romano.)

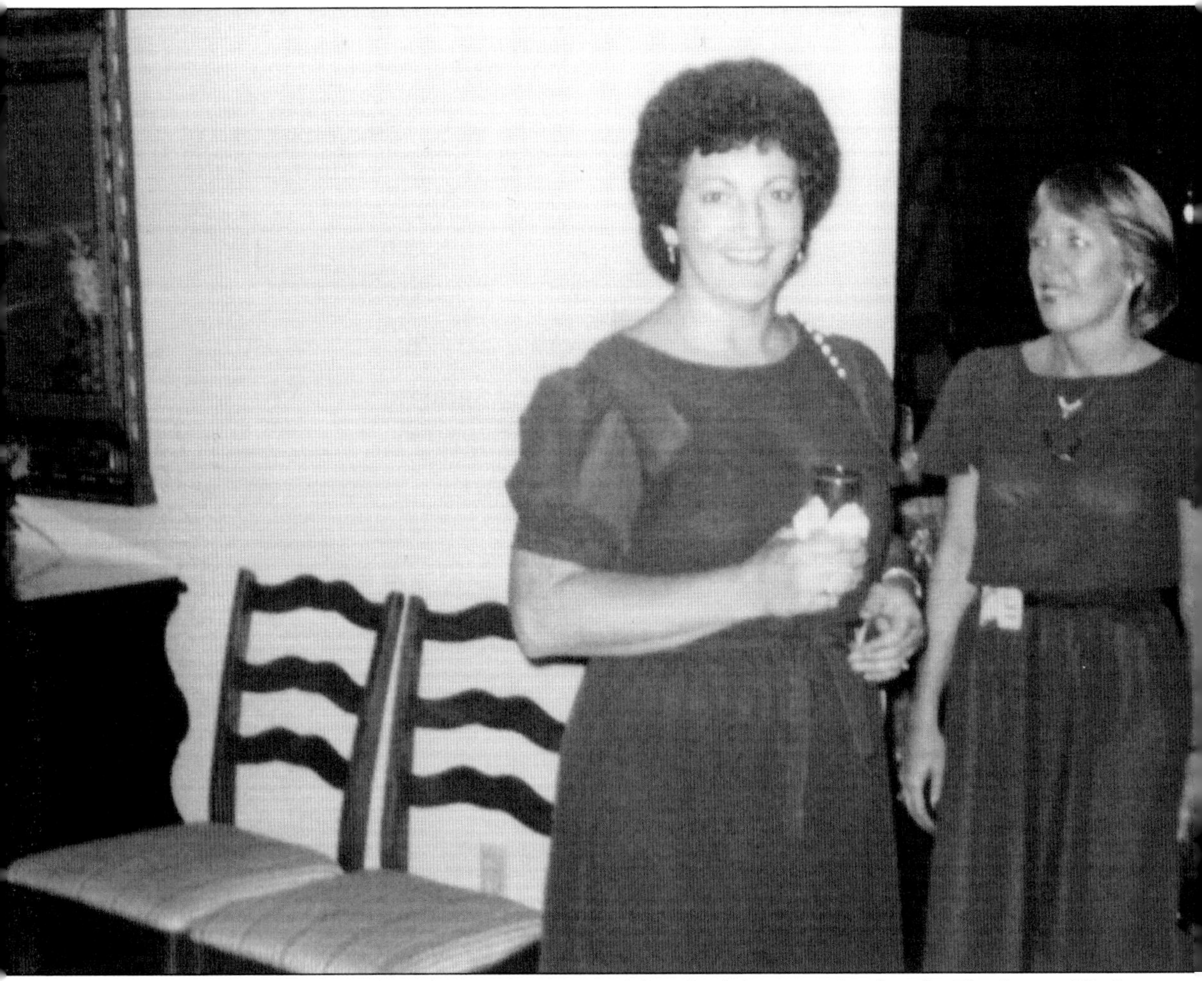

Jackie Frizzell Pauley (left) and Joan Bennett Belcher (right) are at the South Charleston High School 25th reunion at Kanawha Country Club. (Courtesy Judy Romano.)

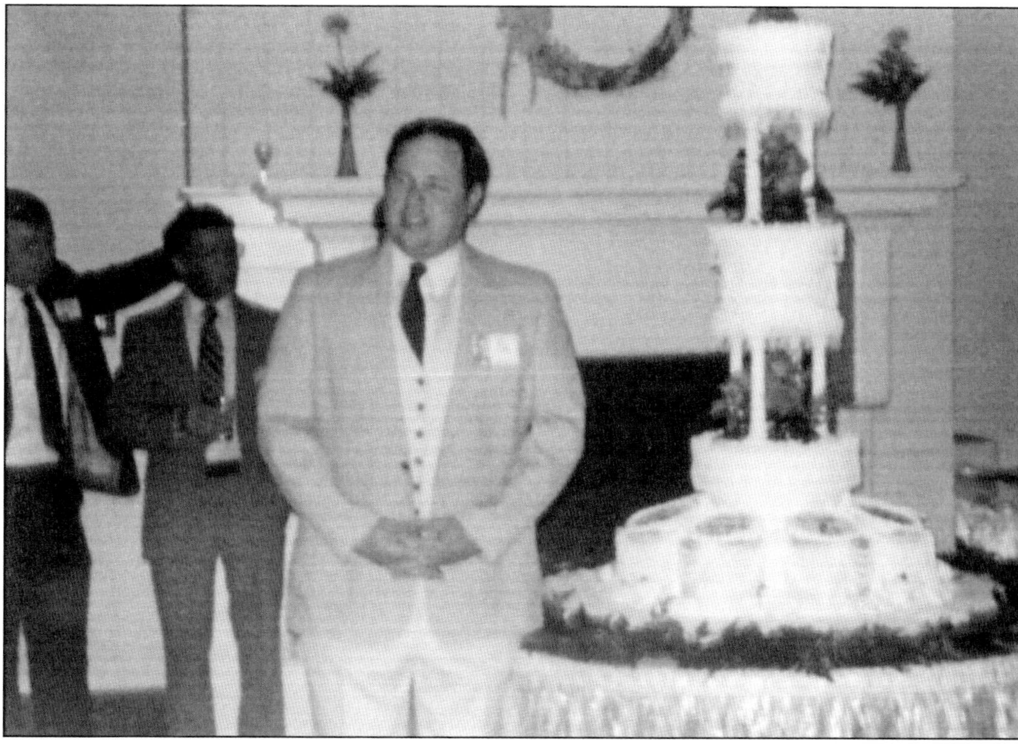

Eric Crane (above) poses with the cake that he baked for the 25th reunion. (Courtesy Judy Romano.)

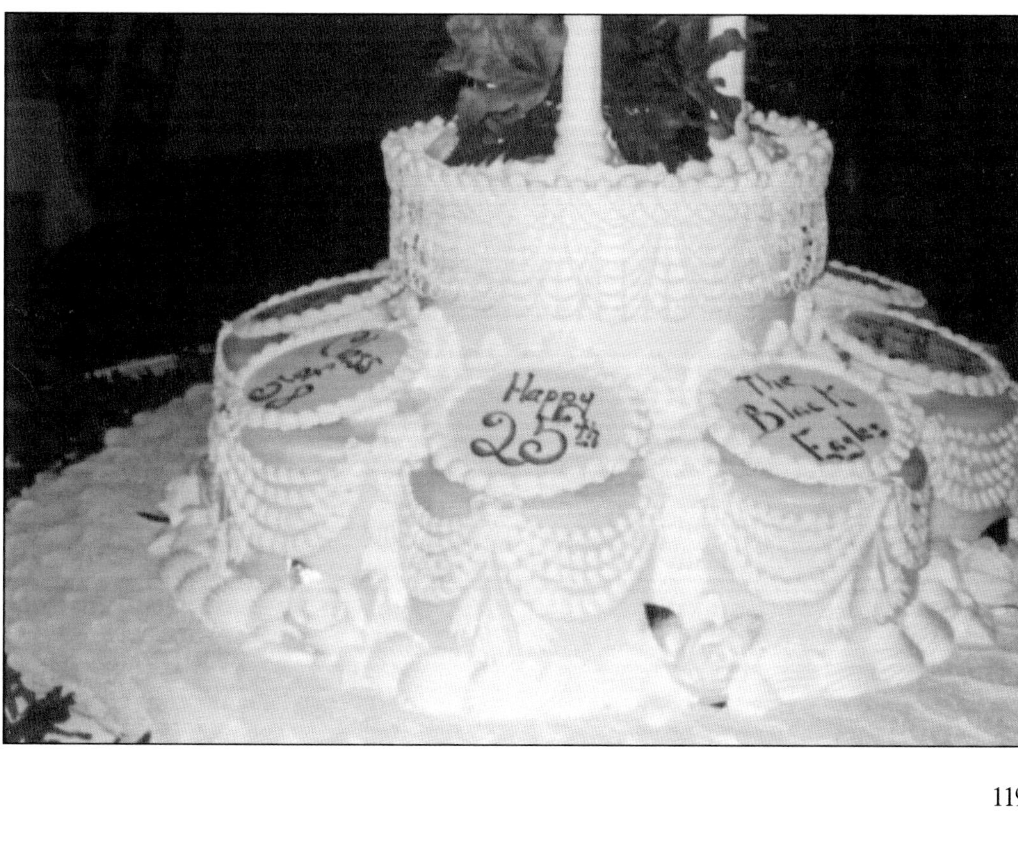

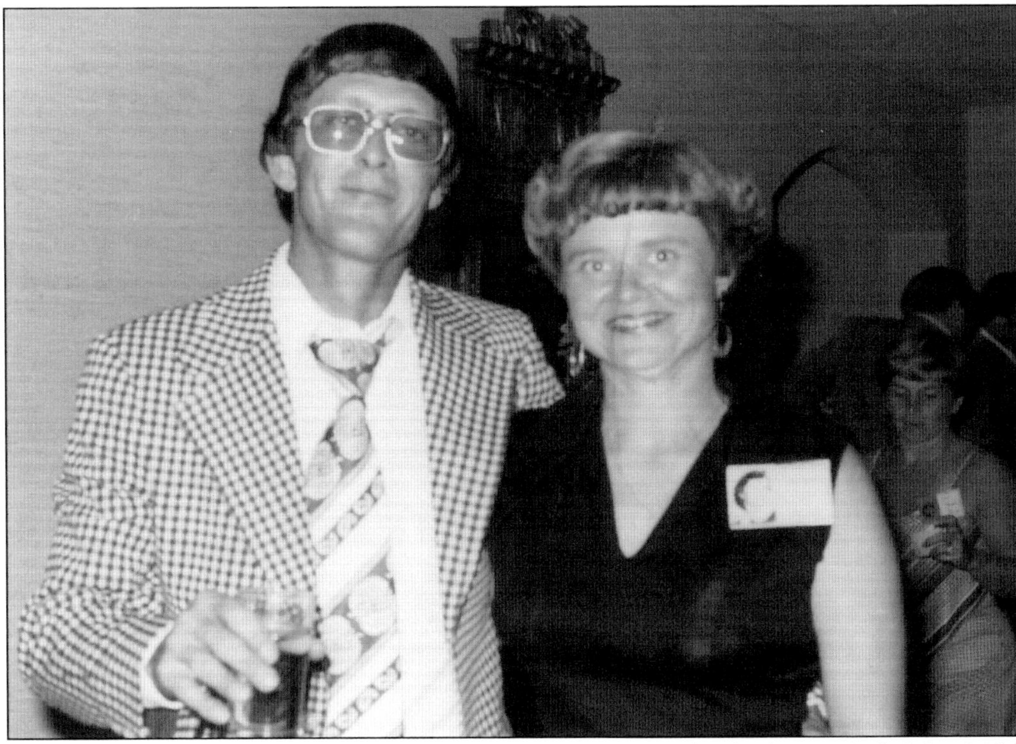

Dean Rollins and Barbara Bates Rollins are pictured at the South Charleston High School 25th reunion; Susie Thewes Brewer is pictured in the background. (Courtesy Judy Romano.)

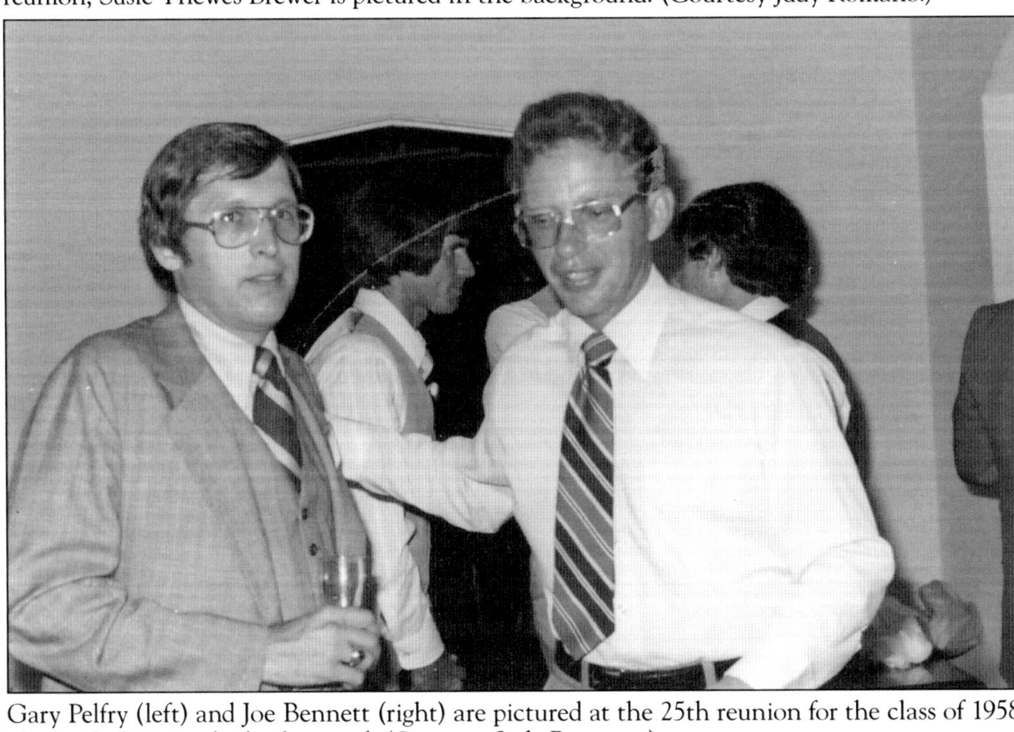

Gary Pelfry (left) and Joe Bennett (right) are pictured at the 25th reunion for the class of 1958. Greg Schultz is in the background. (Courtesy Judy Romano.)

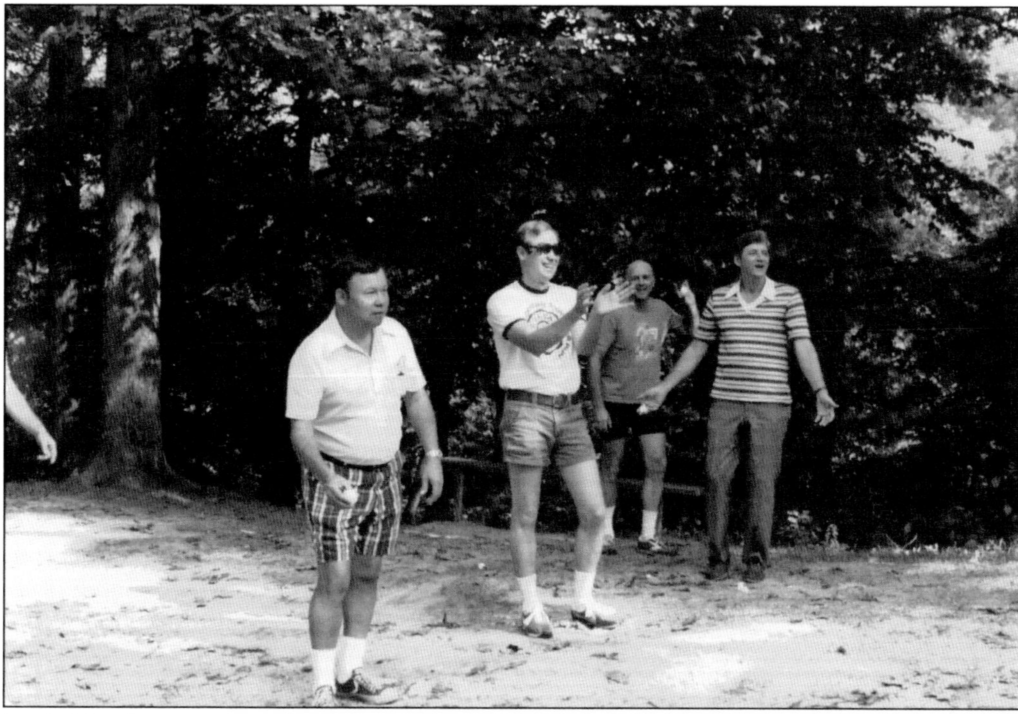

Looks like the guys are winning the egg toss at Little Creek Park. Participants include, from left to right, R. M. Brewer, Dicky Meeks, Frank Turley, and Dieter Garrett. (Courtesy Judy Romano.)

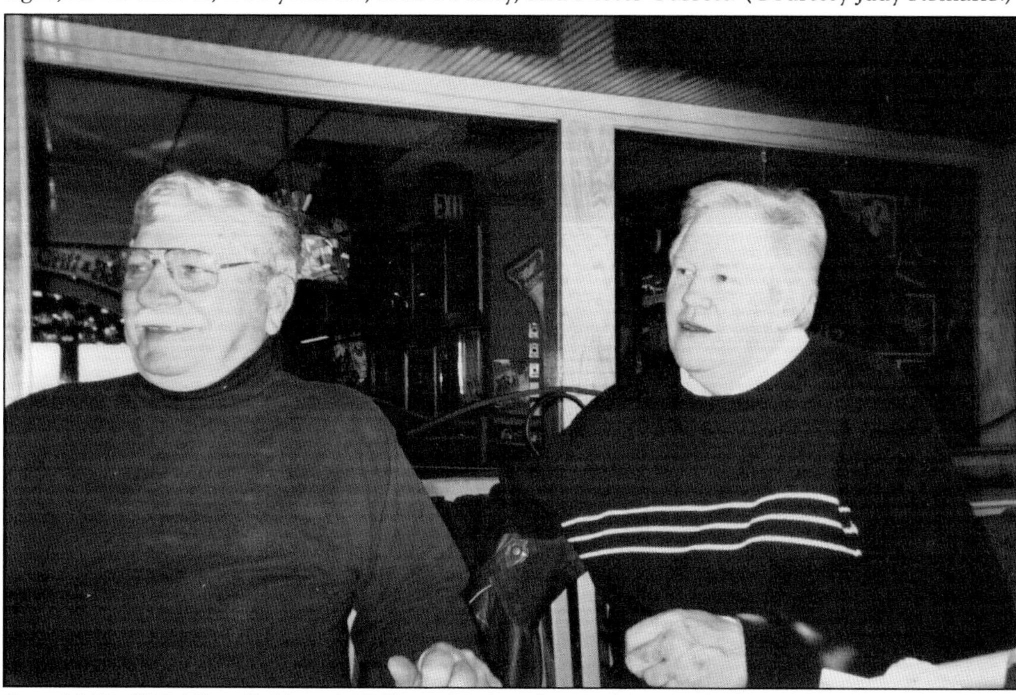

Donald "Bull" Miller (left) and William E. "Butch" Buckley (right) attend a class luncheon at Applebee's on Corridor G. The class of 1958 meets the third Saturday of each month for lunch. (Courtesy Judy Romano.)

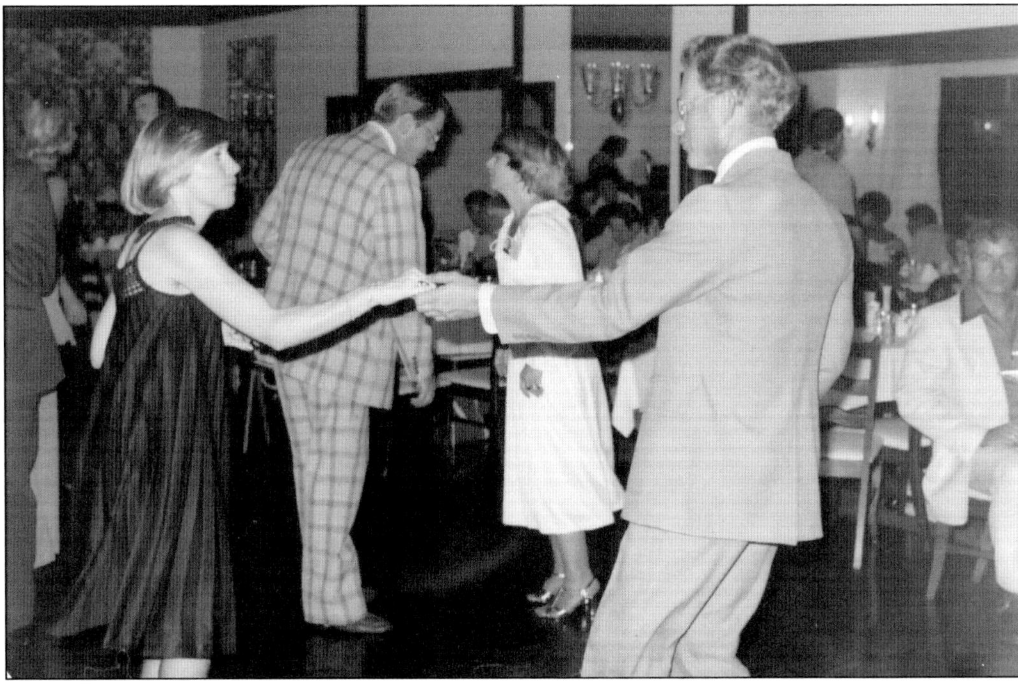

Sister and brother Joan Bennett Belcher and Joe Bennett dance at the 25th reunion at Kanawha Country Club. Leo Mallory is on the right, and Wayne Pritt and his wife Barbara Webb Pritt are behind Joe and Joan. (Courtesy Judy Romano.)

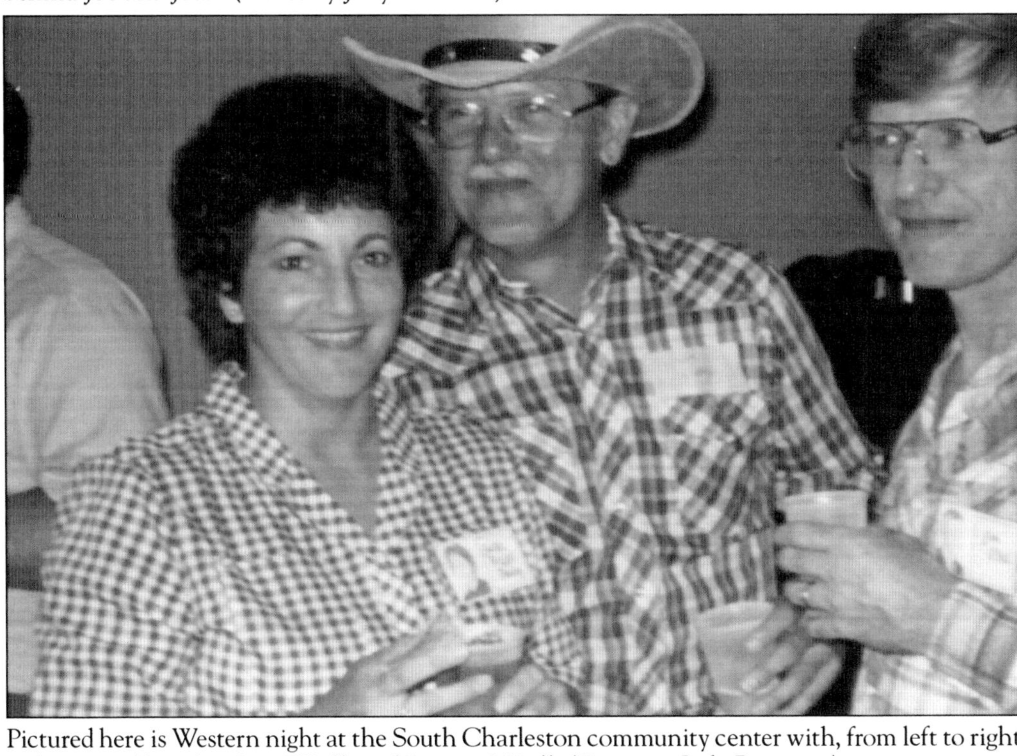

Pictured here is Western night at the South Charleston community center with, from left to right, Jackie Frizzell Pauley, Joe O'Dell, and Jimmy O'Dell. (Courtesy Judy Romano.)

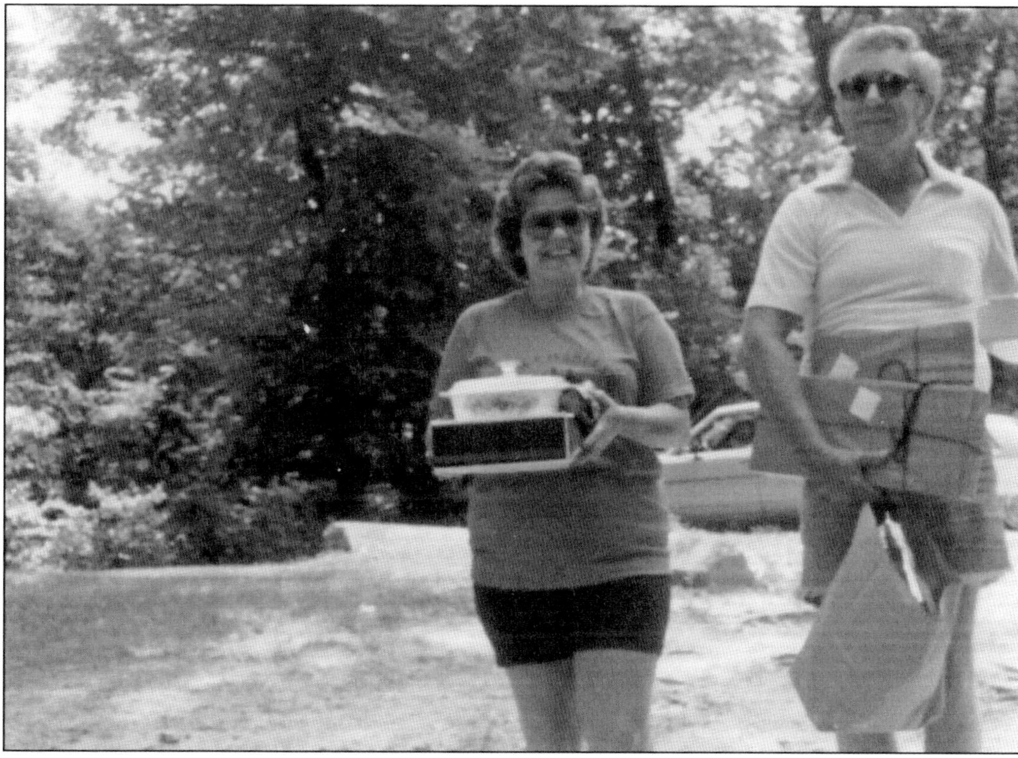

Faye and Jerry Collins are bringing the goodies for the class picnic at Little Creek Park. (Courtesy Judy Romano.)

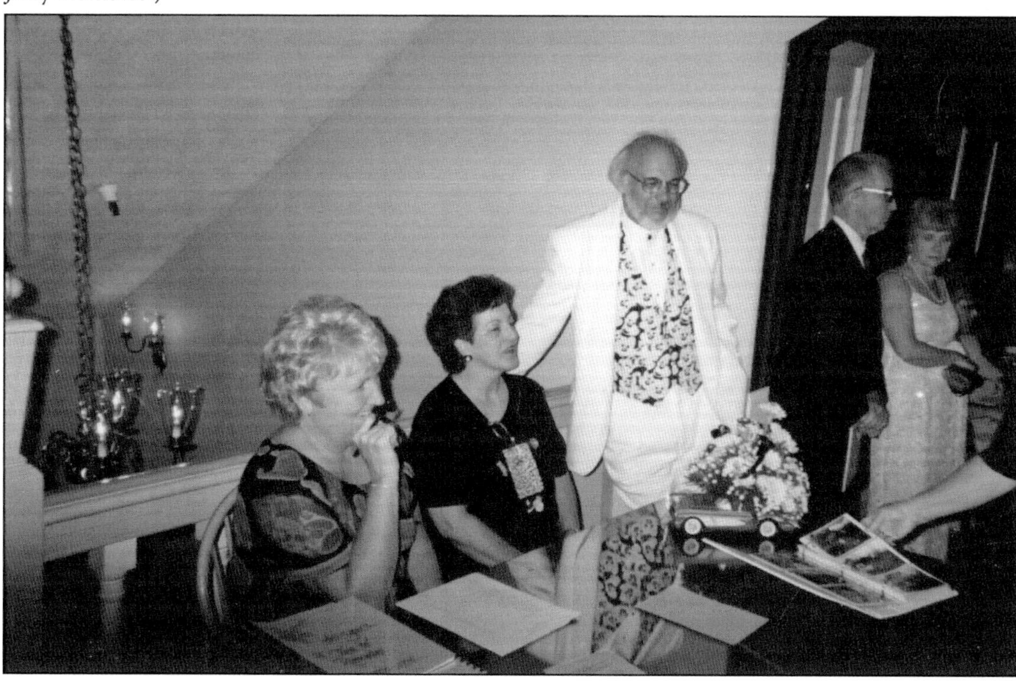

From left to right, Phyllis Rumbaugh Fenwick, Jackie Frizzell Pauley, and Don Evans are at the registration table for their 25th class reunion. (Courtesy Judy Romano.)

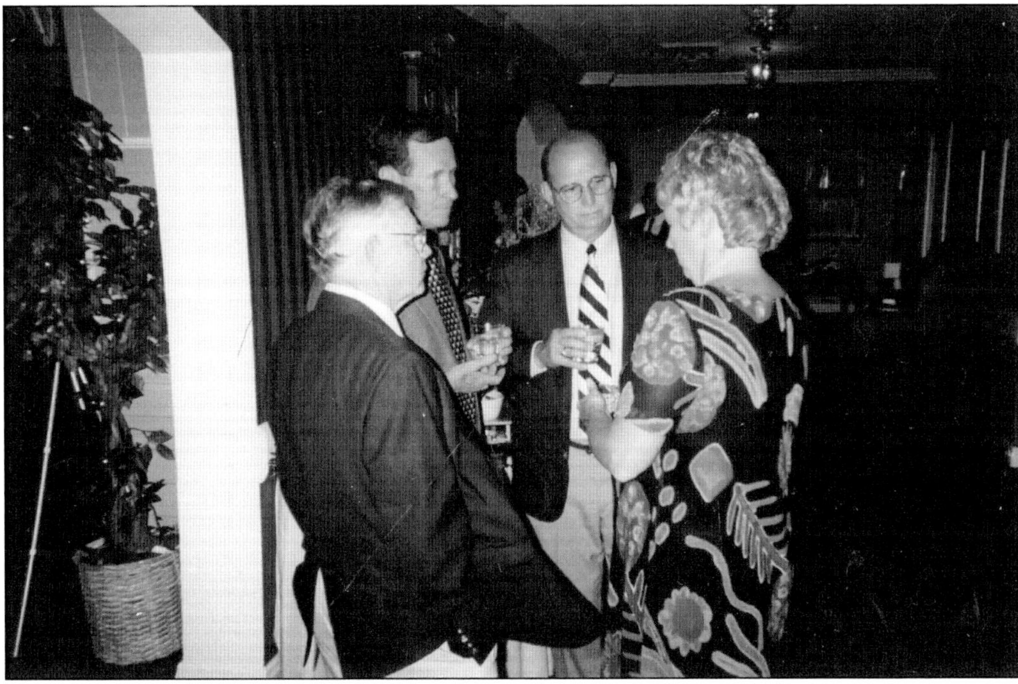

From left to right, Gus Belcher, Dicky Meeks, Dicky Campbell, and Phyllis Fenwick go over the evening's schedule. (Courtesy Judy Romano.)

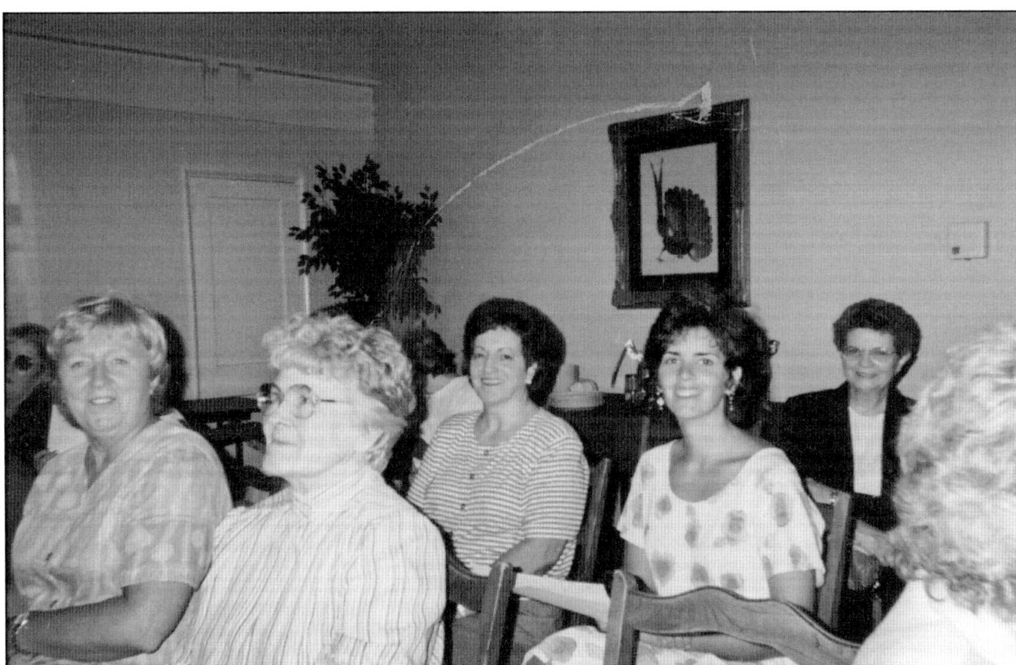

Attending Eric Crane's cooking class at Kanawha Country Club are, from left to right, Phyllis Fenwick, Ruby Rumbaugh, Jackie Pauley, Scarlett Hutchison, and Vesta Grinstead.

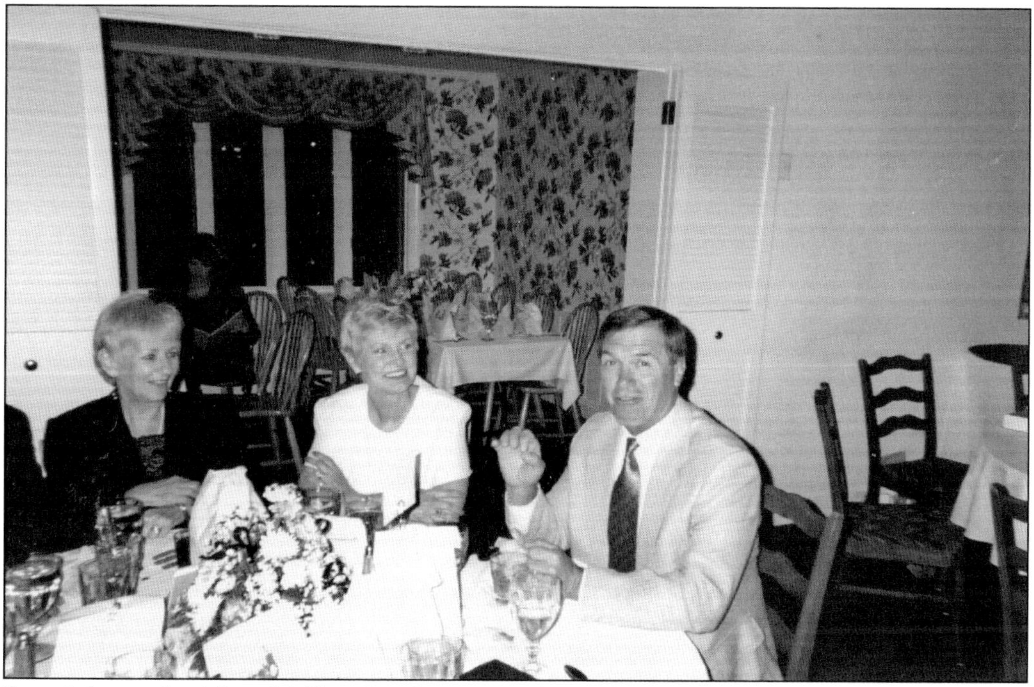

From left to right, Mona Mallory, Linda Loos, and David Loos are at their 25th class reunion at Kanawha Country Club. (Courtesy Judy Romano.)

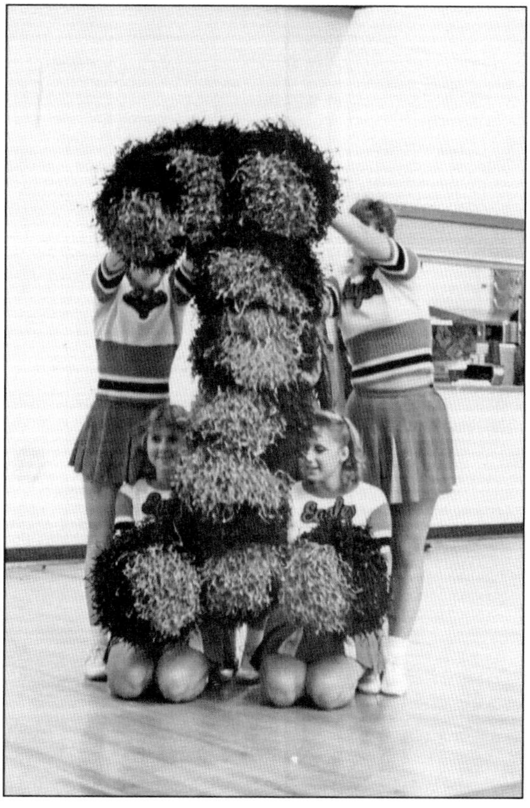

In the 1980s, South Charleston High School cheerleaders are making the number one with their pom-poms. (Courtesy Paula Potter.)

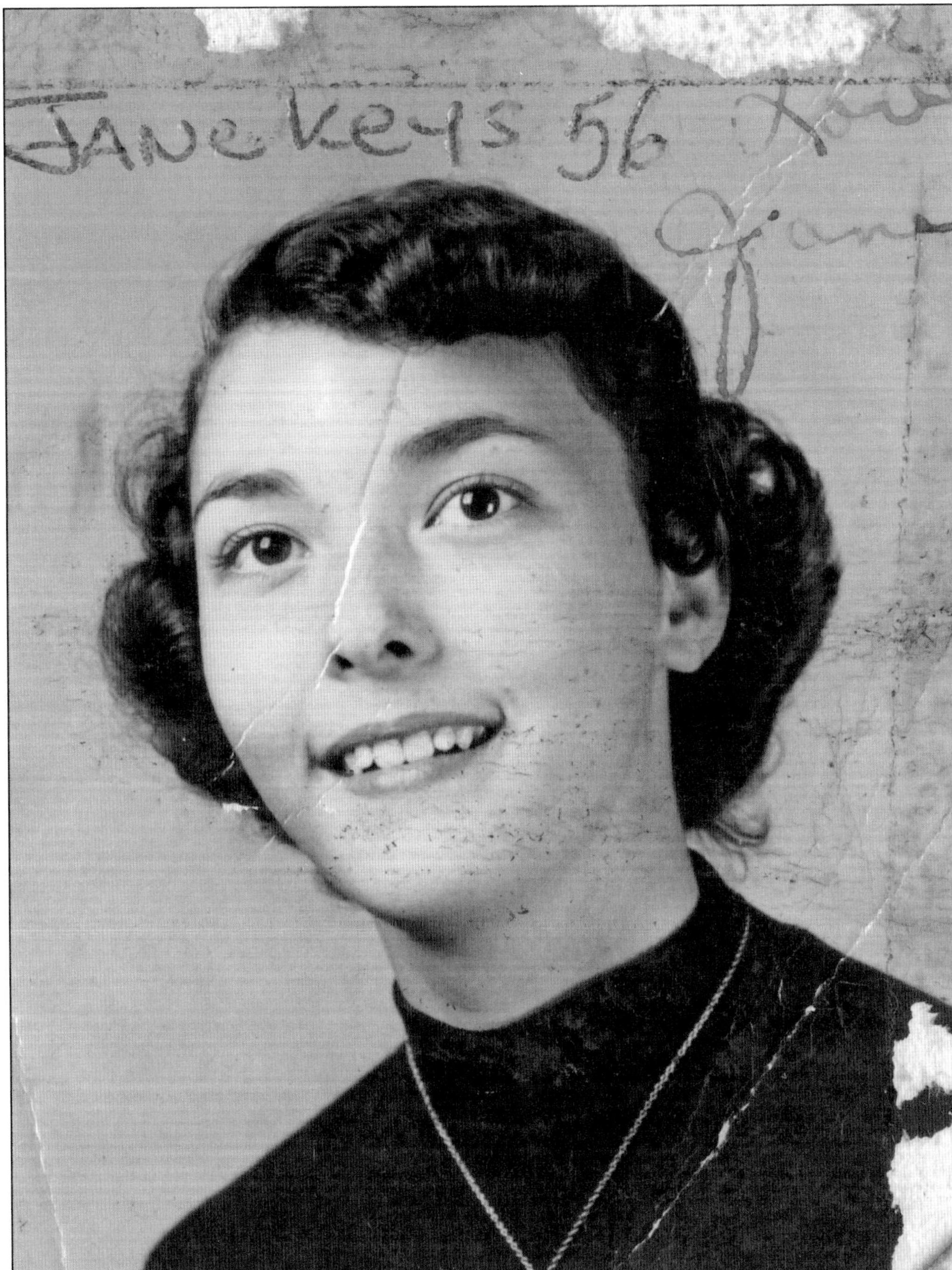

Pictured here in 1955–1956, Jane Keys graduated from South Charleston High School in 1958. (Courtesy Judy Romano.)

About the Organization

The South Charleston Museum Foundation was formed in 1989 to preserve the past for the present and the future generations. The museum offers tours, movies, and monthly events. They have also sponsored a new Interpretive Center exhibit depicting the city's first industry, the Banner Plate Glass Window Factory.

The museum foundation's professional expertise includes Ken Farmer, a noted expert and appraiser of antiques; Steve Fesenmaier, program chairman who previews West Virginia movie makers throughout the year; and Dr. Fred Barkey, who wrote *Cinderheads in the Hills*. The South Charleston Museum is located in the historic La Belle Theater at 311 D Street and shares a space with the convention bureau. Lura Watkins and Steve Fesenmaier handle press releases.

Consistent with our mission to preserve history on a local level, this book was printed in South Carolina on American-made paper and manufactured entirely in the United States. Products carrying the accredited Forest Stewardship Council (FSC) label are printed on 100 percent FSC-certified paper.

MADE IN THE USA